RABBIT IN THE MOON

Rabbit in the Moon

A Memoir

Heather Diamond

A Camphor Press book

Published by Camphor Press Ltd
83 Ducie Street, Manchester, M1 2JQ
United Kingdom

www.camphorpress.com

ISBN   978-1-78869-234-2 (paperback)
         978-1-78869-235-9 (hardcover)

The moral right of the author has been asserted.

Set in 11 pt Linux Libertine

for my grandmother, Ksenia Diamond,
who told me her stories

Contents

Author's Note

Like all memoirs, my story is a composite of relative truths. Parts are drawn from notes and photos, and much of it is constructed from recollection. Because my memory is what it is — a mercurial creature fascinated with certain kinds of moments and ho-hummed by others — I have no doubt that there are people I've included who may remember these events differently. This memoir represents my view, which I have tried to convey with as much accuracy as is possible given time, distance, and subjectivity. I've taken a few writerly liberties with conversations and the order of events, and any errors in the telling are mine alone.

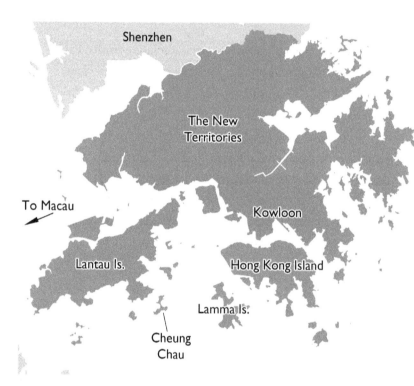

Shenzhen

The New
Territories

To Macau

Kowloon

Lantau Is.

Hong Kong Island

Lamma Is.

Cheung
Chau

Map of Hong Kong, with Cheung Chau indicated

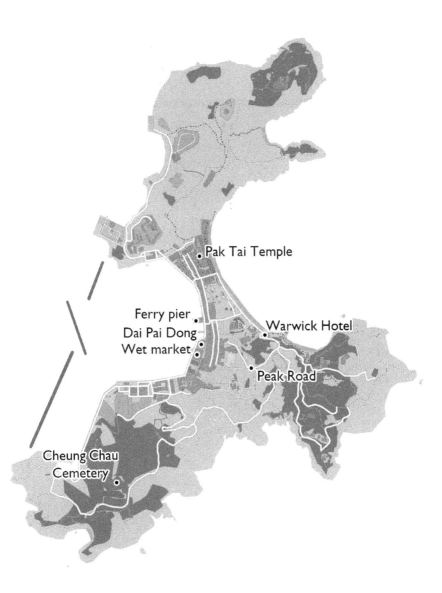

Pak Tai Temple

Ferry pier
Dai Pai Dong
Wet market

Warwick Hotel

Peak Road

Cheung Chau
Cemetery

Map of Cheung Chau

RABBIT IN THE MOON

Prologue: Jade

In Hong Kong, everything about me seems wrong, so I obsess over jade bracelets. I eye them in the windows of fancy jewelry stores. Entranced by the marbled greens, milky whites, and translucent lavenders as much as by jade's alleged magical properties, I imagine how a jade bangle will slip over my wrist and slide against my arm — a small but visible link to this foreign world where I feel so out of place. If jade can also bring me luck, healing, and harmony, all the better.

We're spending two weeks in Fred's childhood home on the small island of Cheung Chau. Since we arrived, my dependence on Fred for translations, directions, and instructions for everything from table manners to shared bathroom protocol has catapulted me back to my shy and surly teens. In our Hawaii life, I'm an articulate, accomplished PhD student, still thrilled by my mid-life reinvention. In America, in English, I'm in charge of my life. In the midst of Fred's family, I'm a beginner, a bumbler, an untrained extra in a crowd scene.

Fred has heard tales about people getting scammed with fake or dyed jade, so he wants to consult with his mother, the shopping expert. There are eight of us packed into the tiny dining room for lunch when he asks her where to go. His parents and two pairs of aunts and uncles start talking at once. Under the loud cross-currents, Fred translates while plopping steamed bok choy and chunks of chicken on top of my rice. He says they're amused I want something so old-fashioned. "Taitai jewelry," he says, using the Cantonese term for wives to imply rich women who spend their days shopping and playing mahjong. More American eccentricity for them to talk about, I think.

As the discussion swirls around me, I sink from feeling invisible to wanting to disappear, mortified to have my shopping under scrutiny. If I could crawl under the table, I would. Why couldn't he have asked her privately? And why does everyone here feel entitled to give advice? I left home at eighteen to escape my family telling me what to do. Fred, on the other hand, seems unconcerned about all the interference.

I'd imagined sitting side by side in Luk Fook or Chow Tai Fook, elegant jewelry stores in the city. Instead, the family decides that we should go to a local jade shop because the Laus know and trust the Cheng family that owns the shop. Fred's mother and Second Aunt will accompany us to make sure they sell us the real thing at the best price. I smile while resolving to humor them. After the past few days, I should know that activities within the Lau family take on a momentum of their own. So far this has not been the trip I imagined, nor have I been the kind of enlightened and adaptable traveler I presumed myself to be. Not even close.

* * *

The next afternoon, the four of us descend steep staircases and walkways to a narrow, shop-lined backstreet that tourists from Hong Kong Island seldom visit. The two old women, married to brothers and living together for half a century, could easily be mistaken for sisters with their tightly permed, dyed-black hair, mismatched polyester clothing, and unfashionable umbrellas that doubled as walking sticks and shields from the sun. Fred's mother, a head shorter, holds the elbow of Second Aunt as they stroll along the narrow street, greeting neighbors at every turn. I've never considered walking like that with my sister, mother, or daughter. I imagine them jerking away in surprise if I reached for a hand or arm.

Fred and I follow behind, holding hands. Beside him, I'm a sojourner, not a tourist. As usual, I notice that our steps match, as if we're running a three-legged race in slow motion. Such a welcome change after two tall husbands to be with a man close to my own size, our conversations always on the same level. I squeeze the hand of this foreign man who wants to protect me, who makes me laugh out loud, who has welcomed me into his world. Now I'm the foreigner.

We walk past mounds of pomelos and dragon fruit, stacks of bok choy, *choy sum*, and *gai lan*. Past cases stacked with raisin twists, egg tarts, and wife cakes filled with melon paste (the first gift Fred gave me when we met in Hawaii), the sundries shop with plastic baskets and toys hanging from the ceiling, and the rag shop where a tortoiseshell cat sleeps atop piles of discarded clothing. Laundry and fish hang on overhead balconies beside large, flat baskets of shrimp. The aromas of baking bread and drying fish are undercut with occasional whiffs of sewage.

I wonder aloud if the laundry ends up smelling like fish, or if anyone would notice if it did. "Don't make fun of my island," Fred says, only half joking. He's proud of his humble origins in "the country" outside metropolitan Hong Kong, but prickly about it too. I make a mental note that what's funny in Hawaii is serious stuff here. There we revel in our differences — his fearlessness to my watchfulness, my counterculture America to his Asian cosmopolitan, his frugality to my spending, his rice to my potatoes — but here, on his home turf, I sense cracks beneath our usual play.

Unlike the gold shops in the city, with their velvet-backed window displays of orangey, 24-karat gold and jade carved into fantastic flora and fauna, the Cheung Chau jade shop is a cubicle in one of the white-tile buildings that line the street. Out front is a display table on wheels topped with jadeite zodiac animals and charms. Through the window, I glimpse a pegboard on the right-hand wall displaying gold necklaces and earrings. Farther back is a glass-topped display case with trays of rings and bracelets arranged on black velvet. I try not to show my disappointment at the dowdy surroundings and skimpy selection.

Mr. and Mrs. Cheng, a middle-aged couple, are eating a late lunch behind the counter. They set aside bowls of noodles and stand when we enter. "Neih ho! Neih ho!" they say.

As Fred's mother and Second Aunt strike up a conversation with the shopkeepers, Fred explains, "Mom and Second Aunt are saying that they know the grandfather who owns the shop and they've known the Cheng family for a long time. They're saying they know this shop will give us real jade and a good price." Their exchange is teasing and friendly. I imagine it as a flirty and loud version of the infamous "we know where you live" threat from gangster movies.

Mrs. Cheng points me to a red plastic stool in front of the counter. When I sit down, she reaches into the back of the case and pulls out a tray of jade bracelets that she sets in front of me.

While I look half-heartedly through the tray, Fred's mother and Second Aunt exclaim over ornate multi-tiered gold necklaces hanging on the wall; yet from what I've seen, neither of them dresses up much, even to go into the city. For a dinner out they might add a scarf or a string of pearls, but the gold on display includes the kind of showy necklaces given to brides-to-be by their wealthy mothers-in-law in pre-nuptial rituals. Mr. Cheng takes the necklaces down one by one, and the women try them on in front of the countertop mirrors, turning this way and that to admire the shimmer and flash of gold against their printed polyester blouses.

When I raise an eyebrow, Fred says, "It's part of the process. They're pretending they might come back to buy something else if we get a good deal."

"Like a reverse bait and switch?" I ask in a whisper, but Fred's standard volume indicates that no one but us understands English.

"Something like that," he says, listening more to them than me. I'm pretty sure he has no idea what this means. Even after two decades in the United States, he's sometimes baffled by American idioms although he's a master of Cantonese proverbs, swearing, and slang.

I point to a circlet the color of seafoam mixed with cream. "Can I see this one?" Mrs. Cheng lifts it out of the tray and hands it to me. I hold it in my palm, admiring the smooth coolness of the stone, the play of light in its delicate veins. "Pretty," I say to Fred, "but it looks like it was made for a child."

I set it down, so she pulls a few more bracelets out of the tray, some wider than others, some cylindrical and others flat on the inside, all in different shades of green — fern, mint, emerald, seaweed — some translucent and others more opaque, some veined and some clear.

We are the only customers, and Fred perches on a blue stool next to mine. Over our heads, Fred's mother and Second Aunt banter and laugh with Mr. Cheng, who occasionally consults with his wife. My plan to look and leave appears less and less possible.

I whisper to Fred, "What about the price? How are we supposed to know how much they cost?" There are no price tags on any of the bracelets.

"Don't worry about it," he answers. "They'll agree on a price, and we'll figure it out later."

"You mean pay her back?" Uneasy, I imagine a replay of the discussion at lunch, only this time about how much we spent.

He talks to his mother and then tells me, "She wants to buy it for you as a gift." Embarrassed by her generosity and annoyed that my romantic fantasy has been co-opted, I suck in my breath and decide to choose a skinny band in hopes it will be less expensive than the wider ones I prefer. I don't want to be labeled the extravagant girlfriend on top of the eccentric American.

The conversation swirls above and around me, making me feel like a small child. I fidget as I wait for translation. Mrs. Cheng lifts my left hand in hers and kneads it, gently pressing my fingers and thumb together while talking to Fred. I assume she's trying to determine my size. He says, "She's saying your hands are soft like a little girl's. Some women's hands aren't so soft." I beam at her, flattered that my nearly fifty-year-old hands have garnered such a compliment.

Mrs. Cheng waves her hand over the tray, and Fred says, "She's asking which one you like." Feeling pressured, I look again through the tray. "I like this color and width," I say, pointing to the first one, "but it's way too small." He translates, and Mrs. Cheng smiles and nods while placing the same bracelet over the tips of my fingers, where it comes only to my second set of knuckles. She removes it and leans down to rummage under the counter, where I guess she must have additional stock.

She emerges with a plastic squeeze bottle and beckons her husband to where I'm sitting. She hands him the bracelet and squirts a cool gel onto my hand. Fred is facing away, talking to his mother. I elbow him and hiss, "Translate! What's she doing?"

"Dish soap," he says, reading the Chinese label. Mrs. Cheng positions my elbow on the counter with my hand in the air, then presses my fingers into the shape of a budding tulip. Her husband leans over and, with a single downward thrust that makes me yelp, rams the tiny bracelet from my fingertips to my wrist, where it fits perfectly, and, as it slowly dawns on me, permanently.

Everyone admires the shiny bracelet on my wrist while Fred and I exchange a wide-eyed look. Holding my hand high, Mrs. Cheng motions for me to stand and leads me into a back room. She washes my hand and wrist at a wall sink, pats me dry with a paper towel, and massages oil from a small bottle into the ball of my thumb. I recognize the peppermint and camphor scent of White Flower Oil, what Fred and I always refer to as old-people smell.

She speaks to Fred as we re-enter the front of the shop. He explains, "She's saying the oil helps with bruising. Last week one woman's whole hand turned black." Cradling my tender hand, I watch as Fred's mother pays for the bracelet and thanks the couple, extending greetings to the Cheng family.

Mr. Cheng gives Fred's mother a bonus gift, which she passes to me — a tiny jade monkey on a red string. "Lucky," she says, patting my shoulder.

"Doh jie sai," I say, careful to use the more grateful form of thank you for the gifts and not m goi, which is for expected and small courtesies. I haven't yet learned that what I consider courtesies can also mark me as an outsider.

"She wants to protect you," Fred says. "Jade is supposed to keep you safe from harm."

Toying with the bracelet, I remember the Chinese finger cuffs my siblings and I played with as kids, the kind where we stuck our fingers into each end of a brightly woven raffia tube that entrapped us when we tried to escape.

"Mom says the color will change as you wear it," Fred says. "The jade gets greener the longer it stays in contact with your skin."

"It will look plenty green tomorrow when my hand turns black," I respond.

As we walk home behind his mother and aunt, I gingerly test the bracelet. It locks firmly at the base of my throbbing hand. Knowing it won't come off makes me feel manacled. We've both shed wedding rings in the recent past, and this is way bigger than a ring.

"Did you know it would be permanent?" I ask.

"I had no idea! Hey, at least you're protected!" he adds with a lopsided grin. I can't stop turning the bracelet on my wrist. "I feel like I'm married to your mother!"

"What's wrong with that?" he asks.

PART I: 1998–2007

1

Tropical Itch

M Y thoughts stray during our seminar at the East-West Center. I'm trying to decide whether two of the Chinese men
across the table from me are flirting or just being friendly. Fred
is an ethnomusicologist who teaches in California, and Michael
is a historian who teaches in St. Louis. I catch them looking my
way, and they both seek me out on breaks. I wonder why they
don't have Chinese names and if being short means that they are
attracted only to petite women my size. I wonder if they find the
much younger Taiwanese woman with the waist-length, wavy
hair more attractive. I do. I'm forty-five and a mother and grandmother. Although people tell me I don't look my age, I know every

year requires more artifice. But none of this matters because I'm married and here to study Chinese ethnic minorities, not play.

My minority and international students at Houston Community College have shown me how little I know about their cultural heritages. Now, despite my husband branding my new fascination with Asia as foolhardy, I'm determined to learn more about China than what I can glean from my students and books.

Hawaii looks and smells like my idea of Eden; but even Eden, chock full of marvels, hung on a bargain. Each day double rainbows crown the valley. The blooming cassia trees on East-West Road are a chorus line of yellow petticoats. Staying in Lincoln Hall, the East-West Center guesthouse, I fantasize about living in a place where the ground is littered with blossoms instead of leaves. Mornings, I sit cross-legged in the gilded Thai pavilion near Lincoln Hall, a sacred dollhouse surrounded by snaky banyan roots. Afternoons, I journal in the manicured Japanese garden with its beaded string of koi ponds. I collect creamy plumeria blossoms — yolky at the center, their fragrance like spring grass mixed with peaches. I stick them in my hair and float them in a bowl in my room. I think how much nicer I would be if I lived in languorous Honolulu instead of parched Texas, how even I might find serenity. I've forgotten the cardinal rule from folktales: Don't taste the fruit if you plan to return to wherever you call home.

* * *

Our seminar group watches a video called "Haoles Anonymous" during the second week of our institute. A local Portuguese comedian, dressed as a Hawaiian woman in a long black wig and flowered sarong, strolls down Waikiki Beach with a clipboard. He asks people what proof sunscreen they wear, whether they put butter on their rice, and who they voted for in a local election. If they answer what he declares is "wrong," he tells them they are haole (pronounced *how-lee*) and leads them to some folding chairs near a screen that says "Haoles Anonymous." Although the group is an obvious assortment of ethnicities, he tells them they all have "Haole-itus, Caucasian Syndrome" but not to worry because "it's a stigma" and rehabilitation is possible. The theme song is a version of Randy Newman's "Short People," in which the refrain is "Don't want no Caucasians 'round here."

"Haole" is Hawaiian for foreigner, our leader explains. It's commonly used by locals as a pejorative term for white people. In our group of fifteen, the six of us who are white titter at the skit, but in that squirmy way you do when you suspect a joke is on you, or you know it is, and it stings. I ventured beyond my white, middle-class, suburban upbringing in the Pacific Northwest when I married at eighteen and moved to a small town in Arkansas. I've taught diverse groups of students in Houston for over fifteen years. Hawaii is my first taste of feeling unwelcome and intrusive, and I wonder what it's like to live where one can never belong.

The six ethnic Chinese in our group are from Shanghai, Beijing, Los Angeles, Hong Kong, and Taipei. Debates among them about proper pronunciation (*lie-chee* or *lee-chee* for "lychee") escalate to arguments about politics and policies, such as whether Taiwan is part of China or Tibet is being oppressed by the Chinese government. Listening to them, I realize I, like most Americans, have lumped all Chinese together. I wonder about the Chinese people my Russian grandparents encountered when they moved from Vladivostok, Russia, to Harbin, China, in 1921. I remember how I performed as a "Chinaman" in a dance recital when I was ten. I wore a coolie hat, an orange jacket with a mandarin collar, and wide cotton pants that my mother made.

We bowed and walked in mincing steps, and I forgot the routine halfway through.

I take copious notes and keep my head down in our seminars, hoping I can hide how little I know. With my BFA in studio art and MA in English from a public university, I feel unworthy compared to those in the group with Ivy League educations, PhDs, university positions, and published books. Looking around, I decide that the organizers had quotas: equal numbers of Chinese and not, women and men, community college teachers and university professors. I teach at a two-year college — the same lower tier that needles my marriage to a full professor from Harvard. I've recently had to train new faculty who make more money on their first day than I do after years on the job because they have PhDs. While I'm in Hawaii, I plan to finish my application to an online PhD program I'm considering. I'm determined to change my life, but I don't want to leave home to do it.

* * *

Fred and I are sunning on Magic Island, away from tourist-infested Waikiki Beach with its wall-to-wall beach towels. Our seminar is "*pau*" for the day, as they say in Hawaii, and I'm perfecting a deep tan that will cost me a fortune in skin care products and treatments in another fifteen years, but I don't care about that now. I don't care about anything except the lascivious rays of the sun, the dazzling turquoise water, the sugar-fine white sand, the thrill of being so completely and utterly outside my life in Texas. My life is nothing to complain about, but escape is still delicious.

"Look, we're the same color," Fred says as he places his smooth arm against mine. After two weeks in the sun, I now match his golden brown. On the first day of our summer institute, I noticed his brassy impudence when he entered the seminar room. I flashed on my daughter imitating the slouchy amble of jazz musicians in her college music department. Half a head taller than me, he is wide-shouldered and barrel-chested, his broad face capped by wiry, black hair. The shortest and loudest of the Chinese men in the group, he reminded me of a half-grown bear. Gibbous eyes behind wire-rimmed glasses, deep voice, cartoon character name. Not my type. I prefer tall. I married two men who towered over most of my family and whose shadows provided me the illusion of safety.

Fred made me laugh across the conference table all week, rolling his eyes at long-winded questions, imitating one person's expressive eyebrows, slipping me silly notes. He invited me to group outings, coaxed me out of my comfort zone on the sidelines, provided cover for my shyness in conversations. His social ease was a welcome change from home, where I am the default social glue, forever prodding my painfully shy husband out of corners.

At the beach, I tell Fred about my life in Houston: my house, my cats, my pride in Sorrel — my grown daughter — and my teaching. I talk about my second husband. "He's my best friend," I explain. "The smartest person I know." I'm proud of my husband's many accomplishments but embarrassed to admit he was once my folklore studies professor. I find it difficult to imagine my pale, introverted, scholarly husband in this brilliant sunlight. I've slipped out of our world of books and documentaries, ideas and careful conversations, the small comforts and potholes of ten years of marriage.

"Wow," Fred says when I tell him I married the first time at eighteen, had my daughter at twenty, went to college late and in installments. "You were so wild."

His admiration for my detours makes me squirm. "Not really," I say. "Young and foolish, maybe. It was different back then. I grew up in the hippie era."

He's five years younger than I am, which means he was in boys' schools in Hong Kong while I was nursing a baby in Arkansas. He played flute with a youth orchestra in Europe while I was serving drinks in a bar and learning about betrayal. He says in high school he played guitar in a band that performed American rock music. I laugh at some of the songs he lists. His counterculture and mine overlap then veer off in different directions.

Uncomfortable talking about my past, I change the subject and ask, "Have you been married before?" I'm at an age when many of my American friends have shed and replaced spouses. His Korean wife will arrive from California near the end of our five-week seminar. They will travel to Kauai before he goes to Singapore on sabbatical.

He looks away. "Of course not," he says. "Asians don't get divorced."

I wonder for a moment if he's judging Americans like me who do, then shift directions to something I've wanted to ask since we met. "Why don't you have a Chinese name?"

"My teacher gave me the name Frederick when I was in school. I was Freddy when I lived in England."

"And you accepted that?" As a teacher, I know how foreign students in the United States often choose English names to fit in and to avoid ridicule and mispronunciation.

"I liked it. Brits like to give everyone nicknames. My Chinese name is Cheongkong. It means 'long river.'" He sits up and brushes sand from his Lincoln Hall towel and his muscular calves. "When I was born, my mom took me to a fortune-teller, who said I didn't have enough water in my chart, so my parents named me after a famous river in China, the one you know as the Yangtze. The fortune-teller said I should stay away from water when I was a teenager, but I wouldn't, so my mom made me wear this jade to protect me." He fingers a jade disk on a thin gold chain around his neck. My girlfriends and I make jokes about men who wear gold chains, but I decide this is different.

An elderly white woman unrolls a towel nearby. We both turn to watch her. She's tall, elegant, wearing a royal blue bathing cap. She shrugs off a flowered robe with kimono sleeves to reveal a black one-piece suit over a narrow frame hung with crushed tissue paper skin. She strides into the ocean without hesitation, as if she's alone on the beach and the ocean is hers. "Isn't she beautiful?" I whisper. "I want to be her when I get old."

"Beautiful," he agrees. "I wonder what her story is." I'm used to speculating about strangers' stories only with my friend Sandra, but the more I reveal to Fred, the less I feel the need to edit. Quirky humor and random insights glimmer between us like reflections bouncing off the waves. We're both irreverent and fond of swearing. He's also a product of public schools. He has a PhD and teaches in a university, but his interest in my life story polishes my wrong turns into daring adventures.

When we can no longer stand the heat, we wade into the clear, tepid water. "I'm a lazy swimmer," I say. "Mostly, I prefer to float."

"Then float with me." I lie back, and the water buoys me, first my shoulders and then my feet. His hands starfish the small of my back, and I let him think he's helping me do what I can do just fine alone. I am suspended between sea and sky. Safe. No, unsafe. He's married, I remind myself, failing to notice I'm more protective of his boundaries than mine.

"Just float," he says. "I'll hold you."

What nonsense, I think, but I don't move away.

He'd said something similar the day we went kayaking with the group, and we were together in the only double kayak. "You don't have to paddle. Just ride like a queen." I pictured Cleopatra on a barge, then a flashing red danger light over her head. *A little romance on a tropical holiday,* I reassured myself. *What could it hurt?*

* * *

Our eyes are closed against the afternoon glare when a slender shadow falls across us and we hear, "There you are! I've been looking everywhere for you two." Fred squints at the silhouetted figure and mumbles, "Hey, Michael." He's clearly not happy to see anyone from our program, and definitely not Michael's earnest, choirboy face. Michael is grinning. Fred's ironic tone — so much like my own — is lost on him.

I know from private conversations with each of them that Michael considers Fred, who is from Hong Kong, to be hopelessly colonized, and Fred sees Michael, from Shanghai and a former Red Guard, as brainwashed by the communists. Fred ridicules how Michael pours his tea into his saucer to cool it and the way he misses or misinterprets American slang. That I've attracted these two I attribute to the fact that, other than the Taiwanese woman, I'm the only woman in the group under the age of fifty. Maybe for them my whiteness is a novelty. Whatever their reasons, their attention has undone me. I already regret letting Michael kiss me a few nights back. A momentary slip, the clutch for a familiar wall in the dark and falling instead through an open gate. Since then, he has happily trotted after me wherever I go. Now they size each other up, and I imagine for a moment they're about to drive claim stakes into my flesh.

I scramble to my feet and suggest we all go to dinner. "I could use a drink," I announce. I've grown fond of a pineapple and vodka cocktail called a Tropical Itch that comes with a Chinese back scratcher as a swizzle stick. I suggest Skoozies's, a small café in the Ward Center a few blocks away, where we can sit outside and enjoy the evening air. They agree, neither looking thrilled about being part of a threesome. I pull my wrinkled, blue linen dress over my bathing suit and shake the sand out of my sandals, then walk between Fred and Michael from the beach to the sidewalk that runs along Ala Moana Park. As we stroll down the boulevard lined with king palms and past the thicket of sailboat masts in the marina, I walk backward in front and then fall behind to keep our little triangle friendly. Beside Michael's slenderness, Fred looks burly and robust.

The psychedelic orange sun is setting low and fat over the bulge of the ocean, spreading a flamingo-pink sheen across silver-tinged waves. "I feel like I'm in a postcard, but that's crazy," I muse out loud. "Postcards are reflections of reality, not the other way around." But none of this is real. I'm someone else here, someone younger, someone daring and free, sensuous and impulsive. Someone I haven't been for a long time. I don't recognize her, this changeling. I wonder what she will do next, as if I were a character in a play.

None of us has ever seen the fabled green flash said to occur when the sun sets in Hawaii. We stop for a moment to watch the fiery orb disappear on the horizon and compare notes. So? Not this time. Me either. Maybe it's only the spots you see when you stare at the sun too long.

*   *   *

In the restaurant, I order something with fish. I'm a vegetarian but not a purist. I also order the first of three drinks, all of which come with back scratchers. Fred and Michael eye each other like attack dogs disguised as house pets, so I try to lighten the conversation by talking about myself. "You won't believe this, but when I was little, I used to believe that if I dug a hole in our yard, I would end up in China. My mom said it was on the other side of the earth, and I thought if I got there, everyone would be upside down. I started digging once, but the ground was too hard and I gave up." Michael beams as if I'm a genius, but Fred's smirk says I'm a performing poodle, cute but silly. I'm aware I'm chattering but can't stop. "If we didn't eat our broccoli, my mother would say there were starving children in China who'd love to have it. We always said fine, they could have ours."

Fred saves me from myself by butting in. "Americans are so picky. We ate everything on our plates because we knew it was all we would get." Michael is quiet, and I remember he was in solitary confinement in one of Mao's prisons. Embarrassed, I reach for my cloth beach bag and start digging to find my purse. My leather clutch is there, but no wallet. No credit card. No driver's license. I empty the bag — only towels and sunscreen and an overripe plum. "My wallet's gone!" My vodka buzz is clearing, but I feel light-headed. While I rummage through my bag again, Fred takes charge and pays the bill.

Michael is eager to help. "When did you last use your card? Do you remember seeing your wallet today?"

"I have no idea. I pulled out my wallet on the bus, so I know I had it when we got to the beach."

Fred jumps in, "Maybe you dropped it on the beach or on the way here. Let's walk back the way we came. Don't worry. We'll find it."

It's dark now, and I'm unsteady, wishing I'd stopped at one drink. The three of us cross Ala Moana Boulevard and walk back the way we came, alongside the marina, across the grassy park, with new purpose. We search everywhere and find only discarded picnic items, cigarette butts, and abandoned rubber slippers. The tide has crept in, and the beach is deserted except for a pair of lovers watching the waves from their bench, a family fishing, and a homeless man picking up discarded straw mats and looking through trashcans.

Michael asks, "Did you leave your bag on the beach when you went swimming? I've heard you should never do that." Fred and I glance at each other and look away. I did exactly that, but I deny it.

"There's a cop over there. Come on, let's report it." Fred grabs my arm and tugs me toward the officer patrolling the park. I try to look sober as I give him my name. Fred supplies the address and phone number of Lincoln Hall. All I can think is that I'll have to call my husband to get the information I need to cancel my credit cards, a thought that makes my stomach clench because I know this will require lying of one sort or another, and I hate lying.

My wallet will never be found. When I return to Texas, I will have a new photo taken, this one with a dark, Hawaiian tan. A new identity to go with my new secrets.

A few days later our group leaders send us to the Polynesian Cultural Center, which is operated by the Mormon Church. Our assignment is to critique tourist presentations of minorities. Our group splits up, and after we tour exhibits of the various island nations in Polynesia, Fred and I encounter a pair of wholesome young missionaries in muumuus who ask if we would like to tour the nearby Mormon Temple. We've spent the day deconstructing missionary representations of Polynesian culture, so seeing the underlying structure up close sounds like an adventure. The women lead us to an unmarked bus, where we join a dozen other tourists culled from the crowd. Random selection, we wonder as the bus pulls out, or something special about us?

In the visitor center of the temple, we watch a film that shows white missionaries bringing the message of Joseph Smith to the brown natives of the Pacific, who cluster around them in grateful adoration accompanied by sacred music crescendos. Fred nudges my knee and rolls his eyes. The proselytizing strikes us both as hysterically funny, and I don't dare look at him again until after we leave. Once we're outside, we erupt into peals of laughter.

We rejoin the group at a luau. Everyone but me eats kalua pig, and we all consume poi and rice before holding hands and swaying to Don Ho's hit song, "Tiny Bubbles." The final event of the evening is a Polynesian fire dance in an outdoor amphitheater. Stuck in critique mode, Fred and I mock what others are enjoying. To us, it is all inauthentic. I don't reveal that a younger, more naïve me came to the Polynesian Cultural Center with my family at age fifteen and was thrilled and charmed by her first glimpses of real Pacific culture.

When we crowd into the van to travel back to Lincoln Hall, Fred's arm is hot against mine. The others noisily share what they've seen, but Fred and I can't stop laughing. The more we try to stifle our giddiness, the more we erupt like a shaken bottle of champagne. Tears stream down my face. I've come untethered.

Back in my fourth-floor room in Lincoln Hall, I dial his room, where I've never been, and ask if I can come down. He whispers, "I wish you would." When I get there, he's waiting in the dark, and when he kisses me for the first time, I want to climb inside his skin, to be swallowed whole.

In the days that follow, he hums the aria from *Samson and Delilah* to me in the city bus. He kisses me in Chinatown by the statue that looks like a straw mushroom. He brings me melon pastries from Chinatown, the ones I will later learn are called wife cakes. We drink Baileys liqueur while sitting barefoot under a full moon. He tells me the legend of Chang'e, a beautiful lady who stole a pill of immortality from her husband and took refuge in the moon. He tells me about a rabbit who keeps her company while grinding a magic elixir with his mortar and pestle. I still see only a man in the moon. Fred laughs, stretches the corners of his eyes with his fingers, and says, "You have to have Chinese eyes." Compared to his, my view of the world seems small. I wish whatever this is between us could be my real life, but I know it's transient, a falling star.

The final week of our institute, there are seven of us at a table in a Thai restaurant. Wearing a short dress of turquoise Chinese silk, I sit across from Fred, who sits beside his newly arrived wife. She has plaited her black hair into French braids that accentuate her square face. Her braces and high, childlike voice make her seem even younger than she is, which is five years less than Fred and ten years less than me. She appears watchful. Stunned at my duplicity, I perform the nonchalance of someone I'm not, someone in a racy movie with amoral twists and turns. I have a second glass of wine to quell the jittering in my chest. I look directly at her eyes, my shy-person trick of looking without seeing a thing, while retreating to someplace in the back of my head or outside my body. I count minutes until I can disappear.

Fred's bare foot touches mine, and I'm too shocked by his boldness to move away. What is he thinking? The bigger question is who and what have I become: feminist and wife, or liar and cheat? I order another glass of wine. I swallow hard against the churn of fear and shame and impending loss. I hold off the flood by telling myself stories: *This was all a mistake, a tropical aberration, a summer storm. You can go back to Texas and forget it ever happened. You won't ever have to see these people again.*

2

Fire Gate

I'VE just landed at Singapore's Changi Airport, and the sky hasn't opened up and cast me down to the place I'd deserve if I believed in damnation. I think of myself as a compulsive truth-teller, yet I've allowed Fred to cook up an official invitation for me and two other East-West Center participants to travel to Singapore, where he's spending his sabbatical. Except there are no other participants. I got an official leave of absence from my college. I used my secret slush fund to buy an airline ticket, and I traveled twenty-one hours to see if our connection is real or I'm delusional. A shred of my former self is standing on the other side of the world, shaking her head in disbelief.

Weeks ago I asked my new therapist, whom I adore because she once offered me her Ritalin and might be a little crazy herself, "Should I go? Am I out of my mind? Am I just exchanging one set of problems for another by following a man? What if it's just infatuation? What if he changes his mind about me?"

In my first session, post-Hawaii, I'd shown her a photo of Fred and me looking tanned and happy. "I want to be her," I said. "I want to be the smiling woman in this picture." I left out that I was three sheets to the wind when the photo was taken at our end-of-seminar party and that Fred's unsuspecting wife was standing across the lanai from us when the photo was snapped. My therapist answered my frantic questions with a question: "Is it possible that you're afraid to be happy?" She reassured me that some people get their lessons from relationships, that what matters is that we pay attention to the lessons. I wonder if my therapist is a romantic caught up by my story, yet I cling to the possibility that she could be right. Maybe I am just afraid to be happy. When I asked my grandmother how she decided to marry my grandfather and move to America, she smiled and said: "I met this man, and I thought this is my life." I want her certainty. Like her, I believe in fate and big love. But now? In the middle of my complicated life?

The last time Fred saw me, I sobbed while he held me in the Honolulu airport. Deplaned in Singapore, I want to look perfect when he sees me again. I stop in the first restroom I find to touch up my makeup and brush my teeth. I swipe at my raccoon eyes and fluff my flattened hair before I follow the crowd to the customs area. The line is endless, and when I finally get to the front with my passport, the official asks for my form. "What form?" He points to the tables behind the lines. I retreat in embarrassment, fill out the customs declaration information, and begin again at the end of the line. Maybe I was asleep when they passed out the forms. I've traveled abroad only twice before this and never alone.

I'm one of the last stragglers to exit the customs area, so someone has already removed my suitcase from the carousel. In the main lobby, I see Fred standing alone near the rail. He's shorter and darker than I remember; yet I'm still drawn toward his muscular embrace. "I thought you weren't coming. I was afraid you'd changed your mind," he breathes into my ear.

"How could I?" I respond, my doubts hushed as he folds an arm around me and sweeps me toward the exit. I have a sense of safe mooring, of ballast I didn't know I was missing. We have nine days to ourselves. No hiding, no pretending like in Hawaii. We climb into a taxi, and he instructs the driver to take us to the Raj Hotel. As we hold hands in the back of the cab, my body hums like a beehive.

* * *

Our hotel is a quaint, whitewashed, colonial confection tucked into a small garden. Light from punched metal lanterns reflects off dark, polished wood floors, and picks out patterns in the oriental carpets. We take the antique cage elevator to our floor. When Fred opens the door to our room, I see a cave. I scan the walls. There are no windows. He turns on a table lamp, and as my eyes adjust to the dim light, I notice an elaborately carved headboard, dresser, and chairs in dark wood set against saffron-colored walls. A tasseled crimson print bedspread covers a bed strewn with orange satin pillows. "I feel like we're in India," I say.

"Do you like it?"

"I do, but there're no windows."

"Yeah, I know. We're on the inside of the building. It took me a long time to find this hotel, and all they had were inside rooms. Plus, they were cheaper."

"I'm a little claustrophobic," I admit. Actually, I am a lot claustrophobic, so I breathe deeply. *Cocoon*, I tell myself.

"We'll just be sleeping here anyway." He wants so much for me to be pleased.

"It's our womb with no view," I say with a smile, and when he doesn't laugh, I have to explain my reference to *A Room with a View*. "Never mind, I brought candles." Do I think I'm in a movie?

Off the bedroom is a small bathroom with a step up to a louvered door. We've never even spent a night together, and now we're in a foreign country in a windowless room with a permeable bathroom door. I try not to think about how I will maintain my dignity in such close quarters. He seems unconcerned.

As in the permanent twilight of a casino, our nights and days tumble over each other. We talk and laugh and make love and cry and make love again. Wax from the candles drips onto the furniture and the shiny floor. We bathe together and overflow the bathtub, laughing as the water sloshes and gurgles down the drain in the tiled floor. We tell each other our entire lives and compare timelines. *When I was doing this, where were you?* We construct ourselves as magnets on opposite sides of the globe, moving in tandem, waiting on different shores for this to begin. We wonder at each other's bodies. We glory in our luck at meeting. We turn the television on for background music. Singapore MTV keeps playing Alanis Morrisette singing "Thank U," a song about gratitude for what you gain when you let go. We think it's a sign. We see signs everywhere.

Fred checks the answering machine at his apartment. His sister who lives in Singapore keeps calling and wants him to call her back. His face clouds as he listens to messages from his wife, who will arrive the week after I leave. He's told everyone he's doing fieldwork and can't be reached. My daughter is with her in-laws for Thanksgiving, and my husband will feast with friends, but I feel sad about missing the holiday. I shake off thoughts that I should be cooking, my house should smell like turkey and dressing, and I should be with family.

Mornings when we don't sleep in, we sit in the hotel's tiny courtyard, where explosions of magenta bougainvillea festoon the low, whitewashed walls. Overhead, the sky is an absolute and astonishing blue. We stuff ourselves with flaky croissants slathered in butter and orange marmalade and sip espresso syrupy with raw sugar.

Emerging from the hotel at last, we wander through the city. The afternoon air is sticky hot and sweetly fragrant. Carts in the open-air markets display heaps of fruits I've never tasted. Two years ago, I traveled to Vietnam with a colleague. She had relatives to attend to, and another teacher and I, two bacteria-phobic Americans, were afraid to eat anything fresh. Now I point in wonder, and Fred is my Adam, naming the fruits of the garden. I want to try everything. Flushed-pink rose-apples, fluted Suriname cherries, jackfruit, soursop, hairy rambutan, ponderous and smelly durian. He buys a custard apple and plops the creamy white lobes onto my tongue. They taste like apples mixed with pears and honey.

*   *   *

When we dress for an evening stroll, Fred asks me not to wear the tan miniskirt I've donned with platform wedge sandals. I laugh and twitch my hips. "Seriously? You didn't mind in Hawaii."

"That was Hawaii. It's not the same here. Here I'm a Chinese guy with a white woman. I don't want people to get the wrong idea."

"What are you talking about?" I'm annoyed at being told what to wear.

"What do you think?"

"You mean people will think I'm a hooker and that you're my pimp?"

"Or maybe the tour guide. This is Asia, and you're haole," he says. I think he's being ridiculous, but I change to a longer skirt. I shake off my irritation as we step into the night air. I'm too invested in discovering our similarities to snag on the places where our experiences of the world don't coincide, too focused on us to see me or us in the eyes of others.

The smoky aroma of marinated chicken and beef sizzling on outdoor grills greets us before we arrive at the hawkers' satay stands. It's dusk, and we find a picnic table in a lane draped overhead with strings of light bulbs. Hawkers compete to bring us skewers of meat (for him) and shrimp (for me), which we eat with sauce and juices dribbling down our chins and arms.

I point at a display of large crabs just as one comes to life and begins to spider-walk away from the pile. The crab vendor lifts a cleaver and hacks the crab in half. I gasp and turn away. Fred laughs and says, "That guy was going to be someone's dinner anyway. You didn't flinch when you ate all those shrimps!"

"That's different," I insist. I grew up with a veterinarian father in a house full of animals. I'm attuned to creatures of all kinds and feel apologetic about the ones I still eat. Fred's never had a pet, and he eats everything.

Some days we go to the food court under a nearby shopping mall, taking an escalator down into a kaleidoscope of unfamiliar tastes and choices, some tantalizing, some not. The sign for the

Piggy Porky Pig Organ Soup Company displays a pig wearing a chef's hat. "Serving himself?" I wonder out loud. I avoid that and another stand that advertises frog legs served twenty different ways. At the dessert stand, I point to a picture and get a bowl of shaved ice topped with pomelo, grass jelly, and palm nuts awash in rosewater syrup. Fragrant, slippery, and sweet — I'm sipping flowers. How will I ever go home?

As we stroll through the old city, Fred tells me about the Malays, Indians, and Chinese who make up the population, and about his research on Chinese diaspora music. We eat dim sum in a Chinese restaurant, and I don't ask what is inside the luscious steamed dumplings.

We stop at a sidewalk café in Little India, where a gray tabby cat snoozes near the entrance. I'm the only woman in the teashop. Our tea is served with milk and sugar in tall glasses fitted into filigreed metal holders. The tea is so hot that I choke and spew a mouthful onto the concrete floor, and we laugh so hard my eyes stream. When the bearded men in the café turn to stare at us, we duck out, still laughing. When I catch my breath, I worry that maybe we intruded into a place where women aren't welcome, but Fred, at home anywhere, shrugs it off. We float inside a bubble of light. This city is ours. We head for the temples.

The sky-blue Hindu temple is covered with figures that look like they're made of papier-mâché. Inside, we sit on a bench alongside a courtyard and watch a woman in a green silk sari bathe a statue of Lord Ganesha, the elephant-headed god who removes obstacles. She dips a long-handled ladle into the pool at his feet, then, chanting, pours the water over his head. When she turns, she sees us and smiles. Reaching into a cloth bag, she hands each of us a ball the size of an orange. When we look puzzled, she gestures that we should eat it, then dips her head to us and walks away. I take a tentative nibble, and the treat is both sweet and tart, like dates mixed with lemons. "Tamarind," Fred says after biting into his. "We've been blessed. Let's go get our fortunes at the Guanyin temple." It's only a short walk to Chinatown.

Unlike the tranquil Hindu temple, the dragon-encrusted Guanyin temple in Chinatown bustles with activity. Stands sell long-stemmed lotus blossoms and bundles of incense of all sizes, from sticks to pillars. Petitioners bow and poke incense into bronze censers on either side of the huge open doors. A stratus cloud of sweet smoke hovers over the courtyard. From within comes a rhythmic clatter, like broken dishes being shaken in a bag.

In the deep red interior of the temple, light seems to emanate from the gilded wall at the rear. A towering and many-armed figure of Guanyin, the goddess of mercy, gleams golden in the center. She's surrounded by sword-wielding guardians, also gilded. Every surface behind and around these figures is gold. In front of the gods, rows of kneeling supplicants shake bamboo cylinders the size and shape of oatmeal canisters. "What are they doing?" I whisper.

"Fortunes. I'll show you. Wait here." Fred steps up to a counter on the right side of the temple and comes back with a container filled with narrow bamboo sticks. He hands it to me.

"Just one?" I ask. "Where's yours?"

"We'll share. We're in this together, you know."

"Do you know how to do this?" I've consulted the *I Ching* many times, but always with coins. I have no idea what to do with these sticks.

"I've seen it done a lot, and I asked the guy." Afraid of being judged an ignorant tourist, I would never have asked. Fred is an insider with no such fear. "First, we have to find a spot," he says. "How about over there?"

He finds us two flat cushions in an empty section of the floor. As we kneel, I note that I'm the only non-Chinese in the temple. Afraid of looking like an intruder, I lean toward Fred in case anyone thinks I don't belong here. "Hold it like this," he says, tipping the canister at an angle with the sticks pointing at the gods. "You make a wish or ask a question, then you shake the can gently until one stick falls out."

"What if more than one falls out?"

"Then you start over. Now make sure you wish first." I pause for a moment, then shake and shake along with all the others around us. "Shake harder," he says when I'm making no progress. So I do, and one stick clatters to the floor.

"Now what?" My wish was nebulous, along the lines of *Where do we go from here?*

We walk to the counter where the elderly temple attendant takes my stick and opens one of the many numbered drawers lining the wall behind him. He hands Fred a small pink slip of paper covered in Chinese characters. "What does it say?" I ask.

"It's like poetry, so you have to interpret it." He reads silently, then says, "It says a period of one year and then good fortune." A moment later he adds, "It literally says that the lotus passes through the fire gate but remains unharmed. It's us, baby. We'll be OK." I fold the paper and tuck it into an inner pocket of my new wallet.

* * *

Fred is sitting up in bed and crying when I wake on our last morning together. Having left the Raj Hotel, we're nested in his rented apartment, barely big enough for his single bed and desk. He makes me Nescafé 3-in-1 coffee from a paper tube, and we drink it from cracked mugs while sitting on the bed.

Soon I'm crying too. "I want to live with you," I blurt although I haven't dared to think it. His wife will arrive from California in a few days. My husband and cats wait for me at home. Fred and I have lives and jobs in separate states.

"Me too," he says. He lifts his flute out of its case to play me a piece of classical music. I don't know what to say because I know nothing about classical music, and in the face of the unknown, all we can do is sit still.

3

Eat Vinegar

My husband leans against the kitchen counter, which is too high for someone my size, sighs, and says, "I don't think we can do this anymore."

"Do what?"

"Live together." It's early evening, and he's holding a Miller Lite, his courage in a can. Since I returned from Singapore, we've been riding opposing currents through our small house in the Houston Heights.

I take a deep breath and feel my heart slow from tap dance to trepidation. This is way too easy, so I'm worried. "What do you mean?" I speak slowly, trying to stretch the time before I have to hear him out.

He gazes toward the enclosed porch where his half-blind Catahoula lolls in a sunbeam. "I think we love each other too much to live together anymore." I think that is the most saccharine thing I've ever heard, but it's a lifeline and I take hold. Eventually, its sweetness will seep inside me and sprout stems and leaves. For now I am stunned, a bird frozen on its perch when the cage door is flung open.

That evening, we drive to Auntie Chang's Dumpling House in River Oaks, and the hostess seats us near the door instead of at our standard table by the window. We order our usual: two baskets of steamed vegetable dumplings to share and General Tso's chicken for him, extra hot. He orders a beer, and I have Japanese plum wine over ice because I don't know it doesn't go with Chinese food. We pick at the dumplings as we comb through the debris of our marriage. We shape quiet, tidy sentences, planning whom we must tell, what we will say. We avoid the question of who will leave and who will stay in the house. My daughter from my first marriage, Sorrel, is coming at Christmas with her husband and their toddler, and we have to warn her about our decision.

We continue our conversation the next evening at Jade Sushi. We order sushi plates, and, like a nervous tic, I want to laugh that we are prying our American marriage apart in Asian restaurants. We decide to preserve appearances through Christmas. We'll have a last holiday as a family and split up at New Year. I'll drive to Dallas after Christmas to stay with Sorrel, and he'll move out. We'll talk to someone about our finances and split things half and half. I'll talk to a friend who has a lawyer. We'll be civil, treat each other with love and care. On our remaining nights together, we curl around each other like dead leaves, his face to my back and mine to the window and beyond.

* * *

The day after New Year, I leave Dallas for Houston in the early morning dark because I always love how I feel when sunrise finds me on my way to wherever I'm going. There are few cars on the road, and I have a sense of beginnings. As I hit I-45, that wide band of blacktop that zips through Texas, the rim of the sky gleams; then I see the moon and gasp. Fat and low above the horizon, an enormous blue-black disk rests in a slim silver bowl of light. I pull off the freeway to take it in and hear my husband's learned voice as I name it out loud: the new moon with the old moon in her arm. Me and the moon, here in the pre-dawn of a new year. Thank you, I whisper to the darkness and the coming dawn. I rest my hands on the steering wheel and try to remember. Robert Burns? No, a Child ballad. Something about a shipwreck. My second husband, who has taught me so much about literature and folklore, would know, but I can't ask him now. No matter, I'm fizzing with hope and the thrill of starting fresh. I crank up Lyle Lovett on the radio as I fly across the Texas flatlands, heading for Houston and the future.

* * *

A month after my divorce is final, Fred says, "I can't do this any-more." His voice is husky, barely audible over the phone. I haven't talked to him in three days, a lifetime for us. It's three p.m. Texas time, one o'clock in California. He's in a tiny garage apartment a few blocks from the beach in Morro Bay, the one he rented after his wife threw him out and changed the locks when she found out about us. I'm in my kitchen.

"Can't do what? What do you mean?" My voice sounds too tight, too high. I swallow hard and lean into the tiled counter during the long pause before he answers.

"This. Us."

"What are you saying?" Silence. "Are you there? Where are you?"

"Sitting on the floor."

"You're tired. I know moving out was hard, but it'll get better." Don't plead, I tell myself.

"I. Just. Can't. Mary and Nancy are coming to get me." When the line goes dead, I stand in my empty kitchen with the silent phone in my hand. Sinking to the floor, I put my head on my knees. Nancy is his Japanese-American friend from the local symphony. She and her mother, Mary, have taken him in since his wife started her campaign of public shaming, calling his family and colleagues and friends to expose his lies and infidelity, amassing a moral army against him. "The Korean way," he had sighed when I expressed disbelief that anyone would invite the outside world to take part in what I saw as a private issue. "Shame and blame," he adds. A Vietnamese friend once told me how, in her mother's time, if a woman in the village was discovered in an adulterous affair, the other women would jump her in the marketplace, strip her naked, and cut off her hair. We had laughed at how ludicrous this scene seemed in our modern world. Not so funny now.

It's our first rupture since he confessed that he, too, had been married twice: a lie of omission, but one I wasn't certain I could forgive. In the storm of explanations and apologies that followed, I'd had to consider that perhaps my assumptions that wrong turns are nothing to be ashamed of and screwups should be aired are both generational and Western. That Asian notions of propriety and saving face were reticent apples to my confessional oranges.

When his current wife said she would take him back, I asked, "Why would she want you if you're as terrible as she's been telling everyone?"

"Eating vinegar," he explained. "In Asia, to swallow bitterness is considered noble." The heroic long-suffering woman trope appalls me, yet I have to admit the idea isn't confined to Asia. How many unhappily married former friends have judged me since I left my marriage?

In the bleak days and weeks that follow, Sandra, my older and wiser friend, tells me what I don't want to hear: "You know what you have to do."

"Not call?"

"Exactly. You have to let him go. If he's yours, he'll come back to you."

"I hate that."

"I knew you would."

At the art supply store, I buy stickers — gold stars and an assortment of birds. A star on my calendar for every day I don't call. A bird for not mailing letters I write — not easy when Fred and I have talked more than once every day for months and mailed each other heaps of feverish love letters. My calendar becomes a starry sky, an aviary. I burn incense in front of the concrete Guanyin I purchased at a neighborhood antique store. I have no faith in my choices, so I'm afraid to ask for what I want. Instead, I pray for the strength to go on no matter what. My will to thy will.

My friend Eddie consoles me in the aftermath of the breakup. On the nights I drive him home from the English department to his mysterious apartment under the Chinatown freeway, it's OK to cry. Last year Eddie accompanied me to Houston's Vietnamese and Chinese temples for a fieldwork job I picked up for extra cash, and it was Eddie who persuaded me to apply for the China program where I met Fred. One night, as I blubber about what I'm going to do with my post-divorce life, he reminds me I have dreams bigger than my heartbreak. "What about grad school?" he asks. "I know you gave up on the online idea, but weren't you accepted at the University of Hawai'i last year?"

"Yeah, but with no money. Besides, I chose American Studies because Asian Studies would've required me to learn an Asian language. I'm too old for that."

"You also picked it because it was interdisciplinary. There are plenty of places to look for money." He reminds me he used to work in the university library.

The next day he shows me how to look up fellowships for graduate school. "How about the East-West Center?" he asks. "They have fellowships for the University of Hawai'i."

"I know the directors. I suppose it's worth a try."

"And there's a field study in China too. Apply for both and see what happens!"

Divination

I'VE been weeping every waking hour for three days when my therapist forgets our regular appointment. I'm crushed because she is my life raft right now. She calls to apologize and ask if I can come in tomorrow, Saturday morning. She tells me she had a dream last night about something she wants to try, something she wouldn't do with just any client but that seems right for me. She instructs me to bring four objects when I come to her office: one that represents my past, one for where I am, one for what I want to bring into my life, and one for where I want to go. I choke out my meek assent.

By morning, my face is a red, puffy mess no makeup can disguise. I have lizard eyes, and my sinuses are so clogged I can breathe only through my mouth. I've reverted to my crybaby childhood. My mother, a former nurse, said I was the only child she ever took to a doctor for non-physical reasons. My mother read Dr. Spock's book on child care, her generation's bible for child-rearing, which advised mothers to let babies cry and to feed them on a schedule. There was no chapter on how to quiet a daughter who wailed day and night, who startled at every sound and was born with a hungry heart. She said she couldn't take me anywhere when I was a toddler because everything made me cry. Frustrated with my waterworks, she paddled me with a wooden spoon, saying, "This will give you something to cry about!" In fifth grade, my teacher sent me to the counselor. When he asked, "Why do you cry so much?" I had no answers, no way to say that the world was just too sad, too sharp, too fraught, too much. That everything hurt.

Over the years, I shored up my soggy vulnerability with dry humor and an internal wooden spoon. I still leak tears when I'm angry, but I now hate to cry. It messes up more than my mascara. When I met Fred, the tides surged. Now that we're apart, I'm a sodden mess. I can't stop. I cry because something with corners or claws has come unmoored inside me and is rattling about like a wandering womb.

I shuffle around my recently shared house, picking up and putting down objects, searching for ones that will speak. A little jade Guanyin. A small, balding Indian doll in a beaded buckskin vest. A red resin Chinese dragon. Stymied on the fourth, I choose three objects instead of one: two silver *milagros* from Mexico — a lamb and a pig — and a paintbrush. Nothing feels right.

My therapist arrives at her office just as I do, frowsy in jeans and a T-shirt instead of her usual work attire. She opens the door and turns on the light. I am leaky plumbing.

Inside the small room, she pushes her rocker into a corner, slides the loveseat against the wall. She lights a sage smudge stick and waves its resiny smoke around the room. "Did you bring your objects?"

I nod and blow my nose.

"I'm not sure exactly how this goes," she says as she arranges four pillows in a square on the floor. "I saw it like this — you were here, in the middle." She sets a red silk pillow in the center of the others, plops down a box of tissues, and beckons me over. I kneel on the red pillow, setting my bag in front of me. I feel ridiculous and desperate and small-child hopeful because I am so tired of crying and talking. I want magical intervention, a map.

"You'll have to help me with this," she continues. "I want you to put an object at each of the four points, but you'll have to tell me where the objects go and in what order."

Great, I think, *isn't she the therapist?* But I say, a frog croaking from the bottom of a well, "It's the Celtic cross from the tarot."

"Good. Where do you want to start?" she says.

I empty my bag and arrange my objects on the carpet near my knees. "This is where I am now," I whisper, mopping at my streaming nose.

She prods, "Where are you now, and what represents that to you?"

I reach into my bag and pull out the little goddess figure. I'd given Fred a matching one. "Safe," I say, feeling anything but.

She urges, "Can you say that in a positive sentence?"

What am I? Five? I clutch the cool stone in my palm. I picture a Buddha hand under me, under the world. "I'm safe. I can't fall. I'm protected."

"That's true. Now, where does it go?"

I place the Guanyin on the pillow behind me. A phrase surfaces from various tarot reading instructions: *This is the basis of the situation.*

"What's next?" she asks. I pull out my Indian doll. She is four inches tall, ceramic, dark-skinned with the round face and belly of a toddler, her gaze askance — in coyness, perhaps, or timidity. Her black hair, like her red maryjanes and white socks, is painted on. A few scraggles of black yarn attach to the top of her head. She wears tan leather breeches and a red vest decorated with beads, and I have reattached her legs to her torso with a piece of grosgrain ribbon. Her pants won't stay up. I hold her on my open palm as if she were a cockroach.

"What does this doll mean to you?" the therapist asks.

"She was my first doll. For my first birthday."

"How do you feel about her?"

"I want to smash her. I want to throw her at the wall." *Where did that come from?* I am crying jaggedly, trying to catch my breath.

"Take a deep breath. Now hold her in your hand and come up with a positive sentence about your past."

There is a long silence before anything comes to me. "I'm more than my wounds."

"Yes. You can visit the past, but you can never stay there. You're always beyond the past." I set the doll on the pillow to my left. *This is behind you.* The tarot formula again, but I keep this spark to myself to consider later.

"Now what?" she prompts. "What do you want to bring into your life?"

"I'm not sure." I reach for my paintbrush and *milagros*.

"What are those about?"

I hold up the paintbrush. "Painting? Creativity? Being an artist? And these," holding up the tiny silver pig and lamb, "Maybe not putting a man's needs before my own?" I'd chafed at my ex calling me his lamb when I wanted to be fierce, at how he reverted to the third person and baby talk when I wanted to feel equal. Fred called me his beautiful dragon after my Chinese astrological sign — a water dragon to his fire rooster.

"A sentence?" she prods. I shake my head, dabbing at my eyes and nose. Nothing comes, so I put the *milagros* on the pillow in front of me, and we move on. *This crowns you and could come into being.* For the moment, the top card is my future drawing a big, fat blank.

"And the last thing?" She points to the dragon.

"A dragon for yang energy," I answer with less quaver now.

"In a sentence? What does it suggest to you? You don't have to believe it completely, not yet."

After several false starts, I say, "I want to be fearless. I am fearless." I'm not fearless, and I know it. I'm scared shitless. I place it on the pillow to my right. *This is ahead of you: the card that leads forward even if I don't know where I'm going.*

When I leave the therapist's office, I am muted and parched. I will sleep and sleep. I will not know that what we conjured today will congeal into map and mantra. That each stuck place in the months and years ahead will cause me to revisit and polish my compass points until they gleam.

I am protected.

I am wise.

I am brave.

My north, what I want to bring into my life, will come later and last: *I am worthy.*

I don't believe any of this, but someday, not soon, I will realize my mended doll's expression is more shy than coy. I will place her in a special box beneath my Guanyin altar. Later, I will take her out and give her an honored place in my writing room. For now, I need the courage to face the changes I've set in motion.

5

Water Dragon

IN May, Fred meets me in San Diego, where I've traveled from Houston for a college conference. We spend a long weekend gingerly trying to recover from our silence, careful as if we might shatter apart again. I carefully worded my invitation to meet me at my San Diego conference, our first communication since the breakup, to allow him to turn me down. I bought a guidebook to the city and made plans to entertain myself in the off hours in case he said no.

As we wander through Balboa Park, he tries to explain his retreat. "She said she wanted a second chance, that I wasn't being fair. We had dinners once a week for a while."

"You mean like dates?"

"Dates that always turned into fighting. Now at least she knows it can never work." We sit on a bench near the Japanese garden and hold hands, weighted by the pain we've caused. A hummingbird zooms toward us and stops, whirring inches from our faces before flitting away. *Another sign*, we say, but where will it lead? How will this ever work with half the country between us?

In Hawaii, he'd slipped me a note that said "*Monkey is under the mountain.*" I'd told him I loved the classic Chinese saga *Journey to the West*, in which the king of the monkeys tricks the gods to gain immortality and then brags to Buddha that he's the equal of all the gods. To punish Monkey for his arrogance, Buddha places him under a mountain until he's given a chance to redeem himself by escorting a monk bringing Buddhist scriptures from India across China. Fred felt pinned under the mountain of my hesitations. Now I wonder if we, like Monkey, have dared to jump too high, if we've wanted too much and caused too much collateral damage.

I have two important pieces of news to share with him. The East-West Center has accepted me into a five-week field study in China this summer. I've also received an EWC fellowship for graduate school at the University of Hawai'i. I'm taking a sabbatical from my college and moving to Honolulu for two years. I'm moving on with my life.

* * *

The China field study is a temple tour, and I love sacred spaces despite my being a defector from organized religion. The Scandinavian simplicity of the Lutheran church of my youth — open-trestle ceiling, bare pews, amateur choir — made my spirit squirm. Perhaps it was my grandmother's Russian orthodoxy that sang in my veins when I visited Mexican colonial churches in my twenties. It wasn't God I encountered there so much as a sense of imminence. I soaked up the jeweled light, the flickering candles, the heady incense, the macabre figures in agony or rapture. Still, my itchy-footed soul murmured, *You don't belong here.* It longed for something less mediated, something I'd glimpsed in the Chinese temples of Houston and Singapore. After all the reading and study, I am eager to experience China firsthand. I plan to share every detail with Fred on my return.

When I arrive at the airport in Beijing, students from Peking University whisk me by taxi to the university guesthouse. Our group comprises eight men and four women, all white Americans who teach in the humanities or social sciences. Jenn, my roommate, is a young redhead from Providence. Like her, the leaders of our group — a self-important professor of Chinese history and a quiet, hollow-cheeked Chinese literature grad — are both in their thirties. They are the only Chinese speakers in the group, and we soon discover from the way most Chinese look blankly at the professor when he speaks that we will have to rely on our local guides for communication. The men, a tall, bearded lot, spark curiosity in the narrow streets of the old city when we venture out. People dare their children to tug the hair on their arms and chins.

* * *

Leaving massive Beijing, with its splendid Forbidden City, for Hebei, Anhui, and Fujian provinces, we journey to a Tibetan lamasery and so many Taoist and Buddhist temples we lose track of their names. We pass between gate guardians with ferocious faces and deadly weapons and across courtyards dotted with waist-high incense censers. We're told to step over the high thresholds that keep the qi — life force or energy — from spilling out the temple doors. We stand behind the short railings and cushions where worshippers can kneel before the gods. Coils of incense and embroidered banners dangle from ceilings blackened by decades of rising smoke. I look with longing at the orange-robed monks and praying figures as we traipse back to our bus. The scent of sandalwood clings to my hair and clothes. I want to linger in these spaces, to be more than a voyeur.

At the Taoist temples, gilded dragons slither across tiled roofs, snake up entrance pillars, and hold enormous pearls in their jaws. I spot the monkey king wielding his magic staff. In one village, we visit a temple where painted celestial dragons swarm the ceiling of a small room containing a sacred well. I'm a water dragon in the Chinese zodiac, so I pay the attendant for a fortune. Our guide translates the pink slip of paper to say, "*You must work hard. You think too much.*" I'm disappointed that it says nothing grand about love and upheaval. I asked for divine guidance but got a lecture I'd expect from my mother.

On an overnight train from north to south, we are shelved on narrow bunks stacked three deep, six to a compartment. I have a top bunk near a small window. I try to calm my claustrophobia by staring out the window until an intimidating train matron comes by and snaps all the blinds closed with a long-handled tool that looks like a whip. She will be back to snap them open first thing in the morning, in concert with fluorescent lights and blaring loudspeakers. Seven a.m. sharp. I pass Fred's parting advice on to my bunkmates: "Never put anything in your pockets you wouldn't want to lose, don't look down, and always wear shoes!" When I'd asked him for an explanation, he laughed and said, "You'll see." I put off going to the bathroom as long as I can, but at last I brave the hall as the train creaks and sways. Two of the philosophers sit on benches in the hallway, heads and arms propped on the tiny fold-down tables. One of them looks up and whispers that he's too tall to fit in his bunk.

I open the door to the WC with trepidation and spot the reason for Fred's cautions. The toilet is a hole in the floor, under which is the dizzying rush of tracks. On either side of the hole is a low wall rail, which I assume is to steady passengers and keep us from pitching onto the floor or against a wall while poised above the hole. Pulling down my pants and positioning myself is no easy feat, and it looks like more than a few passengers have tried and failed to hit their target.

"How was it?" Jenn asks when I return.

"Keep your shoes on and your eyes up," I answer, resolved to drink nothing for the rest of the train ride.

At the beginning of the second week of travel in rural areas, Jenn and I start a list we call "Things We Hate About China." We record everything that strikes us as unsavory or just plain weird. As the list expands, we add commentary:

- honking — doesn't anyone use brakes?
- spitting — just swallow!
- staring/laughing/pointing — we are not a freak show
- space issues — why do people have to get so damn close?
- nose picking and blowing — ew!
- hawkers — stop following us and thinking we are rich
- loudspeakers — we can't think!
- gross toilets, etc., no toilet paper — no words for this
- orange towels — they belong in service stations
- coffee issues — Nescafé is not coffee
- beer and no wine — yes, we are spoiled Americans

The truth is, I feel a little ashamed about the list and a teensy bit smug compared to the Asia virgins in our group. I have a Chinese boyfriend, and I've been to Vietnam, where I braved rustic bathrooms, ate in restaurants with in-house pigs, and encountered maimed beggars and aggressive hawkers. There I felt the squeamishness and culture shock my colleagues are now experiencing. My ears rang day and night from the constant blare of horns used for greetings and instead of brakes. Being the same size as the Vietnamese women (in height if not girth) and having similar coloring spared me from the constant attention of rural people spotting their first foreigners. My chubby colleague with prematurely white hair became an unwilling celebrity. Now red-headed Jenn is the exotic other and target of curiosity.

Our hosts serve us banquets with enough dishes to stuff the emperor and his court, obscene amounts of food that we worry will go to waste. We try and fail to clean our plates even after we've been told repeatedly that Chinese hosts would be ashamed to not serve more food than we can eat. Our American mothers' voices in our heads are louder. We're served mountains of dumplings, each neatly pleated into a half-moon and filled with morsels of pork or vegetables. We leave hills of them behind.

Basking in my newly mended relationship with Fred, I prompt Jenn to start a "Perfect Man" list because she has just gone through a breakup. I jest that I always start with the requirement that his mother be dead or in a foreign country. I brag that I scored this time because Fred's family is in Hong Kong. All my previous lists included tall and handsome, and Fred is neither. When I say I wish he and I had met sooner, he says I would never have looked at him back then. He's probably right, but I take it as personal progress that his Happy Buddha face is my new handsome.

Days later and on yet another bus, I whisper, "Bad teeth," to Jenn. "I'm putting it on the China list." Our jovial driver speaks no English, and his grin reveals a few black stumps and a lot of space. In our search for quaint village temples, he drives us down rutted country roads that shake our bones loose. He honks enthusiastically, aggressively at every driver, donkey cart, doddering grandmother, and bicyclist loaded down with sticks or ducks we pass along the way. We greet him each morning with "*Ni hao*," and he beams back at us, baring tobacco-stained gums and running his hand over the spiky black quills of his hair. Using hand gestures, he shows us how to examine bottles of water for pinholes that indicate they've been refilled. At rest stops, he performs. He juggles steel balls for us, making them spin like planets. He twirls a bamboo pole like a drum majorette, then grins and takes a bow as we applaud.

Ashamed of how I pre-judged our entertainer and protector, I remember a talk I heard at my college about "boutique multiculturalism." A literary critic berated educators for their tendency to skim other cultures for their savory, tame, and decorative bits; to congratulate themselves for our tolerance and appreciation while being selective and judgmental about anything too different or unattractive. *Yes* to music and dance and food, *no* to people. *Yes* to juggling, *no* to bad teeth. Isn't this what I've been doing with our list of complaints and judgments? Easy to preach tolerance in my classrooms when I have my American comforts nearby and a decaf latte in my hand.

When our driver stops our van by the side of a dirt road in a small village, our local guide informs us we're scheduled to visit a peasant house. Suddenly everyone talks at once. *What? Do they know we're coming? Won't they be offended? No way! I'm staying in the bus!* We're appalled by the poverty we've seen along the way. No matter how meager our salaries or circumstances at home, we feel rich by comparison, and the thought of educated Americans dropping in on a family of peasants is mortifying. Then I recall an incident in Vietnam where our party of four was invited to a peasant home for an evening. We — the two white American women — worried that we would be out of place and that they couldn't afford to entertain us. Our Vietnamese-American colleague said, "There's no need for you to go. They're only peasants." We abstained, only to be told later that the family had prepared gifts and all the neighbors looked in the windows to see us. We — all of us — had misread the situation, and in trying to be considerate, we'd caused the family to lose face. After I relate my story in the bus, we all climb out and file into the village house. We sit on the floor, smile awkwardly, and drink strong tea so the family can look us over and have a story to tell their neighbors.

The family members sit on a tiled platform that I suspect is heated in the winter, and I wonder if it's like the stoves my great-grand-parents might have had in Russia. I think of my grandmother, who said her father joined the military to send his children to school, that peasants didn't educate their children. I remember her saying that at the end of a meal they washed their dishes in the water left in the samovar at the end of the table. "Such barbarians we were," she laughed. Fred and I have joked about how we both come from peasant stock and working-class backgrounds — my mother grew up on a dairy farm, and my father was the son of an immigrant tailor. Our families made great economic leaps in a generation or two. Might not these Chinese peasants do the same? If we professors were to dig back into our respective genealogies, how many of us would come up carrying the tools of trades we now consider beneath us?

On one of the last days of our journey, we visit a small temple in Fuzhou dedicated to Mazu, the goddess of the sea. We are in her home temple, set into a hillside overlooking the Taiwan Strait. Inside, our guide translates as the temple attendant shows us murals depicting the goddess's life and miracles. In one scene, Mazu appears as a lone figure on a craggy cliff to save sailors from drowning. In another, she offers a soup bowl to an elderly woman. The attendant explains that Mazu was such a filial daughter that she carved out a piece of her own arm to make soup for her sick mother. Steeped in American independence and having lived away from home since I was eighteen, I can't imagine such devotion.

The eldest of four, I pitched toward escape from an early age. From niceness in the form of church, Campfire Girls, home economics, and respectability. From keeping my knees crossed, my emotions in, my questioning in check. It was the sixties, and my friends and I didn't know how to invent ourselves as women, only that we didn't want to be Betty Crocker or live our mothers' lives. At sixteen, I ran away for the first time. At seventeen, I sneaked out every night. At eighteen, I married a hippie musician and waved goodbye from a bus. My emotional armor became a second skin. I forgot how to take it off and eventually forgot it was there at all. All this to say, I have been the opposite of a Chinese filial daughter.

The attendant leads us out of the temple and up a staircase to a smaller building above, where the multipurpose saint-turned-goddess, like a divine Barbie, has her own dressing room, traveling outfits, and a special palanquin. The attendant explains that she even gets her own airline seat when she travels to her satellite temple in Taiwan.

Back at the temple entrance, I ask our local guide if I can burn incense. She questions a tiny old woman, who smiles so deeply the lines in her face swallow her eyes. When I give her a few coins, she pulls a bundle of incense out of a basket beside her and confers with the guide. "She wants to show you how to make offerings," the guide says I dip my head to the old woman as she lights the incense sticks by holding their tips against the ones already burning in the censer until they flare and release tendrils of sweet smoke. Miming, she waves for me to follow her around the courtyard and demonstrates how I must hold the incense high against my forehead and bow low three times before I place each burning stick in a censer. We bow to each of the four directions, then step over the temple threshold. Inside, she shows me how to bow again before the central deity, a seated figure wearing an elaborate headpiece with a beaded veil that falls to her chin. Mazu is both a traveler and a guardian of those who set sail into uncharted waters. I pray for safe passage in my upcoming transitions.

6

Spirit House

HALE MANOA, one of two East-West Center dormitories next to the University of Hawai'i campus, was designed by I.M. Pei for communalism — a concept I would have resisted had I known before I moved in for grad school. At forty-six, I'm a late bloomer, perennially out of synch with most of my peers. I attended college late and later, both times as a single mom. I've never lived in a dorm.

Between every two floors of Hale Manoa's rows of double windows (covered in beige curtains and an occasional beach towel) is an open floor with a taller profile. These openings are a series of lanais (balconies) that run the length of the building, where east and west are translated to landmarks — Diamond Head or Ewa in island terms. The open floors are perforated by passages that run from *mauka* (mountain) to *makai* (ocean). At ground level, surrounded by lush greenery, walls of glass reveal common areas: a large gathering space, a lobby, and game rooms.

On the in-between floors are communal kitchens, sheltered only by the open lanais facing the mountains. Each kitchen has multiple ranges and sinks under banks of cupboards with common, mostly unusable, utensils. Above each sink, its screen trap often clogged with questionable debris, is a paper sign reading, "Do Not Spit in the Sink!" On the rumbly old refrigerator, another sign says, "Do Not Steal Other People's Food!" I live on the twelfth floor, Ewa end, where I share a kitchen with students from around the Pacific Rim and across the United States.

On a typical late-fall evening, a fine soft mist billows in over the railing but deters no one from cooking and eating. A breeze from the Koʻolau Mountains stirs together aromas of fish sauce and ginger, miso and soy sauce, dal, and garlic, lots of garlic. At the stove nearest the entrance, a square-shouldered, taciturn Thai man in his thirties stands over a large wok. He adds lemongrass, garlic stems, and small red peppers to a pungent curry that hisses and sizzles. Midway back, a fortyish Indian woman in a sari unstops the valve on her pressure cooker, releasing a geyser of steam that makes everyone jump. Three young Japanese men stand around the far stove, cooking hot dogs on an electric burner as if it were a hibachi. Another young Japanese man, wearing a white T-shirt and a flowered sarong, saunters in and reprimands them in Japanese. A lone Chinese man sits at the far table on the lanai, slurping ramen noodles from a saucepan. At the other end, a Japanese wife sets out small dishes of fish, pickled vegetables, miso soup, and salad before sitting down to eat with her Japanese-American husband. At a long middle table, several young Vietnamese women laugh while sharing a steaming bowl of pho and a plate of rice-paper-wrapped shrimp rolls. Welcome to the heart of Hale Manoa.

Although I've met several of the people in my unit, I'm as inexpert at inserting myself into counter space as into conversations. I'm not the only white American or older student, but we're a minority, so I'm often the only one of either category in the kitchen. I feel conspicuous and out of place. My years of teaching students from around the world have not prepared me to be a peer. There are people from countries in Asia I've never been, such as Indonesia and Cambodia, and places in the Pacific I've never even heard of, like Yap and Chuuk. Everyone but me seems to speak at least three languages. Twice the age of most of the students and a college-teacher-turned-college-student, I'm between lives and homes, a beginner again in all things, including love and cooking for one. My small-child shyness returns full force, and I retreat to my room and take solo walks.

The week I move in, Fred arrives from California to help. We purchase a small refrigerator that fits under my desk, so I don't have to share the large, unhygienic one in the kitchen. He buys me an against-house-rules Crock-Pot to cook vegetarian stews that I reheat in my room for the rest of the week. He stays through the first week of school, walking me to all my classes, his arm wrapped tight around my shoulders. When he introduces himself to my professors, some younger than either of us, I feel like I'm being escorted by a big brother. I suggest that his presence isn't necessary, that I need to meet my teachers on my own. His eyes widen in surprise, then he looks hurt. "I just wanted to see your new life. I wanted to picture where you'll be." I can't explain how the insecurity of starting school again and his collegiality with my professors stirs up the same sense of insecurity that made me want a PhD.

I'm as unnerved by the bathrooms as I am by the kitchens. Stairways funnel up or down from the kitchen floors to tiny garret rooms arranged in blocks. In the center of each block is a bathroom cube with three sinks, toilet stalls, and showers. On each side is a swinging door, and beside each door is a hanging wooden sign printed "Women" on one side and "Men" on the other. In theory, one flips two signs to the appropriate gender when entering, and those of the opposite gender wait until the room is vacant. In practice, this system seldom works because flipping both signs upon entering and leaving is too much to remember for a student in a hurry. And then there are the cultural differences. Some stalls still have old "Do Not Stand On The Toilet Seat" and "Flush After Every Use" signs to remind students from places with squat and trench toilets to follow American etiquette. We've all heard stories about footprints on toilet seats.

Residents respond to the bathrooms according to cultural experience. A few of the living units have double rooms for which married couples can apply, and the Japanese-American husband with the Japanese wife stands guard each morning because she's too nervous to shower alone. To move out, they must convince the dean that the lack of privacy endangers their marriage. There have twice been reports of young men holding mirrors above or below shower or toilet stalls occupied by women. In both cases, the men came from conservative places where unmarried men and women don't share public spaces, much less bathrooms. Students from extended families and communal cultures, former Peace Corps workers, backpackers, hostel travelers, and students on educational leave from West Point are in their element. I, on the other hand, am fresh out of a house of my own. I rise at five thirty every morning, carefully flip signs on both sides of the bathroom, and speed-shower before anyone else in my unit gets up. I put up a mirror in my room rather than do my grooming at the co-ed sinks.

Single rooms in Hale Manoa are part of our fellowship deal, along with tuition at the University of Hawai'i and a modest stipend. Each room measures fourteen feet deep by seven feet wide. A single bed and a desk fill all but a narrow band of concrete floor between the door and the window. The rooms are bare and spare, and, because sound rises and carries oddly in Hawaii, roaring motorcycles on East-West Road sometimes sound like they are motoring over my bed. I leave the double windows that fill the end wall open to my stunning view of the mountains. Two lime-green geckos, who have taken up residence near the ceiling, keep me company, while the giant roaches that skulk and skitter in the lower-floor kitchens and lanais don't ascend to the upper floors. I create an altar on the single shelf above my bed — a small Guanyin statue and some incense — and hang a poster of Hokusai's *The Great Wave off Kanagawa* on the opposite wall.

My ivy-covered, cat-filled house in Houston seems like a movie or a half-remembered dream. Here in my cubbyhole, there is nothing to plant, nothing to clean, no one to care for. Nothing but the impossible tasks of reading a book per week per class, writing multiple papers, and mastering beginner Mandarin. In the moments when I feel so compressed I can't breathe, I envision myself in one of the Thai spirit houses I've seen in import stores, a miniature building on stilts placed outside a house or village to invite the gods. I imagine being reduced and refined in an alchemist's fire. I write long lonely letters to Fred and sometimes, even though I know I shouldn't, I call my ex. He sends me a blue ceramic desk fountain, but I turn it off after a week because the sound of running water at night sends me down the hall to the communal bathroom. It will be his last gift to me.

Trying to dress myself for a life in limbo, I sort and discard, abandoning my city clothes on the giveaway shelf by the elevator only to see my skirt or shirt looking just right on some Asian girl half my age. In Texas, I still felt attractive enough in my forties to wear short skirts when I was not in boots and tight jeans. I could walk into any of my favorite stores and find the outfits that spoke to my basic black wardrobe accented with silver jewelry. In Hawaii, I have no sense of myself. No one seems to wear black or jewelry. Definitely no jeans or boots. All around me are Polynesian and Asian women, their bodies monumental or sliver-thin, their smooth skin rich browns or creamy ivory, their hair glossy black. I disappear before my own eyes. When I look in the mirror, I'm a ghost of my former self.

In our first weekly seminar, another requirement of our fellowships, we gather in groups for meet-and-greet exercises. When it is my turn to speak, I opt for humor to hide my discomfort: "I got a divorce to go to grad school."

"So did I!" says a tall white woman close to my age. "We need to talk!" It turns out that Jenny and I are a year apart in age. We each have an adult child, and we are both starting a new chapter in our lives. Jenny's parents were in the State Department when she was growing up, so she has lived around the world, but we have many of the same insecurities about going back to school and the same dilemmas about how to relate to fellow students who are younger than our offspring. I feel a little less alone.

When Fred comes to visit at Christmas, he dives into the kitchen chaos with his usual gusto, chatting with the other cooks and diners and sweeping me along so that when he leaves, I feel brave enough to emerge from my room more often. Wherever I stand out, he fits in. Because of his pan-ethnic face — his curly black hair, round eyes, and dark complexion — students guess he is Filipino or Malaysian before they hit on Chinese. Outside the dorm in Hawaii, he passes for local, something I, a haole, can never do. I love how he helps me belong. I rankle at how I can't seem to do that on my own.

Mostly, the students in Hale Manoa are a congenial mini-United Nations. We're here on East-West Center dollars to get degrees at the University of Hawai'i and then spread the mission of global multiculturalism. And we will, but diversity also creates flashpoints.

A portion of the great Sino-Japanese dorm war begins in a bathroom on the ninth floor. It ignites with singing and is fanned by the EWC listserve. It involves teacups — a matched set. It goes like this: living in one of the co-ed units are several young Chinese women and an older Japanese man. He is effeminate, slightly built, balding with a stringy ponytail, a solitary figure who stays on the sidelines of our required activities: culture clubs, the annual East-West Fest, the graduate student conference, and our Wednesday forums. He seldom speaks to anyone, but he tells me he was a schoolteacher and that he feeds feral cats near the Korean Studies Center on campus. He even brushes two tamer cats. As an animal lover, I appreciate him for this. I miss my cats in Houston so much that the pet food aisles in local grocery stores make me teary.

When the grad students get a listserv, the cat man uses it to voice polite complaints. First, he asks about the singing. *Can anyone please explain to me why Chinese make so much noise all the time? Is this a cultural practice? In my kitchen, the Chinese are always talking very loud or singing and it is difficult for me to think. I would appreciate if they could be more quiet in public spaces.* Insulted, the Chinese girls call him a racist and begin singing loudly whenever he enters the kitchen. They wait for a chance to mock and ridicule him when he next appeals to the listserv.

They soon have their opportunity.

On days when the wind gusts down Manoa Valley toward the ocean and hits the barrier wall of Hale Manoa, it jostles and slams the kitchen doors, demanding passage. It's on such a day that he posts: *Today I was coming out of the kitchen with my teacups on a tray and the door hit me in the back and the teacups went flying. It was a matched set and now one is broken. I respectfully request someone to do something about this door!* The Chinese girls respond with: *What kind of person has matched teacups in a dorm? Why don't you just make tea in your room? Maybe you should live in a fancy house.* The judgments crackle down the halls and spark from kitchen to kitchen, where I hear opinions from various people. I try not to take sides, but I relish the sense of belonging I get from being in on the gossip.

His next post makes them livid: *I have seen something that is very concerning. My neighbor is a young Chinese woman, and she is entertaining a young man in her room. She was sitting on her bed under a lamp. Everyone knows what that means. What should I say to her?*

This time the Chinese girls respond directly: *What are you doing looking into her room? Where else is she supposed to sit?* The exchange escalates, formal on his end, indignant on theirs. Through the "coconut wireless," the term for gossip hotlines in Hawaii, I hear that the girls are tormenting him in other ways, like sidling up beside him in the bathroom wearing nothing but towels, so he drops his shaving gear and flees to his room.

I feel worldly discussing the cultural cross-currents with other students. Chinese are loud, we all agree, but Japanese formality is so outdated. It's a gender issue. No, a generational one. The dean of students bans the Japanese man from the listserv. When I hear that the warring factions were sent to a mediator and that the Chinese girls stood him up, I want to slap them for their cruelty.

I feel deeply sorry for this fastidious and lonely man, but I don't reach out to him. He will eventually disappear. I will think of him for years to come whenever I see the feral cats on campus.

* * *

Each weekday I leave my international dorm for classes on the university side of East-West Road. Most of my seminars meet in a gray stone fortress, where I learn the flip side of American nationalism and how different it all looks with the Pacific at the center of the map. I take courses on Hawaii's multiculturalism, culture and colonialism, the anthropology of tourism, and ethnographic history. Although I struggle through the lexicon of cultural studies, my years of teaching serve me well, and I find I'm good at being a grad student. I'm terrible, however, at undergraduate Mandarin Chinese. I speak up in grad classes; but, in Chinese class, I tremble in fear of being called on, and my eyes water when I make mistakes.

I love the conceptual poetry of Chinese characters, and the grammar is child's play compared to what my grandmother had to learn when she emigrated from Russia to America. "At home we speak Russian, and in school I learned French and German. So where do I end up? America — where I can be dumb all my life!" she used to say. Still, she mastered English well enough to speak only that in front of my father and us, her monolingual descendants. Our Chinese teacher tells us about a comparative study on how many weeks of classes, on average, it takes language students to converse on the street and to read a newspaper. Variances of three to four months for Spanish and Italian. Double that for Chinese and toss the newspaper. There are over fifty thousand characters, and an educated person needs to have two or three thousand in their recall bank to read that paper. I wonder if Chinese papers are like American ones, pitched at fourth- through sixth-grade levels. I'd be happy to read just the headlines.

Along with learning vocabulary and grammar in Chinese class, we are expected to master reading and writing characters, hearing and replicating tones. The learning curve ups the ante. Local Chinese students who can speak Cantonese but not read or write characters have the jump on tones, structure, and vocabulary. Local Japanese who can write kanji — Chinese characters imported into Japanese — are light years ahead in writing. Between classes, Chinese words and phrases leak out of my head. My brain is either too full of all the stuff it has taken to get this far, or I am missing a foreign language lobe. Being smart in English doesn't count in Chinese class, so I stumble along, trying to walk and chew gum and juggle all at once. When I try to string together Chinese phrases in my oral exam, I can recall only the word for "and" in Spanish. I'm in tears before I reach the door. I'm thankful there is a "no credit" option for language classes that will allow me to pass the course without deflating my GPA.

*   *   *

Despite Hawaii being in America, my Americanness dislocates me. Graduate fellows are required to belong to clubs based on our national identities. Jenny and I create the American Cultures Club, emphasis on the "s." We offer a film series with discussions, and we spend a lot of those explaining regional or ethnic variations in the United States, which works fine until the clubs have to organize the annual East-West Fest, a fundraiser for student activities. Each club is supposed to cook national dishes, dress in national costumes, and perform national dances. Where does that leave us?

SPIRIT HOUSE

The few Americans — white and Asian American — laugh about serving hamburgers and hot dogs. We know we can't compete with the other clubs' dishes. I am one of two fellows from Texas, so we decide to make an enormous vat of vegetarian chili. Nearly all the ingredients come from cans, but students from elsewhere love it and pour it over rice from the Asian concessions. We have no national dance or music other than patriotic stuff, so a former Peace Corps worker performs some songs he wrote.

What the Americans at the EWC share is our mutual appreciation for cultures other than our own and a desire to be part of the bigger world. The difference between me and most of the others is that I've taken multiple detours to get here.

The East-West Center is a legendary incubator of cross-cultural relationships, and Fred and I soon become part of the EWC romance legacy. In four years and beyond, I will witness the beginnings of many intercultural and transnational marriages and families.

Fred and I are still a question. I have a daughter, grandchild, and friends in Texas. For the first time in my non-linear life, I have a full-time job and a house. I don't want to lose any of that. I'm on sabbatical for a year, and I have promised my dean I will come back and teach summers to pay it off. I plan to ask for leave without pay for the second year and to do fieldwork in the Vietnamese community of Houston when I finish my coursework. Fred has tenure at his college in California, and we assume we'll figure out our relationship along the way. I send him a card with a picture of two people sitting in a beached boat and a caption that reads "Waiting for a Wave."

"Be careful what you ask for," my friend Sandra always reminds me, along with, "You never know how much it will cost until you get the bill." I should know from experience that when the bill for my choices arrives, the cost will be a surprise.

Our wave builds momentum. When Fred visits during my first year in Hale Manoa, he introduces himself to the music department faculty at the University of Hawai'i. In the spring, a job for an ethnomusicologist opens up, and they offer him the position mid-summer. I am too in love to consider how his impending move will change my course by severing my ties to Houston, the city I've called home for twenty-five years. I can't foresee how staying in Hawaii will stretch my friendships, alienate my daughter, infuriate my ex who is living in the house I kept in the divorce and now need to sell, impel me to find homes for my beloved cats, and make me financially dependent on Fred once my stipend ends.

In August, Fred moves into my tiny dorm room, my spirit house, because an apartment in faculty housing isn't available. He doesn't ask if I mind, but I'm thrilled that his divorce is in process and we're together in Hawaii. Before long, however, I need to escape to the library because I feel like his constant presence sucks the air out of my space. Having grown up in a multi-generational household with twenty-two people, he has no issues with space or sharing. He uses my toothbrush when he can't find his own. He is unruffled by the communal bathroom. I can't sleep two to a single bed. I can't study with him coming and going. I want to dress in private. We move to a double room where we tie the legs of the twin beds together to keep them from rolling apart, but it's still one room. Overnight visitors aren't allowed in the dorm, but he makes friends with all the desk attendants and walks in and out as if he belongs. His audacity astounds me. All my life I've apologized for taking up too much space, whereas he not only owns whatever space he's in, he spreads out.

When he gets an apartment in faculty housing, he assumes I will move with him. I want to, and despite fellowship rules about

living in the dorms (I will keep up appearances), I cut short my
one shot at dorm life for a third chance at live-in love.

7

Strings Attached

FRED and I are only a few weeks away from our inaugural trip to Hong Kong as a couple, and I'm in the Hale Manoa lounge listening to my Chinese friend Annie recount her first visit home to Malaysia with her fiancé. Her story is a cautionary tale that strikes terror into my introverted American heart, especially after three months of cohabitation with Fred in a dorm room. First up for her was the language barrier. Annie had to translate between her fiancé and her extended family because her fiancé, a fourth-generation Chinese in Hawaii, speaks only English. "To make matters worse," she says, "he doesn't act Chinese either." When he disappeared from family gatherings, her brothers took Annie aside and asked, "Who is this guy? We don't like him."

When she found her fiancé curled up in another room reading comic books, she told him he needed to get out there with her family and pronto. He protested that it didn't matter if he were present because no one was talking to him anyway, to which she replied, "That's not the point! You have to show you're part of the family, so smile and act interested even if you don't understand anything!"

"Wow, I don't think I can pull that off! I don't speak Cantonese, and I don't do communal," I tell her. "I need sanity tips!"

Annie has a brilliant suggestion: "Plan a retreat in the middle of your trip, a romantic hotel for a couple of days. Then you can get away, just the two of you, and come back and hang out with his family."

I do some research online and come up with Macau as the solution. It's only an hour away from Hong Kong by boat, so I figure we can zip over and back. I make a list of hotels. When Fred gets home from the music department that evening, I explain the plan while he cooks dinner. He doesn't even stop to consider before he shrugs and says, "It won't work."

"What do you mean it won't work? I think it's a great idea. Just explain that we're taking a break to sightsee because it's my first trip and we'll be back."

"I can try, but I'm telling you it won't work. I know my family."

"Promise me you'll at least try." I can see that I will have to take charge of our travel plans.

* * *

We arrive in Hong Kong late on the evening of December 25. Fred's younger brother, Bernie, meets us outside the baggage claim area. Slight, quiet, and earnest to Fred's round, loud, and boisterous, Bernie greets me in British-inflected English. I would never suspect that they, the financial specialist and the musician scholar, are siblings. I climb into the back seat of Bernie's BMW and gawk at the city's vertical landscape while we navigate a series of winding and ascending roads that twist like ribbons suspended in midair, all from what I can only think of as the wrong side of the road. Bernie asks me a few polite questions in English before they lapse into Cantonese. Exhausted, I lean back into the leather seat, relieved to disappear for the time being.

Halfway up the steepest hill, Bernie turns into a driveway that leads to a garage under one of the many spire-like buildings staggered up the mountainside. We climb out and wheel our suitcases into a glass-encased vestibule, past a uniformed guard who nods, and into an elevator that whisks us up twenty-something stories to a polished marble hall with a door on either end. A sweet-faced Filipina woman opens the door.

"Hey, Stella," Fred says. "This is Heather."

"Hello, ma'am," she says, smiling and then ducking back into what I glimpse is the kitchen.

While we remove our shoes inside the foyer, I meet Bernie's family: his wife, Amy; her mother, Auntie Po; and Michelle and Jeffrey, Bernie's pre-teen children. They wear pajamas and robes, waiting to greet us like the receiving line at a wedding. *Hello, hello. How was your flight? Did you sleep on the plane? Have you eaten?* Fred high fives the kids and launches himself at the adults for hugs. I, as usual, try to follow suit and end up somewhere between a stiff embrace and an awkward handshake. From their peremptory back pats, I can tell that these are not hugging people. Neither am I, although I would like to be. Hawaii is a huggy, kissy culture, but some part of me — a cheek, an arm — seems forever in the wrong position.

Amy points to a row of neatly arranged hotel slippers, and I slip on a pair that's so big I must ski-walk to keep them on. At home in Hawaii, we go barefoot in the house, but maybe bare feet are considered unhygienic here. I don't see any Christmas decorations and feel a bit sad to miss my favorite holiday. Amy wipes the wheels of our suitcases with a cloth before we roll them across the shiny wood floor of the entry and down the hall. She opens the first door on the right; we deposit our suitcases between the bed and the closet, filling the only space left in the room except a sliver between the single bed and the desk. Amy and Bernie duck out, leaving Fred and me alone. "Look," I say, "It's my dorm room, only fancy! Well, except for the Mickey Mouse comforter. Whose room is this?"

"It's Jeffrey's room," says Fred.

"But where is Jeffrey going to sleep?"

"In Michelle's room. They both have two beds. See?" He pulls out a lower trundle.

"Is that OK?" My sister and I once shared a room twice this size and fought like ferrets. I'd never considered sleeping in a room with either of my brothers.

"Don't worry. This is what they always do. They don't mind."

Oh boy, I'm thinking. *Trundle beds*. I already feel like a child, and the tight accommodations are not helping.

Fred says, "You can use the bathroom and go to bed first. I need to stay up for a while and talk with Bernie." He sets the desk chair aside so the bottom trundle can be pulled out completely. We're now wall-to-wall in beds. "The hot water switch is outside the door," he says, pointing down the hall as he heads back to the dining room.

Dismissed from family duty, I gather my toiletries and walk down the dark hall to the bathroom, where I confront the mystery of multiple light switches. Unable to figure them out and unwilling to re-enter the knot of family at the dining room table, I take a cold sponge bath in reflected light from the window and then eenie-meenie between the two flush buttons on the Toto toilet. Back in Jeffrey's room, I look down from the bay window to see a what looks like a toy racetrack, street, and cars far, far below. I stretch out on the top trundle, Mickey comforter pulled up to my chin. *Couldn't we have stayed in a hotel?* This is not at all how I imagined our trip.

When I emerge in the morning, I find the adults already sitting around the table. Fred, Bernie, and Auntie Po share sections of the *South China Morning Post* and drink tea or coffee. I don't have a robe, so I'm dressed, but everyone else is still in robes and slippers. Fred wears the same shorts and T-shirt he sleeps in at home. Breakfast is a quiet affair, with Stella flitting in and out, serving us coffee, square white bread, butter and jam, boiled ham slices, and oatmeal. Jeffrey and Michelle appear one at a time, and within minutes individual breakfasts appear before them: eggs for one, oatmeal for the other. I skim the front page of the paper, marveling at their calm indifference to being served. Unused to being waited on, I flinch each time Stella calls me "ma'am." I feel guilty when she picks up my dishes and when I'm told to leave out my dirty clothes for her to wash and iron.

Midmorning, we all head for "Number 10," as Fred and Bernie call their parents' house, for the Lau family's annual Christmas party. Fred and I leave our suitcases behind at Bernie's and bring only our backpacks for staying on Cheung Chau, the island where Fred grew up and his parents live. The first stage of getting to Number 10 requires piling into two taxis that whisk us to down to the harbor and boarding a crowded hydrofoil passenger ferry that bounces us for thirty minutes across the choppy channel and makes my stomach churn. Fred explains that the older, larger, more stable ferry (the one I will much prefer in the future) takes closer to an hour. Then we weave on foot through streets clogged with people and bicycles because, with the exception of miniature emergency vehicles and delivery carts, there are no cars on Cheung Chau. When I complain that even old ladies refuse to yield to pedestrians headed in the opposite direction, Fred says only Americans expect to walk in a straight line. "You have to weave," he says. Finally, we climb up a series of ramps and staircases that leave me huffing for breath.

At a break in the stairs, Fred opens a metal gate into a tiled courtyard overhung with laundry. A din of voices grows louder and louder as we walk past an outdoor sink and through a tiny kitchen before we plunge into a sea of relatives and noise. I am four again, hiding behind my mother's legs from looming adults as I clutch Fred's arm. There must be thirty people in a room the size of my double dorm room, people calling out greetings to Fred and pumping my hand, shouting questions in English and Cantonese. When Fred's mother hugs me, I am startled at how much she and her son look alike, with their square shoulders, broad faces, and round, merry eyes. His father shyly nods at me, and in him I see Bernie's leanness and seriousness. I meet Fred's sisters Susanna and Mimi and their husbands, his cousins, and his nieces and nephews. Fred presents his aunts and uncles to me by numbers rather than names — Big Aunt, Second Aunt, Third Uncle — and I vaguely remember a lesson in my Chinese class about kinship terms for paternal and maternal relatives. The aunts and uncles all look similar to me, and I wonder first if I'll ever be able to tell them apart, then if I'm being racist to think that. Fred tells his second uncle and aunt, who lived in Beijing, that I'm taking Mandarin classes, and they fire questions at me in

Mandarin. I freeze and can't think of a single phrase I've learned beyond "*Ni hao.*"

Over the commotion, I ask him, "Why is everyone so loud?"

"*Renao!*" he shouts in my ear. "Hot and noisy! It's festive! Happening!" He has explained *renao* to me before, but it's my first immersion. As usual, I'm better at theory than practice.

Soon I am relegated to the role of negligible moon as Fred is swept up in the planetary mass of his family, the electromagnetic field of Cantonese. I catch the eye of Josie, the Filipina maid who has whisked away our bags. She smiles widely in what I take as sympathy for a fellow outsider. I smile back in gratitude. Macau is looking like salvation, my secret talisman to get me through the upcoming two weeks.

When everyone leaves at last, we retreat. We get the room at the end of the hall because I am *Meigwokyun* (American). I hear him talking to his mother in Cantonese but using the word "privacy" in English. She looks puzzled then says, "*Hóu, hóu, hóu*" and leads us to the room that Fred explains once belonged to his paternal grandmother. Being at the end of the hall means that we have a bathroom to ourselves, at least in theory. Also, we have mothballs.

"How can they stand it?" I ask once the door is closed.

"Stand what?"

"This room smells like I'm inside a mothball! I'm pretty sure it's toxic to be breathing this."

"They think it smells good. You're too sensitive." He says this with a smile, but I sense it's time to rein in my complaints. I imagine my former students with their horrendous immigration stories, my Peace Corps friends with their tiny backpacks and linguistically talented tongues, Jenny with her internationally stationed parents, my Hale Manoa classmates with their happy communalism. They could all do this. Despite my wishful thinking,

I'm still a middle-aged woman steeped in my mother's germ pho-bias and my Texas-sized sense of space. My sensitivity to smells, noise levels, and crowds exasperates even me and is not helping me to fit in. My sister, the special education teacher, says there are clinical terms for hypersensitive people like me.

Although everyone has treated me with kindness and warmth, I'm painfully aware of not being the first "wife" Fred has brought home to Number 10. I search for traces of his marital past in the photos that appear under glass and in frames on every surface, finding nothing. His past has been excised.

A dark, heavy dresser, an armoire, and oversize bunk beds crowd the room. The top bunk is stuffed from mattress to ceiling with stored blankets and clothes, impermeable to moths. I sink onto the lower bunk and land with a thunk. "Whoa! This bed is like a rock!"

He laughs, patting the bed. "Chinese bed. I love it."

"You grew up sleeping on the floor. I like soft."

"Spoiled haole girl," he says. I detect an unfamiliar edge to his voice. There's a single knock, and before we respond, his mother enters.

She hands him a tall jar full of what looks like brown sludge and urges him to drink. To me, she says "Good! Drink!" pointing to him and miming how he should down the tonic. I sigh. So much for privacy.

After the Christmas gathering, Bernie and Mimi's families ferry back to their apartments and jobs in the city. Susanna, Fred's youngest sister, and her Chinese-Pakistani husband, Gulam, are visiting from Singapore with their two children, and they stay on at Number 10. That makes twelve to fourteen people for meals, depending on who's coming or going, in a room the size of an American walk-in closet. Two framed sets of ancestors gaze down on us from near the ceiling, and a small altar sits on a table near the door beneath a dangling red light bulb. At the table, I am sandwiched against the far wall between Fred and his father, a spot that will be mine from now on. Like clowns in a circus car, we can exit the dining area only in the order we come in.

Before each meal, Josie, Fred's mother, and his aunts pull metal-legged stools from beneath the large round table and place recycled computer paper on the table for placemats. Taking bowls and chopsticks from the hutch in the corner, they set a blue and white rice bowl, a pair of red plastic chopsticks, and a Chinese soup spoon at each place. For our first communal meal, a small plate and a slightly bent salad fork appear at my place at the table. Fred points to the plate and questions his mother, who laughs and quickly provides me with a bowl and chopsticks like everyone else.

"What was that about?" I whisper.

"She thought you might not know how to use chopsticks. I told her everyone in Hawaii knows how to use them."

We pass our bowls to Third Uncle, who sits closest to the rice cooker. He fills the bowls and passes them back. In the center of the table, Josie has placed plates full of chicken, pork, vegetables, shrimp, and two small fish. Fred's mother deftly detaches the head of one of the fish with her chopsticks, then reaches across the table to plop it on top of my rice. The fish and I eye each other for only a moment before Fred scoops the head from my rice and deposits it in his mother's bowl. He says, "She wanted you to have the best part. I told her Americans don't eat that." I duck my head in embarrassment. She shrugs and laughs.

In Asian restaurants in Hawaii, I'm used to eating family style, where everyone shares the dishes. Eating at Number 10 is different in ways that would horrify my mother, the nurse. No serving chopsticks to protect us from germs, everyone reaching across the table to take what they want, all talking at once and with their mouths full. Without knives, everyone but me mysteriously separates chicken and fish bones from meat inside of their mouths and then spits the bones directly onto the paper placemats. I try not to see the mounting piles of bones, not to think about germs moving from mouths to serving dishes and back again. "Home style," Fred has explained. Not restaurant style. Although I am deft with Louisiana crawfish, and I grew up eating Dungeness crabs, I'm baffled about how to eat unshelled shrimp covered in sauce. Paralyzed by my middle-class American upbringing — *Don't talk with your mouth full! Don't reach across the table! Don't raise your voice! Don't spit out food!* — I meekly eat the deboned pieces of fish and the peeled shrimp Fred piles onto my rice. I smile but hate feeling like a toddler or a baby bird.

In the ensuing days, Fred's mother breezes in and out of our room with only a cursory knock as she opens the door. She comes to ask questions, to bring him tonics, to use the bathroom, to see how we're doing. When she leaves, I complain that she's invading my personal space. "She just walks in! What if we're not dressed? Why can't she knock and wait for an answer?"

Fred snorts and says, "This is family! What personal space? There is no personal space in a Chinese family. There isn't even a word for that in Cantonese!"

"That's not true. I learned some words in Mandarin for privacy, so there must be equivalents in Cantonese."

"Those all mean bad things, like secretive and clandestine. Families have nothing to hide, so you don't need it."

I'm getting nowhere with my argument, and there's more. My sweet, passionate, funny lover of two years is somebody else at Number 10. In Cantonese his voice is louder and gruffer, his gestures more theatrical and brisk. In Hong Kong, he shows less affection in public; he stays up late with his family while I go to bed; he instructs me in how to act Chinese: *pour the tea, shake Uncle or Aunt's hand, help clear the table, say good morning / joh sun.* I long to be an ideal traveler, guest, and future wife, so I appreciate him teaching me the cultural ropes. I could have used that kind of instruction in my last marriage, when I was dropped cold into an alcoholic family. Yet here at Number 10, the independent American in me prickles, retreats into hurt silences, and accuses him of making me feel clumsy and stupid. At home, I'm in charge of my life, and I like it that way.

A few days into our visit, I manage to get Fred alone on a walk. We head down toward the main street, where we buy a skewer of fish balls. The size of a quarter and made with mackerel or cod pulverized into a sticky paste combined with soy sauce, chicken broth, and sesame oil, fish balls are a favorite snack on Cheung Chau. I bite into one. *"Hou sik!"* Delicious! Then I prod, "When are you going to tell her?"

"Are you sure? I really don't think this is going to work."

"You promised! Just tell her we'll leave for only two days. It's my first trip here. Tell her you want to show me around." Sighing, he leaves to find his mother. In a few minutes, he's back and shuffling his feet.

"So? Was it OK? What did she say?"

"She thought it was a great idea." He pauses, takes a deep breath. "We're all going the day after tomorrow."

"All of us?" Surely I'd heard that wrong.

"Just Mom and Dad, Bernie and Amy, Sue and Gulam, Mimi and the kids. She called Bernie, and he said he has a hotel deal, so he can get the rooms."

"But...."

"Sorry! Sorry!" he says, turning up his palms. "I told you it wouldn't work. C'mon. It'll be fun." I'm too astonished to sulk.

It's dawning on me that here I have no control over anything, including my time and our relationship.

* * *

Two days later, fifteen of us gather at the terminal in Hong Kong to board a high-speed ferry to Macau. We stay at the Sheraton Grand Macau using Bernie's business connections. When Fred and I close the door to our room and set down our luggage, I take a deep breath and think maybe this won't be so bad after all. At least we have a room to ourselves, and a rather palatial one at that. Immediately, there's a knock at our door. Fred's mother and sisters tumble in, explore our bathroom, lounge on our beds, and rearrange the pillows. They admire my new jade bracelet and recommend White Flower Lotion for the still-visible bruises on my wrist bone. Susannah lifts my arm and says to Fred, "You really didn't know it wouldn't come off?"

Fred says, "How would I know?"

Five minutes after they leave, the phone rings. Fred answers, "Wei?" He talks for a few minutes and hangs up. "That was my mother wanting to know if the kids could sleep in our room." I glare. He throws his hands up in front of him. "Don't worry! I told her it wouldn't work." I suspect he also said something about the antisocial habits of Americans, but I'm stretched so far beyond accommodation I no longer care how that makes me look. *Are they trying to keep us apart? How does anyone manage intimacy in a family like this?*

I'm hoping that perhaps Fred and I can sneak off for dinner alone, but Bernie has made reservations for the family in a Macanese restaurant. The interior is decorated in blue and yellow tile-work that reminds me of Mexico, except Mexico was where I'd had solo adventures in my past life, and this adventure is far from that. Once we're seated at two long tables pushed together end to end, Bernie and Fred confer on the ordering. We eat family style, passing dishes of Portuguese chicken bathed in curry and coconut milk; tamarind pork; and *arroz gordo* with hard-boiled eggs, raisins, and olives. A serious meat-fest. For me, the lone vegetarian/pescatarian, Fred orders steamed fish and bok choy with mushrooms, but even those dishes must be shared. I feel like I'm eating porridge at a feast, but my deprivation looks less pathetic when the waiter brings the pitcher of sangria Fred ordered. Then Fred pours everyone a half glass so all the adults can have a taste. I down mine and look longingly at what's left in the glasses of the others after they take only a single sip. *What a waste*, I think.

Fifteen strong, we're an unwieldy millipede walking together through the old sections of the city, but I'm still charmed by the lovely black and white mosaic pavement covering the main plaza, the yellow and pink colonial buildings with their white piping. It's amazing that we have reached the main plaza at all, given that, at nearly every corner along the way, there have been raucous disagreements, with lots of pointing in different directions. I pull Fred aside to ask, "Why does your family have to fight about everything? They can't even get down the street without yelling at each other!"

"What do you mean, fighting?" he says, leaning back in astonishment. "We're not fighting — just having a discussion! And if I don't go back and participate, they'll think I don't care." He dives back into the flurry as I watch from the sidelines, puzzling over how intense, non-smiling faces, arm-waving, and raised voices can be friendly discussion rather than signals of anger. In my family, yelling at each other resulted in our mouths being washed out with soap or in spankings with a wooden spoon (mostly me, because I yelled the loudest). Once on vacation, when the bickering in the back seat got to be too much, my mother told my brother and sister and me to get out and walk home from the Dakota Badlands. As adults, we resort to indirection and sarcasm when dissension rises between us.

I admire honesty and directness, but I'm programmed to be diplomatic and polite. Once, when I chided Fred for not thanking me for something, he told me it's rude to say thank you all the time in a Cantonese family, that thank you is for strangers. "In a family," he said, "You're expected to say what you mean and take care of each other, so there's no need to be so polite." At the time, I'd reminded him we were in my country, where American custom prevailed.

We stroll through the main plaza, then enter the grounds of a ruined cathedral where at last we can split up and wander in twos and threes. But, before we do, we gather for photos in front of the cathedral facade. We line up, all fifteen of us, for multiple shots on several cameras. In every configuration, I am somewhere in the middle and always in front.

8

Double Happiness

WHEN my daughter Sorrel calls to say she has invited my second husband to take part in her second wedding, I tell her I'm not coming. Then I ask if I can wear a bag over my head. Exasperated, she spouts, "Mom, it's *my* wedding! It's not about you!" She adds that she expects Fred to be there too. That part surprises me.

Fred and I visited her once before her divorce, and, between her marital disputes, her unhappiness with me for moving away, and her eccentric household, it was a disaster that left me feeling embarrassed and ripped apart. I'd raised her during my wayward youth in turbulent times, in an American era of unconventionality and outspokenness, at least among its youth. But after observing how respectful and dutiful the kids in Fred's family are, I wondered how she would have turned out if I'd been a better role model and disciplinarian. I wanted so much for Sorrel and Fred to get along, to like each other. I wanted to show her off, wanted him to appreciate how talented and funny and smart she is, to see past her snippiness and impetuousness as I was trying to do. I wanted him to view our storms within the context of our history, but he comes from a family that judges actions regardless of intent. Worse, he and I couldn't share our honest reactions because I'm a parent and he isn't. And as any mother knows, no matter how critical we might be of our progeny's inability or unwillingness to match our ideals, we go haywire if anyone else dares to criticize them. Fred quickly learned to keep quiet about my American child.

I call out to him that my ex is coming to the wedding, and he yells back from the kitchen, "I'm not going!" After his rocky and expensive divorce, he's done with reminders of our previous marriages.

"Yes, you are. It's her wedding. It's not about you!" Nothing wrong with borrowing a good line, especially if it worked on me. We bat the objections back and forth a few more times until he gives in.

* * *

We arrive in Dallas during an early March ice storm. Two of my girlfriends have driven up from Houston together, and I'm relieved to see them, my troops. My parents, who have flown in from Seattle, are waiting in the church lobby when we arrive. I wear a mushroom-colored jacquard top and skirt that now seem all wrong. Spotting my ex standing alone across the room, I send my friends to talk to him. I leave Fred to fend for himself while I go in search of my daughter.

The Unitarian church is all bleached wood and modern, open spaces, pared down in ways that remind me of the Lutheran church of my childhood and make me feel like the air is too thin. Someone directs me to an anteroom, where a woman I don't know fusses over Sorrel's hair and makeup. My brainy, independent daughter who shuns cosmetics and wears her hair long and straight is wearing makeup and a modest white wedding dress with a long, bouffant skirt. I blink back tears because it's clear there's nothing for me to do. Even though the wedding is a simple affair to celebrate a second marriage, I wish I could have been part of the planning. I should have been the one helping her find a dress and advising on hair and makeup. I might have said that ivory would have better set off her olive complexion, the gold in her hair. And she would have rolled her eyes in annoyance and said that obsessing over visuals is my thing, because she's as rebellious as I was.

I've met my future son-in-law once. He looks eerily like Sorrel's father, the hippie bass player who disappeared from her life, and he is too close to Fred's age for me to feel comfortable in the mother-in-law slot. They seem happy.

The ceremony includes the groom's two daughters, the youngest a toddler, and my six-year-old grandson. The children have decorated the altar with a clutter of meaningful objects they've made or excavated from toy chests. There is no division between the bride's and the groom's sides, so Fred and I sit on the right side of the aisle. My ex sits with my parents on the left. I sneak sidelong looks at the tall, pale, brilliant man with thinning blond hair beside my small, graying parents, a man who once joked that he and his sisters, descended from Swedish immigrants, were the three whitest people in America. The aisle bisects my life between then and now, past and future. My ex stands and reads a passage in Old English that my daughter has selected and no one understands.

* * *

When Fred and I arrive at her apartment with my parents the next morning, Sorrel announces that her stepfather is taking us all to lunch. I thank my ex for his generosity without meeting Fred's eyes. I've never heard her refer to him as her stepfather before.

As soon as we are all seated in a glitzy Tex-Mex franchise off the interstate, Sorrel announces that it's time to hold hands and say grace. We comply, and she, her new husband, and the children sing a song about how God has given them "the sun, the moon, and the apple seed" that ends with "Amen, let's eat." Fred kicks me under the table, and I ignore him because I'm so mortified by the public praying and singing that I'm wishing us invisible to any other diners in our vicinity. Fred orders baby back ribs, and I overhear him explain to my ex that Chinese prefer meat with bones. I congratulate myself on how civilized we all are to have come together to celebrate and eat and act like grown-ups.

* * *

Months later I'm telling the story to my friend Sandra on the phone to illustrate how my ex and I have transcended the animosity of divorce when I see the gathering in my mind's eye more clearly than I did through the nervous haze of the actual moment. I reconstruct the seating arrangement person by person, visualizing Fred and my ex seated across from each other at one end of the long table. "Wait," I say to Sandra, before calling out to Fred, "Hey, at the wedding when we had to pray, were you holding hands with my ex?"

"Yeeeessssss!" he splutters in mock exasperation after months of biting his tongue. "I can't believe I had to have a conversation about bones with your ex-husband *and* hold his hand!"

"Oh, poor you," I tease back. So much for maturity. With me, he will have to navigate the complexities of our fractured, patched, and reconfigured American family. Not for the first time, I'm happy his family lives on another continent, so I don't have to explain mine to the rest of them.

* * *

A year after Sorrel's wedding, Fred still doesn't want to get married, but I do. I buck the system in many ways, but when it comes to love, I think marriage is the way our story should to go. I want to be publicly, legitimately partnered. I want the pledge and the ring. I want to say husband and wife instead of fumbling through terms like domestic partner and significant other. This standoff has become such a problem I've begun sulking and blinking back tears of envy when friends marry. I understand his reluctance. After all, we've both suffered the pain and embarrassment of a second divorce. He asks the classic question about why we need a piece of paper when we've been living together for four years and things are just fine as they are. He's just finished paying alimony, and I know he's afraid of another failure. But I'm a romantic. I want the leap of faith. I shamelessly resort to conjuring disastrous scenarios where one of us is incapacitated in a hospital and the other is refused admittance, but it's a car rental agency that finally decides the issue by not allowing me on his policy because I'm not a relative.

Sitting on the floor beside me in our shared study, Fred says we can get married if I want. It's not a romantic proposal, but I say yes. We set a date for two months later in March. We want a stealth wedding for our third time around, so I call a friend who got married by a justice of the peace and find out that judges marry couples at the Honolulu courthouse during the court's lunch break.

We email invitations for a spring break gumbo party at our apartment in faculty housing. In a Chinatown sundries shop, we pick up traditional "double happiness" wedding decorations, red paper circles that enclose doubled images of the character used in writing the word for happiness. At the lei stand, we order traditional Hawaiian wedding leis: a long garland of maile leaves for him and a thick strand of white pikake buds for me. Fred finds me the perfect dress at Costco — a Hawaiian print of white plumeria blossoms on a background of Chinese red — and we ask three friends to be our witnesses and swear them to secrecy.

On the day of the wedding, we wait on the walkway of what looks like an old motel behind the courthouse. With us on the second-floor balcony are young and very pregnant brides, older couples, and old–young couples. We seem to be the only ones who dressed up for the occasion, although some women wear simple leis of purple orchids. Below us is a bail bond office, and a police van full of prisoners waves to us as they leave the parking lot. A sign on the door of the passport photo office where the ceremonies will take place announces that weddings cost $100.00 and that, for an extra $25.00, we can have the requisite pictures taken: couple, couple with the judge, crossed hands with rings, and kissing. Couples must bring their own cameras and develop their own film.

The first ceremony happens on the grass next to the parking lot below us because the groom is in a wheelchair and the passport photo office has no handicapped access. Everyone leans over the railing to watch and applauds when the ceremony concludes.

When it's our turn, our party of five files inside, where an assistant has us fill out forms before positioning Fred and me in front of a shoji screen. To either side of us is a tall white basket filled with artificial red-and-orange bird of paradise and yellow heliconia. Asked by the judge if he will love, honor, and cherish me, Fred responds, "I will," and adds with a wink to me, "and much more." Laughing, the judge asks whether I want that in writing. We exchange the plain platinum bands we bought online, sign the papers, and head to a fancy Asian fusion buffet for lunch, heavy on the champagne, before we pick up our pre-ordered sheet cake from Leonard's Bakery. On top is "Congratulations, Heather and Fred" in blue piping, surrounded by a floral lei made of orange frosting. We're delighted with ourselves, jubilant that we have circumvented the usual expense and trappings of weddings.

Later I will look at the photos our friends took and see a microcosm of Hawaii in our little wedding party of six: the local Japanese judge, our hapa friend who is half Southeast Asian, our friend's haole boyfriend, our Filipino friend, and haole me with my Chinese husband. We could be an advertisement for Hawaii multiculturalism and the local saying "Lucky We Live Hawaii." Here, unlike Hong Kong and the mainland United States, our mixed marriage is unremarkable. We've perpetuated a trend that dates back to the mixed marriages of Hawaii's early settlers and plantation days.

When our friends and neighbors arrive at our apartment that evening, they need only a few minutes to figure out the occasion from the leis and double happiness decorations. They scold us for being so secretive. In Hawaii, everyone expects to be part of a celebration, but we, still carrying the embarrassment of our marital failures, wanted to keep the ceremony to ourselves. Now, we can relax and share our happiness. We eat gumbo and cake and drink more champagne. We will laugh for years about getting married in front of plastic flowers by a comedian judge while the rest of the world pays a fortune to fly to Hawaii and get married on the beach. Neither of us has ever done it up big, and we both know by now that the fuss and elation of a wedding does little to build the mortar and bricks of a marriage or predict if it will hold or crumble.

Two weeks after our wedding, we are in Chinatown when we run into three women from a Chinese choir Fred conducts. They greet Fred in Mandarin, addressing him as "*laoshi*" (teacher). Fred tells them we just got back from our honeymoon trip to the Big Island. They turn to me, mouths agape, and announce, "Whaaaa! Good thing you got married! We were looking for someone for him. We were going to fix him up with a nice Chinese girl!"

As we walk away, I ask, "Were they serious? They knew we were living together all this time. Why would they be matchmaking?"

"They're just kidding," he says, but I know that they weren't. Unmarried, I was replaceable, temporary in their eyes and maybe in my own. Married, I'm the real thing, a Chinese wife, even if they refuse to acknowledge I've kept my name. To the aunties, I will forever be Mrs. Lau.

9

Clumping Factor

THE year of our wedding is the year of my graduation and two family visits. Bernie, who works for an international bank in a financial job we don't understand, pays for Fred's parents, his family of four, Fred's recently widowed older sister, Mimi, and her two girls to come to Hawaii in the summer. The trip is Mimi's first time in America, so she booked a preliminary tour for herself and the girls before joining the rest of the family in Hawaii. Their first two destinations were Las Vegas and Disneyland, and now they are staying in Waikiki, the center of Hawaii's tourist zone. "Three fantasies in a row," I say to Fred. "The real fake America!" Maybe that is partly why when we point out the mountains and beaches, no one looks out the car windows. Instead, Mimi and Fred's mother are chatting and putting on hand lotion in the back seat.

When his family comes to our apartment, Fred's mother carries a bag that smells like a Chinese medicine shop with its powerful nose of camphor and tree resins mixed with dried bitter herbs. Once, when I visited a Chinese doctor in Honolulu for relief from hot flashes and migraines, the doctor prescribed an assortment of dried sticks, bark, leaves, flowers, and something that looked like a dirt dauber nest. We bought an electric clay cooker to boil the herbs in water until they became a black sludge. I grew to like the earthy smell of the simmering herbs and am proud of my ability to down a large bowl of murky liquid that tastes like dirt laced with pepper. Our Canadian Chinese neighbor, however, once wrinkled his nose and yelled, "What the hell are you cooking over there?" Fred took my prescription to Hong Kong on one of his visits to Hong Kong, and now his mother pulls several bundles of pungent medicine from her bag, each one wrapped in newspaper. Pleased with her gift, she explains how the newspaper keeps the herbs from smelling. Fred, Bernie, and I look at each other and snicker because it's so not working.

She also brings me gold. Wedding gold. In Houston, I saw a Vietnamese friend draped by her future mother-in-law in gleaming necklaces, earrings, and bangles — all the red-orange of 24-karat gold, the color of a ring I have from my Russian grandmother. My mother-in-law — she says I should call her Amah, and to call Fred's father Abah — pats the jade bracelet on my left wrist and tells Fred it looks much greener than before. She then fastens two slender gold link bracelets around my right wrist, one from her and one from Second and Third Aunts. I know they gave gold to Fred's previous wives, so I'm surprised and touched by these gifts. For his second wedding, they also helped him buy the house in California that he lost in his divorce. We have a lot to make up for.

Whenever my parents visit Hawaii, they take long walks in Waikiki and have places they want to explore. They have drinks on their hotel lanai and don't invite us. They tell us they don't want us to have to entertain them. Fred's family wants to be with us all the time, and after three or four days, I run out of ideas. Exasperated, I ask Fred, "What do they want to do? Aside from Bernie's family, no one seems interested in nature or culture or history. That rules out beaches and museums. What else is there? Why did they even come here?"

"They just want to be with us," he says. "They want to see where we live and hang out."

"And why do they have to eat Chinese food all the time? Can't they try something different for a change?"

"Chinese food here is different from Hong Kong. Chinese people like Chinese food," he laughs.

We eat dim sum lunches three days in a row. For dinners, we keep returning to Jackie Chan's Kitchen in the Ala Moana shopping center. With coupons from the hotel, the kids can eat free, and in Chinese restaurants they can order family style, sharing all the entrees. At least I can order wine.

On a day when Amah and Abah are tired, we pick them up from their hotel and bring them to our apartment to rest while Bernie drives the rest of the group around the island. We urge them to take a nap in our bedroom. An hour later, Fred walks in to find Abah lying stiffly on the brown shag carpet instead of on the bed. When Fred asks him why, Abah says he didn't want to get hair oil on our pillows. I feel bad that he sacrificed his comfort for ours, and that he was too embarrassed to ask for a towel. For a moment, I glimpse the gap between our worlds from their side.

*　*　*

For the last few days of their trip, the Laus want to go to the Big
Island and see Hawai'i Volcanoes National Park, where the lava
has been flowing since the 1980s. When Fred and I went to Hawaii
Island for our honeymoon, we rented a charming little house in
the rainforest and spent a long weekend hiking across the lava
fields. Considering how little attention most of his family has been
paying to the glories of nature, I wonder how another island is
going to be any different. Fred and Bernie make reservations at
the Seaside Hotel, a semi-seedy place Fred and I like, and rent a
van. I claim to have a headache, which I do, but mostly the thought
of spending three days in a van together is about a week's worth
more togetherness than I can handle.

Fred comes home laughing about how the old people stayed
in the car while the young people hiked the lava fields, and how
a local restaurant mistook him, with his deep tan and flowered
shirt, for a tour guide and gave him a free meal for bringing in
his group of Chinese tourists. I laugh and think *thank god I wasn't
there*. I would have been miserable. I would have ruined everything.

When Bernie's family and Amah and Abah leave, Mimi and her
girls stay an extra few days with us. Used to living in small spaces
and traveling together, they're content to sleep on a futon in our
crowded study. I try to imagine going with the flow and sharing a
mattress with my mother or daughter. The image refuses to form.

*　*　*

To round out the year, my December graduation from the University of Hawai'i coincides with my father's eightieth birthday. My
father — who at mid-life bought himself a purple TR6 sports car

just big enough for himself and his golden retriever, who takes our mother on lengthy vacations all around the world now that he doesn't have to haul the four of us along, who hands the phone to my mother when I call — has paid for the entire family, even Sorrel's blended family in Texas, to come to Hawaii for the occasion. We are all flabbergasted. We aren't used to grand gestures, and we aren't particularly good at gratitude either. Once we are all together, my sister and I raise our eyebrows and whisper: *Can you believe it? I know — totally out of character!*

In true local style, Fred and I organize a tent party on Magic Island, a park-like spit of land surrounded by sea and beaches near the Honolulu marina. We have folding chairs and an awning, room for the kids to run and swim, and a cake decorated with a lei made of orange icing, just like the one for our wedding. This one has *Diamonds Are Forever* piped in blue icing — a joke my grandmother used to make about old age and one my father will appreciate. We order local Japanese food. Maren, the wife of Brent, my youngest brother, has brought blue T-shirts for everyone, different shades for each subdivision of the family so we can see who we are years later in the photos Fred and I hadn't considered taking. My other brother, Lindsay, has brought Katie, his new girlfriend. The party goes remarkably well. Everyone likes the food, and our friends drop by to meet my parents and eat. A local Chinese couple my parents met on a trip to Turkey shows up with a lei containing eighty pennies stacked inside plastic wrap. We sing happy birthday to my father and present him with a shirt that says "Older than Dirt." He will wear it for almost ten years. We take pictures in the blue shirts and look happy together in paradise.

I'm from a family that can't sit still, apart or together. In the days after the party, Lindsay and Katie, who will later become his wife, disappear into tiki bars. My sister, Holly, spends a lot of time looking for her teenaged daughters who are sun- and boy-struck. The oldest has brought her boyfriend, and they disappear. Hayley, her troubled middle child, sulks and insists on wearing kitten-heeled shoes in the sand while she and the youngest prowl the beach. Something is up with Sorrel, something more than toting a cranky one-year-old, and I barely see her. Fred keeps asking, "Where is everyone?" I keep making excuses. His family clumps liked cooked oatmeal. Mine disperses like dry oats in the wind.

* * *

I've plowed through my dissertation only one semester behind my original plan, and I'm graduating from my department with honors. When I boast to my father, "Not bad for someone who finished high school with a 2.3 average," he quips back with his usual sarcasm, "I don't remember anything that high."

His comment fits in with my ex's warning when I first started looking into programs, "A PhD is going to make you crazy." Maybe it has. I've reclaimed my maiden name in anticipation of this moment, a promise kept to myself. I'd become someone else with the married name I took at eighteen, someone inventing herself without family. I'd kept that name through two divorces and through the years when Sorrel and I were a tribe of two. Then she changed hers, and I bought mine back in time to put it after the Dr. and before the PhD.

Because of my 4.0 GPA, I'm given the job of leading the Arts and Humanities graduates into the auditorium. I get to wear a ribbon of green satin over my robe with the three velvet stripes on each sleeve, and my job is to count off the chairs and people as we enter the rows to make sure everyone has a seat. I lose count, but, to my great relief, no one is left standing. Scanning the auditorium, I find my family sitting together, but Sorrel's family is missing, and my heart sinks. I want her here more than anyone. In 1990 she cheered through my MA ceremony; then my friends and I made a ruckus at her high school graduation a month later. Finally, I see her slip in alone to one of the seats the rest of the family has saved.

Fred has planned a celebratory banquet at Asia Manoa, our favorite neighborhood restaurant. He has pre-ordered the food with the owners, who are also from Hong Kong. We have two tables near the window for the twenty-two of us, but our gathering starts unraveling before we're even seated. Sorrel is outside in tears because my father sent her to sit with her family at the other table when she asked to sit with us. Holly comforts her. I do some shifting and settle Sorrel next to me.

Fred proposes a toast to my accomplishments, but no one at the other table is listening. Despite ordering what we thought were the safest and most familiar items on the menu — sweet-and-sour pork, steamed chicken, walnut shrimp — the kids who have never traveled keep asking what everything is and making faces. Two courses in, Holly's youngest tells her sister that the shredded daikon on her plate is fried worms. She shrieks and refuses to eat anything else.

Holly's husband, whom we don't yet know is bipolar, snaps his fingers and barks orders to the middle-aged waitress we consider a friend. He complains about not having rice, even though we explained that it's served only at the end of a banquet. My son-in-law, who has blown up like an inflatable Michelin Man figure since I saw him last, pours himself extra glasses of wine although last I heard he was a sober alcoholic. My one-year-old granddaughter struggles to escape her high chair, and my grandson drums on the table loudly with his chopsticks.

Fred lifts his glass again, then gives up on the traditional toasts for each course because everyone seems to request something from the harried waitress at once. Soft drinks, extra rice. Hot sauce, soy sauce, forks instead of chopsticks, extra napkins because someone spilled the tea. I wince as my father douses his rice with soy sauce like we did when we were growing up.

In Hong Kong, everyone thanks the host at the end of a banquet, but in the confusion, I hear only my parents thank Fred for the meal. I spend the next week apologizing to Fred for my family, which I can't stop seeing through a borrowed Chinese lens. I can't yet see the folly of plunking my buffet-on-the-beach American family into a Chinese banquet and expecting them to intuit foreign rules of etiquette to which I have a guide. I've conveniently forgotten all the cultural blunders I've made in the past four years and how long I've fled the pull of family.

After a year of family intersections, I'm ready to return to traveling back and forth between my Chinese and American families, visiting them in their natural habitats, with Hawaii as neutral ground in the middle. East. West. Center.

10

Heritage Tour

WHEN Fred and I arrive at Number 10 a week ahead of Amah and Abah's fiftieth wedding anniversary celebration, I feel better prepared than last time. I think I understand my boundaries, and I've made it very clear to Fred that group expeditions are way too much togetherness for an introvert like me. My plan is to balance time alone in the city against the family hubbub of the banquet. As soon as we've said our hellos, Amah informs us we will all leave on a trip together in two days. Fred insists we won't go, but she dismisses his protests with a wave and some rapid Cantonese. He looks at me in defeat. "This tour will take us to Chao'an," he explains. "They're all looking forward to seeing where Dad was born." My Mandarin textbook taught that Chinese everywhere identify with the part of China from which their ancestors hail. Abah's regional heritage is Teochew (Chiuchow in Cantonese, Chaozhou in Mandarin), and Teochew people everywhere trace their origins, dialect, and cuisine to a region of China's eastern Guangdong Province known as Chaoshan. Hong Kong newspapers advertise heritage tours, and the Chaoshan itinerary has the added attraction of being billed as a gourmet eating tour. It's only three days. How can we refuse? They've already purchased tickets.

I shoot eye daggers in Fred's direction and force a resigned smile at Amah. I imagine what my girlfriends in Texas, the ones who vacillate between calling me crazy and heroic, would say. There's so much that doesn't translate. My compliance in a Chinese setting would look like submission in their American feminist frame. In that context, saying no is a milestone of self-care and self-esteem. My American friends would have a hard time understanding that acting independently here would make me appear rude and, well, American. Knowing this lesson from trying not to act haole in Asian- and Polynesian-inflected Hawaii doesn't make agreeing to go any easier.

It's typhoon season and walking outdoors on the day of our departure is like entering a sauna. As we trudge down the hill to the Cheung Chau ferry, Susanna holds Amah's elbow, while Josie helps to tug our suitcases over the stairs and walkways. Fred tells me the Cantonese term for this weather is *chi lap lap* — hot and sticky. My skin feels like a flytrap. We click open umbrellas as the cloying mist becomes a rain shower then shake them out to dry when we arrive at the ferry. When Bernie meets us with the rest of the family on the Hong Kong side, he mentions that there's a category one storm warning in place.

We board the waiting tour bus, sorting ourselves into generational zones with the old people up front, our generation in the middle, and the grandchildren in the back. With twenty-four people, we have the entire bus to ourselves. Bernie and Amy, Susanna and Gulam, and Mimi sit near us. Fred tells me that the trip is partly to cheer up Mimi, who is still reeling from the loss of her husband. She sits across the aisle from us with the elder of her two daughters. Third Uncle stayed home, so Third Aunt has brought along a woman friend, the only non-Lau in the group, and I wonder what she thinks of this rowdy bunch. They sit near the front with Fred's parents, Second Aunt and Uncle, the tall uncle who can't stop talking, the two paternal aunts with matching haircuts, and the soft-spoken uncle who is a high school teacher.

I'm excited to be going to China and annoyed that I'm on a bus with the Lau clan once again. This expedition is not what I had in mind for my second trip to Hong Kong, but, as the only foreigner in the family, I do my best to fit in and not prove the stereotypes. My insights into cultural dynamics don't make me immune from sulking in private, but they do motivate me to minimize my moments of withdrawal and aversion in public. There is little private space or time for sulking anyway; besides, everyone is in infectious high spirits.

As we roll past the border and into Shenzhen, the rain grows steadily heavier, becoming what Texans call a gully washer. The bus windows fog from the body heat inside and the rain outside, so I have to wipe a porthole to see out. The six younger cousins reach and climb over each other's seats, talking, laughing, and sharing headphones. Amah passes snacks from the front of the bus to the back — she seems to have packed an endless supply. Everyone in the middle of the bus speaks Cantonese and shrieks with laughter several decibels above what I consider bearable, and the sound ricochets off the closed windows. Having chosen a window seat on purpose, I pretend to sleep so I can cover at least one ear with no one seeing, but the shrill, nasal quality of Fred's sisters' excited voices, pitched to carry several rows away, makes me flinch. I elbow Fred. "I thought Asian women were supposed to be demure," I whisper.

"Haha. Not Chinese women!"

"I get that they're having a good time, but do they have to yell?"

"They're just having fun. They're happy everyone gets to be together." I make a mental note to bring headphones if I ever do this again. I now know better than to think there won't be future group excursions.

*　*　*

Our gourmet eating tour includes visiting a series of tourist centers devoted to Chinese specialty foods. Our stops include a pork floss factory, a tea farm, and an eel farm where I refuse to get out of the bus. I'll eat eels cooked and on rice, but I have no desire to discover how they're raised, skinned, and smoked. In the bus, Amah passes around a package of sweet, dried, and shredded pork she bought to share along with all the snacks she purchased as gifts for friends. Americans give chocolates; Chinese give pork floss. I have to admit that it's good. I gave up eating vegetarian somewhere between the last trip and this one, partly because of my desire to be a good traveler who can fit easily into a new culture and partly because I tired of being told that there was only a little pork or chicken in Chinese dishes "for flavor." On the last trip, my special vegetarian soup was garnished with a chicken foot, which Fred quickly snatched from my bowl. Being too much trouble is an issue I'm working on.

Because there are so many of us, meals require two large round tables. I have always had a weak stomach when it comes to cleanliness in restaurants. My father liked to tease me about going to his favorite hamburger joint, Mel's Diner, where I once found a crispy fly in my French fries. This trip poses challenges that go beyond my issues with Chinese table etiquette.

In a Teochew restaurant in Shantou, we're squeezed into a tiny upstairs room that holds only four tables. We're seated on stools like the ones at Number 10, and I'm sitting near the wall when I spot a good-sized cockroach lazily ascending. Not wanting to make a scene, I nudge Fred and tip my head toward the roach. Fred calls the waitress and points. She pulls the wet towel out of her apron pocket, smacks it against the wall and the roach, and tucks the rag back into her apron. She then calmly goes back to taking orders from the next table. I tamp down my gag reflex just in time to see a winking chicken head arriving on the next platter.

I have never seen a naked, boiled chicken head, and I do not understand how anyone could think it attractive as a culinary garnish. Yet there it sits, propped up in the middle of its own chopped, steamed, and sauced flesh, one eye closed and its comb flopping left. Fred turns to me with an exaggerated wink, his fingers crooked over his head like the chicken's comb. Stifling a giggle, I nearly choke on my tea. Mimi sees him and says she heard that if you go out with your boss and the chicken head points to you, you'll know you're about to be fired. This strikes me as hilarious, and as Fred plops steamed chicken into my rice bowl, I'm shaking with the effort to contain my laughter.

Back in our hotel room, I put a shower cap on my head and prance around singing a made-up chicken head song in my beginner Mandarin to the tune of "Fish Heads," by Dr. Demento: "*Ji tou, Ji tou, heng pang ji tou.*" We roll on the bed, whooping and wiping our eyes. Humor, it occurs to me, might be my secret weapon for surviving Lau family travel. I already adore this man for making me laugh, for the way he laughs with his entire body — shoulders shaking, head thrown back, snorting and gasping for air. For his playfulness, his silliness, his willingness to be the epicenter of a joke by laughing at his own mistakes and foibles. The first man in my life who makes me laugh out loud and thinks my jokes are as good as his own. Serious people like me are pressure cookers with stuck safety valves. Left to ourselves, we can ferment or implode. Levity lifts the lid, lets out the steam, and connects us to the world.

* * *

The next day in Chao'an, the rain comes down in blinding sheets, and the roads brim with so much water that the bus tires leave a wake. Bicyclists slosh by draped in visored rubber ponchos that cover bike baskets and riders in pastel and primary colors. They make me think of Easter eggs. Inside, the bus windows fog over from the heat and humidity. We're a traveling terrarium suffused with the aroma of bacon. The pummeling of the rain cranks up the gaiety in the bus.

When the bus stops in a parking lot, we roll up our pant legs before clambering out into ankle-deep water. Huddled under our umbrellas, we slosh after Abah and his sisters down side streets and finally a narrow alley, where we turn into a walled courtyard.

Stepping over the high threshold of Fred's great-grandfather's house is like entering the previous century. The three wings of the dark-wood structure intersect at the corners, their tiled roofs sloping toward the courtyard in the center. Built with money sent home from work in Thailand and designed to hold generations of the same family, with sons inhabiting wings according to their birth order status, the house now holds at least one stranger's family in a front section and a vestige of the Lau family in the back. "Who are they?" I ask Fred as we pass a man, woman, and two children who stare at us through an open doorway.

Fred consults with Abah and then says, "They're a family that was assigned to live here during the Cultural Revolution. The government said these houses were too big for one family and told people where they could live."

We duck through the curtain of rain at the back of the courtyard. "And who is she?" I ask. A hunched and ancient old woman no taller than my shoulder is greeting Fred's parents and their siblings on an interior veranda that runs the length of the central wing. Everything about her seems gray, from her skin and hair to her faded clothes. Her whole face crinkles when she smiles.

Fred says, "She was given to our family a long time ago when she was young. She was supposed to marry one of Great Grandmother's brothers, so she was sent to live with the family. But then he married someone else. She never got married and didn't have any children, so he gave her one of his sons to raise. The Lau family still takes care of her." Fred's father hands the woman two large plastic bags of used clothes. As he puts an envelope into her hands, Fred says, "Now he's giving her money." Meanwhile, the young cousins exclaim over snapshots of themselves on a bulletin board on the wall. The old woman serves us strong tea at a wooden table and gestures toward a bowl filled with longans. We slip off their brown husks and pop the translucent globes into our mouths, sucking on their melony sweetness.

As I watch Amah and Abah talk to the old woman who is family but not family, I think of my beloved grandmother living in a nursing home until she passed; of my daughter and grandchildren, whom I see once a year if I'm lucky; of my parents and siblings, whom I seldom call. Here with the Lau family, I see myself as a runaway in the land of family ties, a disconnected mote in a web of connections. I want my space and privacy, but I see what they have and I want that too.

*   *   *

When we return to Number 10, I want to know more about Fred's family history. Fred translates to his father while we wait in the front room for Josie to cook dinner. As usual, the TV is on even though no one is watching Suddenly, Abah, usually shy and quiet, jumps up from his chair and waves at us to stay where we are, ignoring Fred's protests. Fred explains that his father just remembered that he wants to give him an old suitcase that belonged to his grandmother when she left southern China for Hong Kong. "He said he was going to mail it, but since we're here, he wants us to take it back with us. I keep trying to tell him we don't have room."

Abah pulls the case down from the top of a cabinet and sets it on the coffee table. A little larger than a briefcase, it's made of heavy cardboard lacquered a faded reddish brown and has a brass sliding lock and corner caps. The sides are scuffed, and when he opens it, we can see a yellowed newspaper lining. Eager to empty the case, Abah lifts out papers and old photographs that he piles to one side. Fred shakes his head and says to me, "I don't know how I'm supposed to carry that, but he won't listen. He never does. You just have to humor him." I glance nervously at Abah to see if he overheard. I've noticed Abah follows our conversations in English, smiling and sometimes nodding on occasion, but I never know how much he understands, because he's too shy to speak it.

Fred sifts through the pile, showing me pictures of his parents. *Here's my mom when she was young. This is their wedding picture. Here's my grandma.* He stops short at a black-and-white photo of Abah as a young man standing in front of a painted studio backdrop. He's wearing the drab hat and quilted jacket of Mao's communist army — his baggy pants and jacket too large for his slight frame, his right hand resting on the holster of a gun strapped to his leather belt. His slender, unsmiling face with the large ears is that of a pensive dreamer, not a soldier. "What's this?" Fred dangles the photo in front of his father, who chuckles with his hand over his mouth. "I've never seen this one before!" Fred says to me. Abah picks up another photo that shows a group of young soldiers and points to himself in the back row. The same unsmiling expression amid a group of boys in soldier outfits.

As Fred asks questions, I wait for a lull, caught in the lag-time before translation, perpetually out of conversational synch. I watch how his father's facial expressions and gestures accompany the pitches, slides, and falls of his tones, how the drawn-out vowels add drama to the telling. Abah seems agitated and points to a man in the front row. "His friend who helped him escape," Fred explains. As his father's storytelling picks up speed, my after-the-fact version arrives in fits and starts. As usual, I am primed for suspense, drama, and comedy before I know the story. It's as if I'm first watching a movie with the sound turned off before getting a recap of the dialogue. I can feel and see the intensity of this story.

Fred translates: "He says he was young and idealistic. He ran after the communists' truck and told them he wanted to join up. At first, they didn't believe him since he looked like a weak city boy, but he said he wanted to teach the peasants to read, to be one of what they called the 'send-down youth,' so they finally took him. His superior trusted him with a leadership position and a gun, but he says he never wanted to have a gun or be in charge. He wanted out. He says no one trusted anyone to not turn them in, but there was one guy who got nothing from home, and Dad had shared his packages from Grandma with him and loaned him money. When Grandma wrote Dad a fake letter telling him she was sick, he trusted this guy and found out he wanted to leave too. So they came up with a plan to escape together."

Abah waits for Fred to finish, then sounds conspiratorial as he explains what happened next. Fred relates: "At the end of their training, there was a banquet to celebrate their graduation. During the banquet, Dad and the other guy stood up and announced that there wasn't enough food and they were going out for more. As soon as they were out of the banquet hall, they changed from their uniforms into street clothes they'd stashed nearby and ran for the train platform."

Abah stands now, eyes wide and arms waving; then he crouches down to mime a hobbling, bent-over run, bobbing up several times to look over his shoulder. I've never seen him this animated. At last, he finishes talking and sits down, so Fred finishes translating: "When they didn't return, guards were sent to find them. They could see the guards coming, so they ducked behind an old woman with a cart carrying heavy bags and barely made it to the train by staying behind her. Dad had to hide out in Hong Kong for a while after he got back because the commies were still looking for him. They came to the house, but Grandma always said she didn't know where he was."

Abah sits quietly, his hands resting on his pajama-covered knees. "Wow," Fred says, leaning back and shaking his head. "I never knew he was a communist!"

Amah has walked in from the kitchen during the telling; now she points at Abah and speaks in a teasing tone I once thought was accusatory. The men laugh, and Fred explains, "Mom says they were on opposite sides because her father was a general in the Kuomintang, and she could have married a general but instead she ended up with this communist sympathizer." Abah laughs quietly, and I can see how the rough and smooth of their relationship have fit together for fifty years.

In bed that night, I think about our family migrations. My grandfather and his siblings moved to America to escape the pogroms and restrictions on Jews in Ukraine. My grandmother's family dispersed because of the Russian Revolution. Fred's grandparents moved from China to Hong Kong ahead of the communists. Second Uncle got stuck in Beijing, separated from the rest of the family for years. War and political upheaval have shaped our family histories.

Fred's parents' fiftieth-anniversary party, the event for which we traveled to Hong Kong this time, is a grand affair in a hotel ballroom. We arrive at five o'clock, but the mahjong enthusiasts have been playing at tables along one side of the room since two. At least fifteen round dining tables are set for a dozen guests each, and, after an hour of photos, we are finally seated at the head table. On the stage, the grandchildren perform a skit they created that pokes gentle fun of Amah and Abah's habits, and they play a song on their various musical instruments: cello, clarinet, and saxophone. When the parts don't quite come together, they joke that they didn't have time to rehearse. Fred gives a speech that makes everyone laugh; then Abah says a few words and gets so teary that he has to stop for a minute. Others wipe their eyes as well. "So sentimental," Fred says. "He says he is honored to be married to this wonderful woman." At my parents' fiftieth anniversary dinner at the Everett Country Club, my father gave a speech in which he said he owed it all to Viagra and his therapist. No mention of his wife of five decades and no public sentimentality.

As far as I know, my father never saw a therapist, but I did once spot a bottle of Viagra in their medicine cabinet. Public sentiment is not in our family repertoire.

We are served twelve courses at the Lau anniversary banquet. "So much meat! *Bao le!*" I moan to Fred when I am full after the fourth or fifth course.

"Pace yourself! They always serve lots of meat at a formal banquet to show bounty and give guests the best stuff. Remember the rice and noodles show up after the last course." He reminds me, "The rice course is a polite way of saying that we're so sorry there wasn't enough food and you're still hungry. And then there will be sweets for dessert."

"How could anyone still be hungry?"

"You can't. That's the point. It's all ritual. Just for show." I try to nibble on each course as it comes, and Fred eats what I leave on my plate. The plates are whisked away and replaced at intervals.

Full as I am, when Amah and Abah pose like newlyweds next to a three-layer wedding cake, I look forward to having something Western and familiar to top off all that Chinese food. They pose holding the knife but don't cut into the cake. They smile but don't kiss. As they take their seats again, two waiters step forward to take the cake away. They lift the table by its legs, and when the cake tips to one side, I gasp just as a waiter grabs the top and rights it. They tote the plastic cake out of view, and the real Chinese dessert — red bean soup with black sesame mochi balls — is served.

PART II: 2007–2008

11

Number 10

Our new condo in Hawaii, my first stab at renovation, is modern and beautiful and rented to strangers. Our borrowed flat on Cheung Chau is somewhere between basic and outdated. It is, however, free because it belongs to Third Aunt, who lives at Number 10 and has generously allowed us to live in it for the nine months of Fred's sabbatical. To get to our tile-covered, two-story walkup, we must climb one more set of stairs beyond Number 10, walk across the upper road and through an iron gate, and slip past the downstairs neighbors' dogs, who bark like they want to eat us. In reverse, all exits lead past Number 10, if you don't count the long way around. It's August and hot, so we mostly take the shorter route.

"I don't get it. Why do they leave the labels on everything?" I'm standing between the minuscule kitchen and the compact living and dining area. Faded and peeling manufacturer's labels stick to the kitchen wall cabinets, the fan, and the water heater.

"It shows that something's new."

"New? You can't even read the print on these anymore." I can feel myself morphing into my aesthetic cop mode, but I can't stop. "And what's with keeping the plastic on everything? This fan is rusted, and it's still in its original plastic wrap!" I'm pointing to the floor fan, its stand encased in a wrinkled plastic sleeve.

"Just a different way of looking at things."

"But it's so tacky."

"Hey, at least we're not staying at Number 10."

"Ha! That wouldn't have worked." I know it would have worked perfectly for him. "I have my standards."

"Maybe your standards are too high for Cheung Chau. Maybe you should have married somebody rich." There's a tightness to his voice now, a clench in his jaw. I hate it when he goes there, and he does it only when I've pushed too far. I'm always startled when his colorful stories about growing up in "the country" tip into defensiveness. Nothing in my middle-class American experience compares to the class striations of colonial Hong Kong. It's his home island, I remind myself, and I'm a foreign guest.

I try to dial it back. "Sorry. I appreciate Third Aunt letting us stay here. I'm just trying to make it livable." What I don't say is that my friends in Texas and Hawaii think I'm a saint for being here at all. They'd heard my stories, and they had questions. *What will you do for a year? Who will you talk to? Why would you agree to live near his family when you crave privacy? What about the language?* Firmly planted in mid-life, they would never leave their homes, pets, jobs, and stuff to go trailing behind a husband.

After assuring them I could do this, I feel like a big fat failure, and I just got here. No matter how hard I try to be adaptable, I end up sounding high-maintenance.

I size up what I can do to make the place look and function better. I've already moved the flimsy rattan furniture around. We'll need new sheets for the two beds — a tiny double in the cramped bedroom and a twin in the alcove next to the galley kitchen no bigger than an alcove. We have a flowered polyester quilt from Amah. She offered us Number 10 towels — thin and stiff from drying on the line, but I brought my own. Showering with hot water requires forethought in the form of turning on a switch at least twenty minutes before getting wet. I regularly forget and get doused in cold water. In the cabinets are plastic bowls and chopsticks and cheap aluminum pots and pans. We can hit the backstreet sundries store for anything else we need, but Fred keeps reminding me that whatever we accumulate will get left behind. I say I can make do, although the thought of washing dishes in cold water sends me close to the edge. The topic of meals pushes me over.

Amah has just called Fred, and he reports, "Mom's says dinner is almost ready." It's the third or fourth time she has called his mobile phone today, and we were there for lunch. Fred and I are still pre-mobile-phones in Hawaii, and I'm not used to feeling tracked.

"Are we eating at Number 10 again?"

"Of course. They're expecting us."

"Why would that be? What did you tell your mom?"

"I didn't tell her anything. She was excited we were coming, and she assumed we'd stay at Number 10 because they have plenty of room. I said I didn't think that would work for such a long time, so I guess Mom talked to Third Aunt, and she offered us her flat as another option."

"What does that have to do with meals?"

"A trade-off? She assumed we would eat with them since we're so close."

"Did you tell her we would eat all our meals with them?"

He's looking sheepish now. "I guess I didn't tell her we wouldn't. Think of the bright side. Isn't it better than having to cook? I don't see why it's a problem."

"It's a problem because you made a deal with her without even asking me! What if I don't want to eat with them three times a day?" In this battle of principles, I've forgotten that we have only a rudimentary cold-water kitchen and must carry groceries up ramps and stairs that leave me breathless and shimmering with sweat. That we have a two-burner propane stove I'm convinced could blow up. I'm too busy rebelling against imposed communalism and old peoples' eating schedules and rice.

"What if I tell her just dinners?" he asks as we head down the stairs.

"Fine. As long as we can get out if it when we want to." I'm holding out for frequent dinners in the city on our own — and more options than Chinese food in this international city. For now, we are en route to Number 10, announced by the neighbors' deafening dog patrol.

* * *

As a result of what I see as the great eating compromise and what Fred sees as the convenient eating solution, I have frequent headaches in the next few weeks, some real and a few manufactured. My staying home does not mean that he stays with me and cooks for me like he does in Hawaii. Instead, it results in steaming plates of food covered in plastic wrap that arrive with him when he returns from Number 10. The plates are filled with whatever Amah thinks

I like best — never fish because I am now famous for choking on fish bones. Mostly they're filled with home-cooked dishes Fred loves and that I am learning to appreciate: pork hash, drunken chicken, long beans with preserved olives. Fred's cousin, the last remaining young person living in Number 10, has laughingly warned us not to praise any dish too much because everyone will be stuck eating it for a week when Amah has Josie make it again and again. She is that happy to have her eldest son back.

Over dinner at Number 10, Amah watches me closely. Fred translates, "She says you don't eat enough rice." At the beginning of every meal, we pass our bowls to the person sitting next to the rice cooker. Then the filled bowls are passed back. During the meal, everyone plucks bits of vegetables, fish, and meat from the serving dishes with their chopsticks, places these on their rice, and scoops up whatever they are eating with a mouthful of underlying rice. Though other rice bowls are emptied and refilled, my bowl is never empty until Fred takes over at the end of the meal. No wonder he's so round. From the time he was small, he won his grandmother's praise for being a "good eater."

I point to my half-empty bowl. "I eat rice."

"She says you get headaches because you don't eat enough rice." I fake a laugh and finish the bowl.

Amah wants to make me herbal tonics for my headaches. Because the tonics are bitter, and I hate eating alone, I show up at Number 10 more often than I meant to. I try to eat more rice.

Evening meals get more interesting for a while when "the old people," as Fred calls the Number 10 residents, take up drinking red wine with dinner. The bank where Third Uncle used to work has sent him bottles of French wine over the years. No one in the house drinks, so a thin layer of dust films the bottles despite their being kept in the glass-fronted cabinet beside Third Aunt's aquarium. Now Third Uncle pours everyone an inch of wine from a bottle infused with bobbing chunks of onion because someone heard that red wine with onion was good for your heart. They each down their "medicine" with dinner. They grimace and shudder as they drink, so Fred helps them out by opening our own bottle and making some of the wine disappear. We have only tiny sherry glasses, and we don't want them to see us as lushes, but even sips remind me of when I had an independent life without an audience.

After dinner, I help Second and Third Aunts stack the bowls and chopsticks and dump the paper placemats and bones into the trash. Third Uncle makes dinner for the dogs from the leftovers, mostly rice, while we take the dishes outside and wash them in cold water at the outdoor sink. Josie washes while Third Aunt and I dry. They practice their limited English on me. Once the sun has gone down, the air in the tiled courtyard is cool.

* * *

The best part of our second-floor flat is that it includes the rooftop of the building. We reach it by going out our front door and up the interior staircase. Against the stairwell wall on our terra-cotta tiled roof is a rickety green shed that contains an ancient washing machine, some shelves, and a sink. A low wall runs around the perimeter. From our building at the high point of the island, we can see over the tiers of houses, past Number 10, and toward the main harbor, where we can glimpse the masts of fishing boats. On the other side is a sweeping view over the less densely populated back side of the island with its greenery-flanked pathways and beaches, and beyond them, the South China Sea dotted with fishing boats. When the pollution haze lifts, we can see Lantau Island on the horizon. On those days, the sky is a cerulean blue glorious for its rarity, although it never matches the intensity of the Hawaii skies we took for granted. We hang our laundry from the double clothesline that runs the length of the roof and clean off the plastic chairs stacked against the wall so we can lounge in the shade of the sheets.

Away from home and in a borrowed flat, I need a project. The online American Studies class I am teaching for the University of Hawai'i is off to a slow start, and when Fred takes the ferry into town for his visiting professor job at Hong Kong University, I am marooned on Cheung Chau. He tells me to go to Number 10 for lunch, but I feel awkward going there without him to translate, so I make peanut butter sandwiches and work on setting up a blog. I feel like a ham radio operator tinkering with the device that will connect me to the world.

A row of tiled planters lines the opposite end of our roof. Some rangy weeds and a few sticks that were once shrubs poke out of dirt so parched and pale it looks like cracked concrete. With a rusty trowel and a short steel bar I discover in the shed, I chip at it until it comes away in dusty clods. Wearing an old pair of gardening gloves, I yank on the dead shrubs until their withered roots break loose. Among the weeds, I find what I think are canna lilies. I set them aside in a plastic bucket with some water.

Once started, I continue through the weekend. "We aren't staying forever, you know," says Fred, content to lean back in his plastic chair with his shirt off. It's Saturday, after all.

"We're staying long enough that I need to make a garden."

"What about Third Aunt?"

"It will be our contribution, a thank you for loaning us her flat."

"*Tai mafan,*" he says, shaking his head and using the Mandarin phrase for too much trouble. "A lot of work for something temporary."

Despite his reluctance, I coax him to the garden shop where we've often stopped to admire the plants while walking with Amah and Abah. When we pass, Amah always greets the pleasant young woman who runs the shop. Despite Fred's misgivings, we purchase two large bags of potting soil and four bougainvillea starter plants in shades from white to hot pink. I envision a blaze of color that will be my mark on the flat.

That afternoon, the shop-owner's brother delivers our purchases using one of the few vehicles allowed on Cheung Chau. It's a mini flatbed truck minus the cab; instead, it has an engine, a steering wheel, and a seat for the driver, who arrives via the single road that winds up the hillside to the upper road. The few other vehicles I've seen include a miniature ambulance, fire truck, and police wagon, all the size of a Smart car, some with extensions and all skinny enough to fit through narrow streets packed with vendors' wares and pedestrians. I've even seen a miniature senior van with open sides carrying four elderly people tightly packed together.

With my nursery supplies delivered, I do my best to aerate the parched soil by driving my steel bar into the packed dirt. I cover it with the topsoil and set in the new plants. Using an old, leaky hose, I water and water, but the bougainvillea shed all of their colorful bracts in the first week and soon look like the dead plants I worked so hard to remove. Gardening has always seemed such a transparent metaphor for whatever I'm doing or not doing in my life — weeding, transplanting, pruning, waiting, occasionally blooming — that the bougainvillea seems a gloomy comment on my inability to root myself in this new place. The rescued lilies, one of my least favorite flowers, unfurl like torn scarves.

* * *

Each time we make the trek downhill to the ferry or back home again, we pass a collection of one-room tarpaper shacks with galvanized tin roofs, low-slung structures that look as if they grew out of castoff materials rather than being intentionally built. They remind me of carrier shells I had in a childhood collection, ocean snails who camouflage themselves by attaching debris to their exteriors. These buildings hug the walkway, patterned tiles at their entrances. The doorways are decorated with tattered red and gold lucky paper and dented canisters spiked with stumps of incense sticks. A couple have sprouted air conditioning units and outdoor sinks, although none has actual plumbing. Sometimes we hear a television and see an old woman sitting on a stool near her door. When I ask about these dwellings, Fred says, "Those are the boat people houses. A few generations ago, some fishermen dragged their boats inland and made them into houses. Now the government wants to tear them all down because they're unsanitary. No plumbing."

"Where do they wash? Where do they go to the bathroom?"

He points down the hill, and says, "They have to use the public restrooms for all their water-related needs." I try to imagine bathing and washing my clothes in a public restroom and come up with an image of the homeless people in Hawaii.

There is something of the barnacle to these structures, seagoing vessels now cemented to rock. When we walk along the street or ride the ferry, Fred points out weathered old people who speak as if they were shouting over the wind and dress in layers of sunfaded clothes. He refers to them as "former boat people," their fishy origins never forgotten.

"How did they get their boats so far inland?" I ask.

"It's the shore that's moved, not the houses. Over there, all this," Fred says as he waves his arm toward the harbor and front streets, "The main street, the wet market, the ferry terminal, the restaurants, and the funeral space are all on reclaimed land. The boat people's houses mark the island's former shoreline."

When we take our evening stroll with Amah and Abah on the upper road, Fred points to a three-story concrete block apartment building and explains that the government moved the boat people to new apartments. He's heard that there are former boat people who come down the hill to stay in their former homes. I wonder if they missed their proximity to the street market, their short walk to the sea, having doorsteps where everyone walked by. I know how the familiar can tug us like a tide.

12

Parade

ON Cheung Chau, we're governed by the moon as much as by the sun. On the twenty-first day of the seventh lunar cycle, which falls in September this year, Fred and I accompany Abah on a day trip to the neighboring island of Peng Chau for an annual festival. Abah is treasurer of the Cheung Chau Teochew Association, and the association members are all going. Fred grew up hearing the Teochew dialect spoken by his paternal grandmother and among his father's siblings. I assumed he would be excited about joining the group. Instead, he resisted. He complained that he had grading to do, that he didn't want to be gone all day, that it was supposed to rain. I suspected that the prospect of spending an entire day with his father was the real reason. I pushed him to say yes because I was excited about seeing another island and using my folklore fieldwork training to gather information and photos for my blog.

The three of us head out in the early morning, walking down the hill to the main street, where we climb a narrow staircase to the Teochew Association hall. Five men are already there in an upstairs room decorated in red and black. The air is laced with sandalwood incense burning on an altar table near the far wall. The men all wear yellow polo shirts, each with Cheung Chau Teochew Association printed on the front pocket and Blue Girl Beer emblazoned across the back. "*Joh sun! Joh sun!*" they greet us. We wish everyone good morning, and, as Abah introduces us to his friends, his usually serious expression gives way to smiles because his eldest son, the one who lives so far away and is usually missing from family activities, stands by his side.

I'm the only non-Chinese in the hall and the only woman. I wave my camera and smile to show the men I will be their photojournalist for the day. Abah nods in approval. Donning a yellow sports shirt, he bustles about with the other association members who are assembling bronze gongs and cymbals on a long side table. They load the instruments onto a bright-yellow pushcart decorated with the association name and holding a thigh-high kettle-shaped drum with a head the size of a manhole cover. Abah explains that the Cheung Chau association is assisting the Peng Chau association, which is too small to have its own drum. Fred reminds me that noise is an essential component of any Chinese festival, so we are bringing the *renao*, the "hot and noisy." Too late I realize that I forgot to bring earplugs.

While the men ready their equipment, Fred inspects a series of black-and-white photos on the wall nearest the door and calls me over. "Look, here's my grandfather," he says. I recognize the face that floats above the dining room door in Number 10. "Grandpa was the head of the association. Dad is the treasurer now." He leads me to the end of the long room, where tiers of black wooden plaques hang against a vermilion wall. "Our family's ancestral tablets," he says, pointing to a lower row.

"Everyone?" I ask.

"Just the men, I think," he replies.

The tablets look like miniature gravestones. On the altar sits an assortment of pink and white feather and silk flowers, bottles of oil, and a tall oil lamp with an open flame. Abah appears behind us with a fistful of incense. He points his chin at the Lau family tablets, then hands Fred three sticks. Side by side, they light the sticks from the oil lamp and bow three times toward the tablets before placing the incense in a sand-filled bowl. The smoke curls upward.

I feel an affinity for Fred's shy, quiet father, so often accused of being moody by the rest of the family, but I've learned to keep my observations to myself most of the time. When I sympathize, Fred says, "You don't know how he used to be. You haven't seen his temper. He used to drive everyone crazy." He still storms out of rooms and sulks from time to time, but I suspect that his moody silences and retreats, what the family calls his temper, are signs of a short fuse for frustration and the coiling inward of an introvert in an environment where pulling away from others is considered abnormal and antisocial. I see a listener and a watcher like myself.

I often chide Fred for saying "I told you so," but today I can't resist whispering, "See, it's good we came. Your father is so happy." Amah remained at home because a parade meant too much walking, so today Abah occupies the foreground, and we are his guests. *No competition or commentary*, I think.

"We'll see," says Fred.

Having paid our respects to the dead, we're ready to go. Two younger men tote the drum on its cart down the steep stairs while others carry the cymbals and gongs. When we're joined by a few family members at the ferry pier, I'm happy to see that there are other women coming along. We board a pint-sized ferry with a single deck and an open cabin and settle into rows of green plastic chairs.

"So what's this festival about," I ask Fred, who is used to my constant stream of questions, my endless curiosity about traditions. He confers with Abah, launching the usual conversational dance in which I am never satisfied with his abbreviated answers.

"It's a procession around the island," he says. I'm prepared for walking; I'm wearing a new pair of cream and green Ecco sandals, and I brought my umbrella. Amah doesn't let me out of the house without an umbrella for sun or rain.

"But what does it celebrate? Is this part of the Ghost Festival?" In the past few days, colorful Ghost Festival banners and an outdoor opera stage have sprung up on Cheung Chau.

"No, this is different. This is to thank the god for saving the people from a plague."

"Which god?" It seems there are gods for everything; I can't keep them straight, though I revel in the multiplicity. I like the idea of hedging cosmic bets.

"This procession is for Tin Hau."

"Isn't she the same as Mazu? The protector of sailors?"

"Tin Hau for Cantonese. She saves people from drowning, but she does other stuff too. Mostly saving people." I met Mazu in China, where she appeared relatively normal compared to the pantheon of male gods, many of which have visages so terrifying they look more like demons: black or red faces and bulging eyes, ready to bellow and thrash. Mazu, on the other hand, sat serene behind a beaded veil.

"Tin Hau is the patron god of Peng Chau. This festival thanks her for saving the people from a plague." Another heavenly intervention to add to the list of her selfless deeds, like saving sailors and healing her mother.

After twenty minutes, we see the harbor at Peng Chau, Cheung Chau's sleepy smaller brother. A sign at the pier claims the island has only six thousand people to Cheung Chau's thirty thousand. Several members of the Peng Chau Teochew Association — easy to spot in their yellow shirts — meet us at the pier. There are noisy greetings as the group congeals then crosses the open plaza to a squat temple sandwiched between taller buildings. I've been worrying that members will wonder why I am here with the group, but so far no one seems to notice or care.

In front of the temple, a small crowd forms under a striped plastic awning. Three Taoist priests, wearing long red satin robes and black hats like slouchy mortarboards, bow and chant while circling an altar covered in piles of bananas, oranges, and pomelos pricked with burning incense sticks. I can't see Tin Hau, but I know she must be inside, impassively receiving her tributes, perhaps smiling demurely as she is fanned by heavenly attendants. One priest periodically strikes a large gong. Another priest punctuates the chanting by clanging a large pair of cymbals.

We are joined by more men in yellow shirts, and when the priests wind down their ritual, the combined Teochew Association picks up where the priests left off. The men form a double line in front of the temple with the big drum cart in the middle. On each side of the drummer stand members with hand gongs and cymbals. One Peng Chau member pulls a cart topped by a crude noisemaking ensemble: two yellow paint buckets with lids and an enormous metal dishpan. No wonder they needed Cheung Chau backup. The players erupt into a metallic cacophony that makes my head feel like a struck gong. My heart races and slows with the drumbeats. Two horns add a piercing minor drone over the top, sounding eerie and insistent, like a bagpipe married to a kazoo. "*Suona*," Fred shouts into my ear. The tune snakes over the deep booms of the drum, the clanging cymbals, and the reverberating gongs. The gods must be hard of hearing. They will be stone deaf by the end of the day. With my fingers in my ears, I notice several small children and some of the adults have cotton in theirs. I wonder how I can take pictures and cover my ears at the same time. The Teochew group's greeting to Tin Hau crests in a frenzied explosion of noise, and in the momentary lull afterward, voices sound tinny and distant. Not that it matters since no one around me is speaking English.

This festival is the last place I would ever expect to find myself — the girl with hearing like a cat, who gets agitated by noises no one else notices. When I was a toddler, my mother complained that she couldn't take me anywhere because crowds and noise made me hysterical. Parades and fireworks were the worst. Vietnam, China, Hong Kong, Peng Chau: all deafening. Somewhere, even before the East-West Center, my life path took a crazy turn and ended up in the wrong hemisphere. That I've committed myself to someone who wouldn't flinch if a brass band played in his car or blush if his pants fell down on a public bus still astonishes me. That I ended up in a culture that uses ear-splitting dins to celebrate must be either a karmic joke or a lesson yet to be revealed.

* * *

After the temple ritual, our hosts lead us down a side street to their regional association hall. Inside the tiled building are tables spread with sausage buns, *char siu* pork, noodles, and cans of soda. The men pour from bottles of Blue Girl Beer provided by their official sponsor. Abah chats and laughs. He seems to know everyone. The only outsider, I'm afraid of looking like a tourist who has wandered in, but the women smile and beckon, urging us to eat: *"Sik faan!"* We finish quickly, and when we go back outside, the sky is dark and threatening rain. One of the men fetches a sheet of plastic to tuck over the top of the drum. We retrace our steps to the plaza, which has filled with noise and people in our absence. As light rain begins to fall, umbrellas unfurl like clumps of mushrooms.

The general disorder shapes itself into a horseshoe and, as with urban break dancing, groups burst into the space in the center to perform before the temple. Several lion-dance troupes in succession writhe and clown. The papier-mâché heads, more massive mythical beast than any real lion ever seen, are furred and spangled, with rolling eyes, wagging ears, and flapping jaws. The dancer in the front end of each lion rears the head above the crowd, using internal levers to roll its bulging eyes and snap its articulated lower jaw while the dancer in the rear gyrates his hips to wag the lion's tufted tail. Replacement dancers hover on the sidelines dressed in T-shirts and satin lion leg pants ruffled by furry stripes. A multi-colored *qilin*, the grotesque East Asian answer to the unicorn, leaps into center stage, spinning and ducking its horned head. Then a troop of small Boy Scouts snakes a long, yellow dragon around and over the crowd on tall poles. Next comes a group of women whose costumes include cloth horses hung over wooden frames and draped to the ground so that the women appear to be riding. The horse dancers, with their long black ponytails and red and black makeup, look like depictions of

Mongolians in Chinese art. Finally, two hand trucks full of gleeful little girls stuffed into gold and silver lamé leotards jump and gyrate to Canto-pop songs blasting from a boom box.

After the performances, the Teochew Association bangs its drums and gongs once more. Someone lights a yards-long string of firecrackers that explodes like a machine gun as smoke and bits of red paper fill the air. Even with my fingers jammed into my ears, my head feels like a shattered vase.

When Tin Hau has had enough human adoration and the ground is littered with shards of red paper, the crowd somehow knows that it's time to take this show on the road. Joining Abah and the rest of the Teochew Association, we are no longer just part of the entourage; we are part of a parade. As we march down a street leading out of the plaza, I am dismayed to find that bystanders are now looking at us instead of me looking at them. I nudge Fred, "I feel so out of place!"

"Don't worry," he assures me with a grin. "You're the right size."

"The right size but wrong face and not in a costume."

"Think of it as blessing their festival by being here."

Invading is more what I'm thinking, but it's too late for that. We're being swept along.

We funnel into an awning-covered street so narrow we can walk only two across, no small feat with pennants, mythical beasts, horses, and drums. Shopkeepers and residents stand in their open doorways to watch us file past. I'm on the wrong side of the action to take pictures. Heat spreads over my neck and face just like it did in all the onstage moments I've tried to forget — falling up the stage stairs when I was the reader for a grade-school play, flubbing dance and piano recitals when I blanked out on directions and notes, opening my mouth to no sound at a teen audition to sing with a band. Where is my cloak of invisibility when I need it? A costume would have made this better, preferably one with a mask to hide my non-Chinese face.

We emerge into another plaza, where more people wait. The rain has stopped for the moment, so the dancers and musicians perform once again. As we make our way around the island through more skinny streets, along a seawall, across a narrow bridge, and up a hill, we lose our audience. We're a procession now, not a parade. Relaxing my jaw, I roll the knots out of my shoulders. The rain lifts and showers. Water seeps between my toes. Our umbrellaed heads are dry, but wet pants cling to everyone's legs from the knees down. My new shoes are caked with red mud. I mind, and then I don't because even with a plastic-covered drum and rain-soaked feet and legs, Abah is a steady fizz of good cheer.

At the top of another hill, we stop to buy canned tea and sodas at a shop across from a small bar. Beside it is a stone grotto lined with empty liquor bottles. I joke to Fred about this being a spirit shrine of a different sort than the many spirit shrines we've passed along the way. When he looks at me blankly, I have to explain the humor, turning the translation tables for a change. No one has been watching us for the last hour of our procession, and without an audience to worry about, I've finally stopped watching myself and let my discomfort wash away.

The rain fizzles to a stop, and my feet and calves are protesting by the time we come to a stop in front of a school. Groups of per-formers peel off to go to their homes, the ferry, or their association halls. We stroll with the local Teochew group to a small restaurant near the pier, where they treat us to a dinner that includes heaps of freshly caught shrimp. Here on Peng Chau, where no one is watching me, I shuck the shrimp like I would Texas crawfish and do a fair job of keeping up with Fred and Abah.

On the short ferry ride home, I close my eyes and try not to think of climbing the many steps home once we're back on Cheung Chau. Fred chats with his father, and I hear none of his usual tight impaticncc. That alone, I muse as I slide down and rest my head against the molded plastic seat, is worth ruining a new pair of shoes and maybe a portion of my hearing.

13

Dragon and Phoenix

Two weeks ago, a red-and-gold invitation was hand delivered to Number 10 from Fred's cousin's house down the hill. It featured intertwined hearts with the English names of the bride and groom and cartoon graphics of two large-headed children dressed in Qing dynasty wedding attire. Inside was a *lai see*, a small red envelope containing a bill worth less than an American dollar. "Token money for the symbolic ritual exchange," Fred says when I hold up the paltry amount. "The big bucks are for gifts and New Year."

Number 10 is once removed from this wedding, so I am surprised by how much everyone is involved. We attend a small banquet lunch given for close family by the groom's parents at one of the seafood restaurants near the pier. Then there is the important business of gifts to navigate. Fred says Amah always knows the right gift or amount of money to give for weddings: 24-karat gold jewelry for women in the immediate family, otherwise money in amounts that decrease with relational distance. For this wedding, Fred and I are dispatched to the bank to get a special gift check for several hundred Hong Kong dollars. Third Uncle writes out a list of traditional greetings, so Fred will know what to write on the card. Then the check is hand-delivered to Fred's uncle, the father of the groom. I am aghast at the amount we're expected to spend, but Fred explains that guests are expected to pay their way at the banquet, and family must pay gift money on top of that.

* * *

Although I've had more than my share of weddings, they've each been simple affairs with minimal family involvement from my side and none from the other. The first two times around, I was guilty of thinking of in-laws as extra baggage if I thought of them at all. When hard times hit my first marriage, it didn't occur to me — in my desperation at twenty-five — that moving the three of us across state lines meant leaving his family as well as trying to escape destitution. My daughter would see her Arkansas grandparents only twice more in their short and overworked lives. The second time around, at a jaded thirty-eight, I told my friends, "Good thing I'm not marrying his family! It's perfect that they're so far away." I didn't yet understand the presence of absence, the way we carry our families within us and shape our relationships according to the relationships that shaped us.

Given my marital history, I could be cynical about weddings, but I'm a romantic. Even TV weddings make me cry. Between my two brothers, my sister, and me, we've racked up eight weddings and five divorces, yet I still love weddings and believe in marriage. I'm thrilled at the opportunity to see a Chinese wedding.

* * *

My first taste of Chinese wedding traditions was last month, when we heard loud voices from next door to our flat. We watched from our balcony as a groom and his friends came to fetch his bride. From where we stood, we could see the young men below and the bridesmaids above. Fred said the bride was probably at her upstairs window, hidden behind the curtains. "Courtship games," he explained. "Listen." Clumped at the door, the groomsmen called up to the house while the bridesmaids hung over the balcony railing, calling back and doubling over with laughter. Fred said, "The groom has to beg to be let in, and the bride's friends make him pay first." The girls went into a huddle and scribbled something on a piece of paper. A minute later, two of them appeared in the courtyard and handed it to one of the groomsmen. The boys started hooting and pushing each other to the front while the girls above and below pointed and yelled back.

"What are they saying?"

"The girls are saying, 'You're his brothers, so you must do this for him! If you cheat, we'll start over! Push-ups! One hand behind your back!' The groom's friends are considered his brothers and have to do the stuff for him."

Several men complied while the groom, dressed in a red-brocade vest, stood safely behind his friends. The go-between girls demanded that the boys in front do more push-ups while the other boys clapped, and the girls counted. When the boys collapsed, the front door opened and one of the girls held out a bowl full of something that caused the boys to protest and pretend to gag. Fred said, "It's probably fish balls covered with syrup or marshmallows soaked in soy sauce." The groom grabbed the man nearest to him and thrust him in front. Fred continued, "He's saying 'Eat for me!'"

The boy who ate exclaimed "*Aiyaaa!*" and ran out of the courtyard to spit the food in the bushes.

"The girls are saying, 'Your real brothers will help you! The ones who run away aren't your real brothers! Do you think it's easy to get a wife?'"

Next, the girls grilled the groom.

"They're making him answer questions about her favorite food and flowers and colors." The groom must have passed, because the girls finally opened the door. I was thrilled to witness living traditions. Now I get to be a wedding guest and see even more.

* * *

On the day of the wedding, we walk to the pier with the Number 10 crew in our fancier-than-usual clothes, and I ask Fred what to expect. He reminds me that, although his cousin is from Cheung Chau, he's marrying a city girl, who might think traditional games are too old-fashioned. We know from Amah's family hotline that yesterday the groom got up early to take the 5:45 ferry to Hong Kong. His city friends met him at the pier with a decorated car, and together they went to collect the bride and bring her to the Cheung Chau ferry. When they arrived on Cheung Chau, the group walked to the groom's house, two stairways below Number 10. Fred speculates about what might have happened. The bride would have worn a red silk cheongsam, and her family would have sent sprouted coconuts and other symbolic gifts to the groom's family. The couple would have bowed to the groom's family altar, requesting the ancestors' blessings on the union. The bride would have served tea to her future in-laws to show respect for his parents. His mother would have gifted her with gold, each necklace and bracelet linking the bride-to-be to her new family.

We ride the fast ferry to the Hong Kong side, disembark, and pile into multiple taxis that whisk us up the hills to the office building where the legal ceremonies take place. I'm surprised to see the couple posing on the steps in full wedding attire and greeting people as they arrive. I've always heard it is bad luck to see the bride before the ceremony. The bride, professionally made up with false eyelashes, silver sparkles in her face powder, and an elaborate updo, wears a voluminous white satin dress with a train. The groom reminds me of a drum major or a magician in his top-stitched gray jacket with tails and a silver metallic tie and vest, his hair stylishly spiked. They look breathtakingly young.

We parade up the steps and into the lift in batches. We rejoin in an office lobby where long strips of pink tulle festoon the ceiling tiles, and portable easels display portraits of the day's wedding couples. An attendant directs our party down a hall to a waiting room already packed with family and friends. While we wait, we admire the pastel dresses and coifed hair of the aunts and mother of the groom. The groom's mother has streaks of silver glitter in her hair, and the rest of the aunties shimmer like figures in a shaken snow globe. One of the bride's friends dashes in to grab a bouquet of plastic roses off a chair.

Soon a clerk motions us into the wedding hall, a pink extravaganza. "I feel like we're in a Barbie house," I whisper to Fred. At one end of the hall is a long table covered in pink flowered fabric and lace, and at the other end are matching floor-to-ceiling flowered curtains. Rows of chairs, each topped with a little capelet of the same pink fabric, fill the rest of the room. Tall plastic vases holding bunches of long-stemmed plastic roses line the center aisle. Yards of pink tulle and garlands of plastic flowers swoop across the ceiling. I wish my daughter and girlfriends could see this.

A few moments after everyone is seated, the curtains part at the back of the room, and the couple enters to a crackly recording of "Here Comes the Bride." The bride carries the plastic bouquet and wears a veil. When she and the groom reach the front, an expressionless lawyer drones something we can't hear because a young guest's phone is ringing. After rummaging for the phone in her huge handbag, the guest answers the call, further drowning out the lawyer. Other guests, dressed in jeans and T-shirts, stand to snap photos with their phones. The bride and groom giggle as they lift rings from the table to place on each other's hands. They read aloud from cards the lawyer hands them and sign a paper, their friends chattering loudly throughout. When the lawyer pronounces the couple married, they kiss briefly, then again for photo ops that are cut short by staff reminding the group that another wedding party is waiting. The couple files back down the aisle and disappears behind the curtains. We crowd back into the lift by generations and descend, old people first. We've been inside for less than twenty minutes.

Back on the street, I ask Fred, "That's it? No real ceremony? No real flowers? Fake everything? Now we just hang out until the banquet?"

"That's just the legal part," says Fred. "They want the Western stuff; but the stuff before and the banquet, that's the real part."

It's barely noon, but the banquet hall isn't scheduled until dinnertime. The family is headed to Bernie's apartment to rest, so we trail along, all dressed up, as they say, with nowhere to go.

* * *

Hours later we reconvene at a restaurant in luxurious Times Square, a shopping complex in the Causeway Bay district, which is not to say that the banquet hall is fancy in a Western sense. From what I've seen, the banquet halls in big Chinese restaurants all look the same: megawatt chandeliers glaring off an endless expanse of round tables and a garish backdrop. The red-draped entrance to this one, decorated with a golden dragon and phoenix arranged as symbols of yin and yang, makes me think of the tunnel of love in a creepy amusement park movie scene. We see on the seating chart that our party has twenty-seven tables. The hall has been reserved from late afternoon on, and the mahjong players are hard at it when we arrive, tiles noisily clacking at a row of tables along one side of the room. At the far end, the newlyweds sit on a stage in front of a wall-length banner with their English names spelled out in blue glitter.

The bride has changed into a lavender satin ball gown whose hooped skirt would make Cinderella or Scarlett O'Hara proud. "C'mon," says Fred. "Everyone has to pour tea for the couple."

"Including us?"

"Of course, we're family."

"What do we do?"

"I have no idea," Fred says. "I know we have to give them the *licee*," he says, waving red envelopes Amah has stuffed with crisp new bills. An old woman with a single visible tooth watches us, grinning because she can see we're clueless. She calls out instructions to Fred, and we make our way to the stage, where we sit side by side on chairs. The bride and groom kneel on cushions in front of us, and an assistant pours four cups of tea, each with a red Chinese date floating in the cup. "A date for sweetness," Fred whispers. One at a time, the bride and groom each offer us cups of tea, which we drink. I have to repeat the motions because I sip my tea without pausing for the photographer, but we pull off the rest of our performance without a glitch, posing in mid-pour. Then we "pay" for the tea by handing each of them two *licee*. The assistant hands us a pair of tea towels with double happiness symbols on them when we step down from the stage. On our way back to our table, the old woman calls to Fred that the towels are because "you are so happy that you drool and need to mop up." Later we learn that she is the "matchmaker," now only a protocol expert in this modern era of love matches.

We are waiting at our banquet table for the bride and groom to reappear when the grumbling reaches us: Abah is peeved with the seating arrangement. Out of all the breaks with tradition so far today, it's the seating plan that incenses him the most. "Insulting!" he mutters. "Disrespectful!" In the rectangular restaurant ballroom, we sit midway between the head tables and the back of the room. Fred's generation is assigned to table number 19 with the rest of the Number 10 party — Amah and Abah, Second Uncle and Aunt, Third Uncle and Aunt — at tables nearby. According to Abah, close family should be up front near the wedding party. Fred and his siblings try to coax Abah out of his sour mood, but I can tell we will be hearing about protocol transgressions for some time to come.

More than once, Fred has explained the intricacies of Chinese relationship connections, each with their own kinship terms, but I've given up on trying to understand more than the basics. In my family we just say "cousin," and we mostly don't stay in touch. In his family, connections are honored and come with obligations. At least that is the expectation. In the days to come, Abah will stew over what he sees as a breach of familial propriety: *It's the parents' fault. They left the arrangements to the young people, and they put their friends in the front. This is not how things are done. The parents should know better.*

I tell Fred that this is why everyone I know does their best to avoid having parents involved in wedding planning. As usual, he reminds me he's from a communal culture. "It's all about the community for us. For you guys, it's all about yourselves."

"Big talk for someone who lives a continent away from his family and who married me in a passport photo office."

"OK, you have a point." As the absentee eldest son of the eldest son and someone straddling Chinese and American cultures, he must be a shape-shifter as well as translator.

We're still waiting for the meal to begin when another drama unfolds. We hear that the groom's mother tripped at the edge of the stage and fell, cutting herself. First the story is that she hurt her arm, and then no, it was her leg. She was taken to the government hospital, where they told her to wait, so she went to a private hospital where they stitched her up and told her she had to be observed for three hours despite her glitter-streaked hair and rhinestone-encrusted pink satin sheath. Thanks to the omnipresent cell phones at the banquet, a paramedic guest was dispatched to fetch her and pledge observation.

Meanwhile, the bride and groom pose for photographs in the hall. At one point they pose cutting a fake wedding cake, like the one at Amah and Abah's anniversary banquet. There was a real cake, a flat one, but it was served while people wandered around the banquet room before dinner. "Cake before dinner?" I'd asked, but I knew the answer. Cake is for afternoon tea, and most Chinese don't even like cake. Besides, no one ever lingers after a banquet. I'm hopeful when I see the bride and groom pose drinking champagne with linked arms, but the guests are offered a choice of tea, red wine, beer, or soft drinks.

"It probably wasn't even real champagne," Fred mutters.

At long last, the groom's mother returns, and the meal is served. The ten courses, which everyone at our table complains are uniformly bad, end with marshmallow rabbits — a Chinese version of Peeps. Throughout the meal, I wait for Western-style toasts and speeches that never come. Instead, while we eat, we watch videos of the couple's childhoods and courtship, interviews with friends and the groom, and pre-wedding pictures taken in Taiwan. The soundtrack is saccharine love songs in English. The bride puts on a fashion show, changing from her lavender gown to a pink, then a yellow, poufy dress, each with a matching feathered hat perched on one side of her bouffant hair. Near the end of the banquet, the wedding party makes its way from table to table for the ritual "*gambai!*" toasting — quickly because it's almost nine o'clock. Fred notes that while toasts are traditionally done with cognac, in his family the circulating group carries tea in wine glasses to look like the real thing.

At last, the couple make their way to the door accompanied by the recorded sound of firecrackers. From her large cloth purse, Amah produces plastic bags to take home the leftover desserts and oranges, after which everyone parades past the wedding party and their families to shake hands.

The rush to the ten p.m. ferry always makes me feel like Cinderella, more so on a day when I'm wearing a dress and heels. Abah is still fuming about the seating arrangement and the "cheap" food, so Fred and I amuse ourselves by counting up the fakes: fake flowers, fake wedding pictures, fake cake, fake scallops, fake music, fake cognac, fake firecrackers. The traditional toasts and games I'd hoped to see were replaced by video interviews despite the people on the screen being present at the wedding. Even traditional activities like pouring tea were stop-actioned by photographers. Traditional seating arrangements had been overlooked because the son and not the father had orchestrated the wedding. Still, I had to admit it wasn't all fake. "Did you notice that every one of the videotaped interviews wished for babies? That's pretty traditional, don't you think?"

"Yeah, and the bride is moving to Cheung Chau to live in the family house. You can't get much more traditional than that!" says Fred.

"I guess we aren't exactly in a position to be sticklers for authenticity. We got married in front of fake flowers in Hawaii."

"True," he replies.

My defections from tradition and organized religion meant I never got to walk down an aisle or wear an outrageously fanciful and expensive white dress (although I wore my mother's handmade, tea-length satin dress for wedding number two). Instead, I invented traditions, or tried to: a park wedding in my teens, dancing the hora in a Legion Hall after my second wedding, then number three, the wedding for keeps, in the passport photo office in Honolulu. I still got gold bracelets. I still bowed to Fred's ancestors and poured tea for my mother-in-law. Just not in order and without the fanfare.

14

Hungry Ghosts

WHEN Fred and I walk into Number 10 an hour before dinner, Josie and Amah are busy in the kitchen and Abah is sitting on the green vinyl sofa. In front of him are piles of paper squares he's folding into three-dimensional rectangles and stacking in a basket on the floor. I recognize the paper as a kind I once purchased in Texas for an art project: tissue-thin, newsprint-colored squares washed with orange ink and stamped with metallic silver and gold blocks. "What's he doing?" I ask Fred.

"Folding ghost money for the Hungry Ghosts Festival," he says. "Plus, they always keep some money folded and ready to burn on the fifteenth day of each lunar month." I've seen the covered basket in a corner of the dining room, and I flush to think that I once used ghost money to make handmade Christmas cards. What other cultural faux pas did I make before I came here? I take a chair across the coffee table from Abah.

"Why's he folding it?"

"To make it look like bars of gold. What do you call those in English?"

"Ingots. Can I help?" It looks like easy origami, and I'm eager to try my hand. Fred translates to Abah, whose usually sober face crinkles into a smile. Abah demonstrates how to fold the paper lengthwise and tuck the ends. I take a few tries to make my first ingots, and when I get the hang of it, I can turn them out just as fast as Abah.

I'm zipping along when Amah comes into the room and is surprised to see me working alongside Abah. *"Whaaaa! Lek neoi!"* she says, calling me smart girl. I beam and keep folding. Finally, a family activity that doesn't require talking. A welcome change after weeks of family lunches and dinners where I'm left out of discussions unless Third Uncle or Fred takes time to translate. The Cantonese term for people like me is *gweilo*. It means white ghost, and, like a ghost, I hover outside the circle of family conversations, translucent and detached.

* * *

That evening Fred and I go for a walk and see preparations for the festival everywhere. Smoke shrouds the backstreet and stairs, making me squint. I'm used to seeing small offerings of incense and oranges outside local shops, but today joss sticks and red candles smolder beside plates of peanuts, crackers, and oranges at every door. In the narrow walkways, people burn stacks of colored paper. Flecks of ash drift through the air, and the smoke tickles the back of my throat and stings my eyes and nose. I have a moment of panic about house fires on an island with no way to get a fire-truck through the alleys and stairways, then realize that a village made of tile-covered concrete would be tough to ignite.

In the folklore course I'm teaching online, my Hawaii students are reading about Samhain, the Celtic precursor of Halloween, when the seams between the realms of the living and the dead open and spirits roam among the living for a day. They've also read about Dias de los Muertes in Mexico, when food is placed on graves and altars to welcome the dead on the first and second of November. Here on Cheung Chau, Fred explains, wandering ghosts roam among the living for the entire seventh lunar month, hungry for supplies from the living. Gold and silver paper is spirit money to help them pay their way, and food is sustenance, just as it is for the living.

"Why are they hungry?" I ask Fred.

"These ghosts don't have anyone to make offerings for them when they die."

"Do they cause trouble?" I'm thinking of how jack-o'-lanterns and trick-or-treating emerged from notions that ghosts were up to no good.

"Only if you've done something bad. There's a Chinese saying that, if you've done bad things, the ghosts will come looking for you."

"Sounds like the bogeyman to me. Or maybe karma."

"Same idea," he says.

When we return to Number 10, Amah and Abah have filled three big baskets with paper ingots.

* * *

On the day set for burning paper at Number 10, Fred and I hurry to catch an early ferry back from the city. Fred's phone rings while we are en route, and I can tell from his increased volume he's talking to Amah. "Mom says you should take pictures tonight and write about it," he tells me after he hangs up. Fred has shown Bernie and Third Uncle my blog. Then someone showed it to Amah. Even though she can't read English, she has understood from the pictures that I'm interested in Chinese traditions.

At first, I'm uncomfortable with the family's attention. To have anyone in the Lau family reading my invitation-only blog meant I had to up my game. I'd started the blog to process my culture shock and record my experiences, and my initial intent was to write only for my family and friends because I wasn't brave enough to go public. Once Third Uncle and Bernie signed on, I had to squelch my tendencies toward comic relief. No more silly posts where I made jokes like the one about pressed duck looking like road kill. No more exaggerating, complaining, or venting to let off steam. And I have to get my cultural and historical facts straight. Fortunately, I have plenty of material at hand, and I enjoy a research challenge.

It's dusk when we climb the staircase to Number 10 and find that the family is starting early because of impending rain. They assemble supplies into four containers in the courtyard. Fred helps Abah to carry a large washbasin, candles, incense, and baskets of folded paper to the front gate. They will take care of the upper house corners. Josie helps Amah and Second Aunt carry a smaller container to the back gate. Third Aunt picks up the last container and tells me to follow her downstairs to the lower corner of the house. Third Uncle heads to the far lower corner with the last of the containers.

At our spot near the stairs, Third Aunt sets out a metal basin and a tin can filled with sand. She squats to light three thin red candles and three sticks of incense, which she pokes into the sand. One bunch at a time, she holds fanned stacks of colored paper to the candle flames until they ignite. As the paper flares and crumples, she drops each stack into the basin or the narrow gutter that runs along the walkway. She explains, "We have to put food at the gates and corners to keep the ghosts happy." After the colored paper, she feeds million dollar "hell notes" into the flames, "to make sure the ghosts have money to pay their way through the underworld." When all the paper is gone, she dusts off her hands and we stand. She lights six sticks of incense and hands three to me. "Now we bow three times," she says. I follow her lead, bending three times from the waist, and she says a few quick prayers in Cantonese before we hurry up the stairs as the first raindrops pelt our heads and arms.

In the courtyard, Josie clicks open umbrellas and hands them around, and everyone is gleeful that we beat the rain. Third Aunt, a devout Catholic from Macau, jokes to me that the family conscripted a Christian to burn ghost money and that this is her community service to the Lau family. "The ghosts are now very rich, and we are very lucky because the money burned fast. Now we can eat dinner," she laughs.

* * *

Over dinner, the conversation turns more serious than usual, so I elbow Fred for translation. He says, "Mom wants to know if you'll write about the offerings. They're talking about how these things have been passed down for many generations. She says that when they die, no one in the family will do it anymore." She looks at me expectantly while he explains, and I nod at her to show I understand. She smiles back. In English, Third Uncle comments that people used to put out lots of food and now they offer only a few packaged items that they clean up later. He says poor children used to come and take the food — their big opportunity for a feast they couldn't otherwise have. He adds, "Now that we have government benefits, there's no built-in cleanup crew."

I've been so focused on trying to understand what's going on that I haven't stopped to consider how it's only the older generation mediating between the past and the present. All but one of Fred's Number 10 generation has moved to Hong Kong Island or beyond, and none of the younger generation came home for this festival to honor the wandering ghosts. The young people attended Western-style schools, many run by Christian organizations. Bernie's children go to Canadian schools in Hong Kong, and Susanna's attended American schools in New York and Singapore. They'll all go to American Ivy League colleges. Mimi's girls are growing up in the city. Third Uncle and Aunt's children are Catholic, and Second Aunt and Uncle's oldest son and his family have converted to Mormonism.

Fred tells me, "Mom says she hopes the kids will read your blog and get interested enough in their heritage to carry on the traditions." That, I realize, makes me a family anthropologist. I can't speak Cantonese, but I do have my folklore training and a million questions. Maybe being the family ghost, forever floating on the sidelines, has its advantages. I warm to having a responsibility to which I can graft a sense of mission. I can't save the traditions, but maybe I can help with Lau family collective memory.

* * *

That Friday, we ferry back to Cheung Chau after seeing a French film in an upscale cinema and eating dinner in a trendy Japanese restaurant. It's close to eleven p.m., and the harbor is awash in the yellow glow of dim street lamps. Clusters of fashionably dressed young people returning from work melt into the pre-weekend crowd near the pier. Locals stroll, talk to each other and on cell phones, sit in sidewalk cafés, and eat snacks from the illegal street stands that appear only after the sun goes down. As usual, arriving in Cheung Chau feels like transiting between parallel worlds.

Garlic-and-ginger-saturated steam rises off skewers of fish balls and chicken wings and mingles with the smell of incense. Near the water, we spot a stage, made of tied bamboo poles covered in brilliantly colored banners, that wasn't there in the morning. "What's that?" I ask, pointing. How many times a day do I ask that question?

"Maybe a set for street opera," Fred guesses. Walking closer, we enter a cloud of incense smoke, out of which looms a paper deity with fierce red eyes and a flamingo-pink face. A smaller figure perches on his protruding belly. "That's the King of the Ghosts," says Fred. "And Tin Hau," he adds pointing to the smaller figure.

"Gatekeepers for the dead?" I ask.

"Something like that. They live in the spirit world." Old men and women fill a cluster of plastic chairs on the sidewalk. Hundreds of burning sticks of incense spike a long berm of sand near the railing at the water's edge. A woman crouches there, sticking more incense into the mound. Behind us is an enclosure where five Taoist priests sit at a table covered in objects before an altar decorated with paper scrolls displaying painted figures of more monks. Sweet smoke wreaths around the paper and human figures, reflecting off a string of bare light bulbs. The familiar street looks ethereal.

As we stand at the edge of the light, the robed priests — four in blue and one in red embroidered with circular patterns — rise from their chairs. Two *suona* players blow a wavery drone while the priests chant a phrase that opens with a loud "om" and repeats in sets of three. They circle the table, picking up ritual objects as they chant, then form a procession that carries a crown and various other items to the nearby paper giant.

"Amateurs," Fred whispers, the educated critic judging the musicians.

I don't want the spell broken. "Stop it. What are they chanting?" I want to know.

Fred listens for a bit. "It's called *chao du*, a ritual to help spirits who die a sudden death to move on. Like when there is a car accident where someone gets killed, and the next day the family and the priest come and perform *chao du* to tell the spirit to come home."

"Why would they want a ghost to come home with them?" I come from a culture that prefers to keep ghosts at a distance.

"It's not home in a literal way. It's part of the process of releasing them to go home in a spiritual sense, so they don't just wander around where they died. The family brings a favorite shirt or food and invites them to come home." I teach about *descansos*, the roadside crosses that mark places of death in America. Now I wonder if those spirits are forever staked to calamity. A year earlier my sister's middle daughter, Hayley, had died in a car accident, and I shudder to think of her lingering anywhere near the site where her car went up in flames.

We walk to the water's edge, where a man pulls handfuls of colored paper out of baskets and throws them into the water. In the breeze, some of the paper spirals up under the lights and flutters down near his feet. He has several bundles to go. Two people empty bags of rice the size of small children and other foods over the rail. Debris bobs against the hulls of the moored boats.

"Are they really dumping all that stuff in the water? So much trash and waste!" I'm entranced by the rituals but appalled at the littering of ground and sea.

"I know, I know. It's for the ghosts. They're inviting and gathering the ghosts and making offerings to the sea."

I shake my head. How can I be an ethnographer if I'm so quick to judge? But how can I not judge when I think things people do are destructive or wrong? To distract myself, I ask, "Is that why Tin Hau is here?"

"Cheung Chau is a fishing village, and Tin Hau protects fishermen, so she's important to the boat people. And there are a lot of drowned ghosts too." I imagine water ghosts forever afloat. More hungry ghost mouths to be fed. Ghosts I had presumed malicious I now see as sad and lost. Homeless and adrift in the netherworld, they wait for the gates to open, for this annual outpouring of charity.

A lone photographer takes pictures. The restaurants along the waterfront are closed, and what's left of the evening crowd threads around and through the smoke and activity, intent on their own pursuits. Chanting and *suona* trail after us as we walk away. When we come back down to the pier on Saturday morning, only the shell of the enclosure remains. Later in the day, even that will disappear.

* * *

A few days later, Fred and I head to Times Square in Hong Kong for a family dinner. We are over an hour early because we're coming from Hong Kong University, so we plan to *hang hang kei kei*, literally to "walk walk, stand stand," mingling with the throngs of people shopping and socializing on the street. When we reach an overpass, Fred points to a median where two old women sit on plastic stools in enclosures they've created with woven mats and cardboard. They look like homeless people to me, a common sight in Honolulu, but Fred says, "Those are the women who beat the little people."

"What does that mean?" It sounds menacing.

"If someone is bothering you, you can pay these aunties to take care of the bad spirits."

"Won't that come back at you, like bad karma?"

"You don't beat the person. You beat the bad spirits."

"The bad spirits are the little people?" I like how this is sounding more like a community service than revenge.

"Something like that." His pat phrase that makes me wonder if I ever get the whole story.

"Hmmm. I can think of someone you might want to take care of." I'm referring to an obstructionist colleague he has at the University of Hawai'i.

"Haha. Me too."

"Can we try?"

"Sure, if you want to."

As we approach the median, we see that one woman is already engaged with a customer, so we head to the one on the left. She nods her wizened face toward the plastic stools when Fred greets her. We sit. Between her and us is a mat with the tools of her trade: buckets of sand, bundles of incense, a group of paper tigers, a red plastic bowl of raw rice, ceramic figures of Guanyin and the Monkey King, stacks of paper fortunes, and bowls of amulets. When Fred asks if I may take pictures, she nods again without looking at me.

The woman asks Fred his name and comments that his parents did well to name him Long River. Lighting incense, she asks him to bow to the deities, so he bobs his head to Guanyin and the

Monkey King. She then hands him two pieces of paper — one with a figure of a woman on it and one inscribed with Chinese characters — and tells him to write the name of the person bothering him on the papers. When he finishes, she takes the papers in one hand and circles them around his head a few times while she chants. Next, she places the papers on a low wooden platform and picks up a detached shoe sole. With a vigor that startles both Fred and me, she beats the pieces of paper with the shoe sole until they are shredded. *Thwack! Thwack! Thwack!* With each lift of her arm, she tells the evil spirits what she is doing to them: "I am hitting you! I am telling you to go away! I am beating you! I am telling you to leave!"

She ignites the tatters with a lighter, fanning the smoke toward the paper tigers near her feet. "The tiger is eating you!" Discarding the burning paper into a large tin can, she draws out some paper fortunes, which she also lights, waving the smoke over Fred several times to cleanse him of evil spirits. She tosses several handfuls of raw rice toward the paper tigers. Finally, she throws the traditional divining tool — two comma-shaped pieces of wood that fit together on their flat sides. They fall one up and one down on the mat, a positive *yes* that the cleansing was successful.

Fred thanks the old woman and pays her a hundred Hong Kong dollars. We head for the restaurant as I observe that even paper tigers must be fed, evidence that the Chinese obsession with food extends to the spirit world.

* * *

The restaurant is upstairs in a fancy mall, and when we arrive, Amy and the kids are waiting in the vestibule. Bernie arrives from his job a few minutes later, still dressed in a tailored suit and red tie.

"Sorry, sorry," he says, "the traffic was bad." Then to Fred, he says, "On the way here, I saw those old women who beat the little people. They're still there under the freeway, and they had customers. I can't believe that some people are still so superstitious!"

Fred glances at me and his eyes spark mischief, "You'll never guess where we just were," he says to Bernie. To me, he says, "Show him your pictures."

I pull out my phone and start the video of the shoe-beating and tiger-feeding.

"Whaaaa! You actually went there?" Bernie's eyes widen behind his glasses.

"Of course!" says Fred. "Whatever works!"

15

Ancestors

THE *dai pai dong*, an assortment of open-air cafés sheltered by tarps, is more crowded than usual because today is a public holiday. It's Chung Yeung, or Double Ninth, one of two annual grave-sweeping days, which falls on the ninth day of the ninth lunar month in the Chinese calendar. I've ordered Chinese-style French toast, which is a decadent and delicious two pieces of egg-dipped bread with peanut butter in between, deep fried and slathered with sweetened condensed milk. Fred has ordered *yauh-jigwai* (long crullers whose Cantonese name translates to oil-fried ghosts) to dip into his bowl of warm *jok* (rice porridge). When the plate of *yauhjigwai* is plunked on the table in front of us, I look up to see a motor cart exiting the wet market for the main street.

On the cart's flat bed are stacks of plastic-and cloth-wrapped bundles tied down with twine. Balanced on top is a large, whole roast pig. As the cart putters away, another cart appears in the market's entrance. This one has a blue tarp tied over a lumpy mound. Sticking out from under the tarp are four stiff and hairy pig legs. My mouth full, I nudge Fred and jab a finger at the pigs. "Offerings," he says. "They're going to the cemetery."

"I'd hate to be a pig in China or Hong Kong," I say, thinking of all the dismembered and roasted pigs I've encountered since I arrived. Porcine innards, feet, and legs dangling on meat hooks inside the market; ears, snouts, and heads displayed on tables: crispy baby pigs splayed on banquet platters with their skin glazed and their eyes replaced by battery-powered red light bulbs. I wedge my camera and my research brain between the ongoing pig-fest and my animal-tuned heart. Fred has no such filter.

"Yum," he says between spoonfuls of *jok*. "That's what we're having tonight!" The pork will be delicious because my taste buds have no conscience.

After breakfast, we walk to the pier to meet Bernie and Mimi at the ferry. The four of us stroll back uphill to Number 10 where Abah, Second and Third Uncles, and two of Fred's cousins gather in the courtyard along with another aunt and uncle who arrived on an early ferry. Together, we all funnel back out through the gate, Abah and Second Uncle each carrying a big plastic bag filled with incense, paper money, flowers, and cleaning tools.

We climb the stairs to the Peak Road, round the hillside, and then ascend the long hill road to the Cheung Chau cemetery. I'm excited because, along with museums and bookstores, cemeteries are among my favorite places to visit. Museums of the dead, they soothe me with their stillness and fascinate me with their combination of history and ritual. Fred offers to help his father and uncle with their loads, but they shoo him away, insisting they can carry the bags themselves. Halfway up the hill, an old man by the roadside sells metal canisters for paper-burning. As we walk, we catch up to other Ko Shan Village families, and more families appear behind us. A man in front of us has long strings of gold paper ingots draped over his shoulder like kite tails. The scent of roast pork and steamed buns signals that some people are carrying bags of food. We see a few roast piglets wrapped in pink plastic and toted in raffia slings or rolled on handcarts. Greetings and conversations swell as the group grows. It looks like the entire village is setting off on a picnic. It sounds like a party.

At the end of the hill road, we turn right and wind along the back side of the island, where a paved esplanade runs along a ridge overlooking the ocean. Third Uncle carries a stick in case the wild dogs that live in the cemetery get too close. Above and away from the village, the air grows noticeably cooler and the fresh scent of greenery replaces the faint odor of sewage in Ko Shan Village.

The walkway slopes to the cemetery outskirts. Unlike the village below, with its hodgepodge of concrete-block and tile buildings draped with fish and laundry, its milling pedestrians, and its weaving, bell-dinging bicyclists, the cemetery is orderly and quiet. The oldest graves have arched low walls that curve into graceful arms around the headstones. Graves from this century display porcelain cameo photos of the dead. In front of each gravestone is a small concrete platform for offerings.

Unlike graves in the park-like cemeteries I know in the United States, with their lawns and trees, the Cheung Chau dead are packed together in tiers, elbow to elbow. As we walk the narrow pathways between levels, Third Uncle sweeps his arm across the rows of markers and says, "See? The cemetery is just like Hong

Kong — crowded and full of concrete." Pointing at the ocean, he adds with a grin, "And, if you're rich, you get the best view." Because land is at a premium, in recent years the government has encouraged cremation. Third Uncle points to the new niche walls for urns and adds, "It's so crowded that the dead used to have houses, and now they have apartments!"

When we pass a section of the cemetery with shattered stones, I ask Fred if they've been vandalized. He explains that this is a first burial section and that traditional Chinese burial doesn't involve embalming. Instead, the dead are buried and allowed to decompose naturally. After seven years, they're exhumed. Specialists clean and arrange the bones in a burial urn, which is then buried in a permanent location. I try to picture Americans gathering for a ritual exhumation and can envision only creepy scenes in horror movies. Most Americans I know don't have that kind of comfort with death. We no longer wash or sit with the bodies of our dearly departed; we turn our loved ones over to funeral homes and tuck our cemeteries out of sight. Some people avoid cemeteries altogether. Just last week there was an exhibition of biodegradable coffins in Hong Kong, and the local news showed elderly people climbing inside to try them on for size. I'm not sure if the coffins were for cremation or burial, but either way, I can't imagine my friends or family at a coffin fitting.

* * *

Unlike the rest of my family, I go to cemeteries wherever I travel. In Mexico, I visited the mummy museum. In Paris, the catacombs. In Texas, I collected Day of the Dead skeletons. I took my Houston students to a funeral museum and showed them afterlife feature films and documentaries about funeral customs. They told me I was weird. Here on Cheung Chau, I love how the funerals happen in plain view, amid people living their everyday lives.

At least twice a month on the main street there is activity in Cheung Chau's equivalent of a funeral parlor: an awning-covered enclosure erected in front of a building that reminds me of a double garage and says Cheung Chau Pig Herders Association across the top. On any given day, we stroll past and through funerals in various stages. In the days leading up to a funeral, we see banners announcing who has died, the date of the funeral, and who has donated money for the service. We watch paper offerings accumulate. When a funeral is in progress, we see groups of white-clad mourners sitting on folding chairs. Neighbors out shopping or on their way home lean into the enclosure to chat with the bereaved.

One evening we watched a Taoist priest chanting and spitting wine into the incinerator, making the flames inside roar and surge as he ritually lifted a paper effigy over a knee-high paper bridge. Fred said he was conducting a soul over the bridge to the Western Kingdom. He read the banners announcing who had died and pointed to the back of the enclosure, where the deceased rested in his coffin. Next to the incinerator were a paper car, boat, and mahjong table. In the car's window was a reproduction of the dead man's Hong Kong ID card, and on its license plate was the lucky number 8888.

Fred asked if I wanted to watch.

"I do, but I feel like I'm invading their privacy," I said.

"Your kind always pretend you aren't looking at something or someone when you really want to look," he teases. We've had this conversation many times.

"I was taught that it's rude to stare. I don't want to offend anyone."

"So silly. Chinese are just more honest about it."

"I guess dead people don't care if I look."

"Exactly!" He grinned as he always does when he thinks he's proven Chinese are smarter. We stood in the deepening dusk, watching until the last of the paper went up in smoke.

* * *

In the cemetery, we walk along the center road and then turn off and follow Abah and Fred's uncles single file through an older section. As they navigate the familiar paths, they identify the graves of former neighbors and friends. At Fred's great-grandmother's grave, Abah and Second Uncle stop to kneel. Abah has brought scissors to trim the grass creeping over the edge of the base. He uses his trowel to push back the grass while Second Uncle sweeps away fallen leaves and dried blossoms with a small whisk broom. When the grave is clean, they carry a cup of water from a nearby tap and pour it into the metal vase where they place flowers from Amah's garden — just like my mother occasionally does for her family graves on Memorial Day. The graves of my paternal grandparents rest in a walled set of rolling lawns between my hometown and theirs, out of sight and on no one's way to anywhere.

We aren't done here with just flowers. Abah lights red candles and inserts them into cans of sand decorated with paper symbols. He adds sticks of incense. From the walkway, Third Uncle retrieves a canister that looks like an office wastebasket. Fred's cousin Gabriel opens a sack and pulls out thick packets of hell notes with rows of zeros. Fanning then lighting each stack with a lighter, he drops them into the canister, where they flare and shrivel to ash. He calls out, "OK, Great Grandmother, we're burning lots of money for you! Here's a million dollars so you can help us win the lottery!" He pulls a stack of colored paper out of the bag and lights that as well, several sheets at a time.

"Cloth for new clothes," Fred says. I've been eyeing the funeral paper shop near the pier, where they sell packages with paper shirts and ties, jewelry, remote controls, sneakers, and even dim sum: ready-made goods for the dead. I guess the Lau family dead have to sew their own clothes.

In birth and gender order, family members step up to the stone and bow three times to greet each ancestor. Wives bow beside husbands. Fred is the eldest son of the eldest son, so Second Uncle motions for us to go first after his father's generation. Fred takes my hand and we step in front of the headstone. "Hello, Great Grandmother," he says to the stone, "This is my wife, Heather. She's here to meet you." Then he tells me, "Now we bow to her." We dip three times; then it's Mimi's turn.

When everyone has paid their respects, we repeat these actions at the graves of Fred's maternal grandmother, say hello in passing to a deceased uncle, then head to the columbarium to pay respects to his grandparents. Fred's grandfather died between our first visit and this one, and I'm remembering how we visited him in the nursing home on Cheung Chau, where his dutiful sons stopped by every day. Although his father was comatose, Abah stroked his hand and talked to him in the same gentle tone with which he greets these stones.

Near the niche wall displaying Fred's grandparents' pictures, Gabriel burns more paper money and colored paper in a big collective bin. We all bow before the niches, and Third Aunt points out several people who have died since Fred left Cheung Chau. They read the niches in the wall like a chronicle of village history. A little farther down the wall, a family is telling a little boy who was who in his family by pointing to the pictures on the niches. I wish there was such a resting place for my niece, who has only a roadside shrine to mark the site of her departure. In the years to come, we won't make offerings to indulge her sweet tooth or update her wardrobe. With her ashes divided and dispersed, we will be without a place to lodge our grief or offer our greetings.

* * *

As we leave, smoke billows over this city of the dead. We pass graves where some families have laid out meals on plastic plates. At Number 10, an offering of a fish, a roast chicken, and a piece of roast pork wait on the dining room table next to three bowls of rice and pairs of chopsticks. The food will be eaten by the practical living once the dead get their fill of its essence.

Growing up in America, I learned that Chinese worshipped ancestors, but here I see dead relatives remembered, honored, and incorporated into the fabric of daily life. Taking care of the dead connects the generations, reinforcing interdependence between the old and young. In American nuclear families like mine, our focus is the other way around, our attention on our children and our elders less and less relevant. It strikes me that if we focus entirely on the young, we will be forgotten once our children have children.

Amah talks to her children on the phone every day, even if just for a few minutes. Sometimes I've gone months without calling home, and my daughter has done the same. My grandmother lived her last decade in a nursing home. It's a lot to mull over, and the mulling makes me feel guilty and sad. I miss my grandmother and my daughter. I think of all the years I've devoted to unraveling the threads of family, and now part of me wishes I could knit up the holes and tighten the strands.

16

Foreigners

In the lobby of the Salisbury YMCA in Kowloon, my parents look like they've stepped out of a TravelSmith catalog — all breezy, bright, and wrinkle-free. Only they are too short to be models. My mother wears crisp white trousers and a tasteful coral tee topped by a white cardigan. My father sports long khakis and a turquoise print shirt, a step up from his standard travel uniform: khaki shorts, an aloha shirt, and Birkenstock sandals with white socks. They both wear sturdy sneakers, and I remind myself that they're on vacation. This visit will be the first meeting between Fred's parents and my own, so I catch myself anxiously inspecting mine as if they're my children upon whose behavior I will be judged.

Lunch is at the Craigengower Cricket Club in Happy Valley, where Bernie is a member. Hong Kong clubs are vestiges of British colonialism, and membership is often conferred as part of hiring packages in the professional sector. In the early colonial era, these bastions of British elitism excluded Chinese and Eurasians. Not to be outdone, wealthy Chinese created their own class-conscious counterparts. Although my family had a club membership when I was young, the British version makes me squirm. My family belonged to the Everett Country Club, named for my hometown in Washington State. Membership was by invitation and granted us access to a good-sized pool in the summer and golf for the adults. My parents, both from working-class backgrounds, felt privileged to belong. Built in a paper-mill town, our country club was all recent construction with functional spaces. The Craigengower Cricket Club, with its dark paneling, tennis courts, pools, uniformed waiters, and multiple chandeliered dining rooms, makes the Everett Country Club look small-town provincial. The carpeted floors, muted lighting, and white tablecloths of the Craigengower dining room transcend the usual clamor of Chinese restaurants. The diners are mostly Chinese, and, with my parents in tow, I feel even more out of place than usual in this rarified environment.

Bernie and Amy, Mimi, Amah and Abah, and the kids — Jeffrey, Michelle, Clara, and Anna — are already seated at a banquet table when we enter the restaurant. As everyone stands to greet my parents, Fred makes introductions all the way around. I notice that my parents, now in their early eighties, are the same size as Amah and Abah. Amah holds my mother's hand, looks into her eyes, and says in her halting English, "Very. Happy. To meet you." She pats the chair beside her for my mother, and everyone takes a seat. My parents smile awkwardly at these people to whom they cannot speak. I think *If they only knew how much they have in common.* My mother may be a long way from the farm now, but she has country roots. My father may be a Seattle city boy, but he grew up with frugality and his Jewish cousins' hand-me-downs.

Shy Abah shifts in his chair and looks away, but Amah is undaunted by any social situation. Digging in her satchel, she pulls out a small blue satin pouch, which she hands to my mother. Fred translates that his mother welcomes my parents and wants to give my mother a gift. My mother looks embarrassed, and I'm horrified. I should have told my parents to bring gifts, which didn't even cross my mind. How could I have forgotten? I try to deflect this thought by palming the blame onto my mother for not thinking of this courtesy, but I know that I'm the one at fault. I didn't grow up in a culture of reciprocity. I learned about house gifts and *omiyage*, the Japanese term for gifts brought by travelers, in Hawaii. My mother unsnaps the little pouch and pulls out a bracelet made of jadeite beads, which Amah insists on putting on my mother's wrist. "So happy," says Amah, smiling and patting my mother's hand. My mother thanks her, and I make a mental note to have them send something to Fred's family the minute they get home so the Laus won't think the Diamonds have no social graces.

Amy has ordered the food, which is dim sum followed by beef noodles and red bean dessert soup. My father persists in calling it "din sun," despite all my previous corrections. I cringe, but no one seems to notice. When Bernie offers to get them forks, my father shakes his head and says, "No, no, we're fine with chopsticks," and I'm happy to see that Fred's instructions in Honolulu's Chinatown have paid off. I try to turn off my overactive embarrassment radar. Maybe it's the language barrier or the importance of the occasion that puts my father on his best behavior. Both he and my mother are charming and sociable even though my father dislikes anyone else paying for his meals.

Fred puts out a hand to stop my father when he reaches for his wallet at the end of the meal. "It's taken care of," Fred explains.

Outside the dining room, someone says we need to take pictures, so my parents line up beside Amah and Abah while Bernie snaps photos on his phone and then on Fred's. Looking at the four of them standing together, I realize that the Laus have done more than meet my parents. They've welcomed them as part of their extended family. My parents are family because I'm family. We're a package deal.

* * *

This is not my parents' first visit to Hong Kong, and as we sightsee on Hong Kong and Lantau islands, my mother remarks on how the city has changed in the thirty years since they were last here. She reminisces about visiting George and Vera Gavriloff, my Russian grandmother's cousin and his wife, who moved from Russia to Hong Kong in the 1920s. She remembers that George was an engineer who showed them bridges he'd designed and told the story of one he'd blown up when he served with the Hong Kong Volunteer Defence Corps. He'd been imprisoned in 1941 when the British surrendered Hong Kong to the Japanese. When I press for more, my mother recalls only a beautiful house filled with "oriental" art, a sweeping view of the harbor, and Vera imperiously flagging taxis with a white-gloved hand. Enough for Fred and I to know that they'd been part of Hong Kong's elite. I know from Fred that most wealthy Westerners considered the Chinese uncivilized and low-class.

It's not just my Russian relatives who'd been here. My first husband, a country boy from Arkansas, had flown in on R & R from Vietnam. From him I'd heard shocking details about the brothels that filled the Wanchai district, and from Fred I heard about the drunken carousing and blatant racism of American GIs. Stories about the disrespect of entitled foreigners toward people who looked like my in-laws always make me feel guilty by association.

My parents want to see where we live, so we meet them at the Kowloon YMCA in the morning, grab a quick breakfast in the lobby café, and take a taxi to the Cheung Chau ferry. My father is back in his shorts, Birkenstocks, and white socks, but today I don't care because Cheung Chau is country. If anything, my mother is overdressed in her matching pants and top. On the ferry ride, Fred and I warn them about the walking, but my world-traveler parents are not easily daunted.

My father's bad knees are too rickety for the stairs up to Number 10, so Fred and I opt for the long road that slopes up the hill to meet the peak road. My father refuses to use a walking stick. On level ground, he's fairly steady, but it's hard not to notice how my parents are shrinking into miniature versions of themselves. My father's back bows forward, so he is now the same height as Fred's five feet and six inches although he used to be three inches taller. My mother, who was the same height as I, is now hunched enough that I can see the top of her cropped silver hair. My father walks with Fred, who grabs his arm from time to time to keep him from being run over by the bicycles whose dinging bells he cannot hear.

My parents have questions about everything, and I can see that I've finally hit the jackpot in the husband market by bringing home an "exotic" man who piques their interest in the world. Not that they didn't love my second husband; they just found his cryptic introversion hard to understand. Ironically, Fred, the outgoing, genial foreigner, makes more sense to them. Seeing him alongside my father, the boisterous type of man I once avoided, I realize that they have more than size in common.

When we get to our flat, we have the dog gauntlet to run and the stairs to climb. My father is out of breath, but we pretend not to notice so he can pretend to be his old hale and hearty self. I'm as relieved as they are when they finally drop onto the rattan sofa. Within fifteen minutes of our arrival, Third Aunt knocks on the door and hands us a plate of chilled red and white dragon fruit that she's cut into wedges. Was she alerted by the barking dogs? My parents, who have never tasted dragon fruit, are delighted. We invite Third Aunt to stay and visit, but she is off to the market to select fish for tonight's Cheung Chau banquet in my parents' honor.

We make a quick tour of the roof, where I proudly show my mother my little hedge of bougainvillea, which has revived into glorious bloom. Both parents are more interested in hearing Fred point out the South China Sea and various locations on the horizon. For once the haze has lifted, and the sky is a fine periwinkle laced with clouds. Then it's time to head back downstairs so we can descend the hill to Number 10.

I am beside my father on the stairs as he lurches and teeters on his bad knees. When I reach out to take his arm, something all younger people in the Lau family do when they walk with elders, he swipes my hand aside. "I'm fine," he quips as he wobbles down another step. I glance down the incline and imagine him flipping end over end until he plops into the harbor. My mother seems oblivious. Fred and I look at each other in alarm. Two more steps and Fred grabs his arm. My father rebuffs him too. I stop holding my breath when we reach the gate.

Inside Number 10, everyone is gathered in the front room, waiting for us to arrive. Amah and Abah pump my parents' hands, and Amah says to each of them, "Very happy." Fred introduces Second

Aunt and Uncle and Third Uncle. My parents wave to Third Aunt, who has just returned from the market. My father says, "Where's the fish?" and she laughs and explains that it will be delivered to the restaurant and cooked to her specifications. Josie serves us tea, and Third Uncle becomes the family spokesperson because his English is best.

Once we've finished our tea, we set out for a seafood restaurant near the pier. Third Uncle reaches out to take my father's arm when he sways on the first set of stairs. My father looks at him in surprise for a second and then smiles and thanks him for the assistance, allowing Third Uncle to hold his arm the rest of the way down the many steps. Fred and I exchange glances. When we reach the bottom and my father steps ahead with my mother, I ask Third Uncle, "How did you do that? He wouldn't let us help him at all today!"

Third Uncle chuckles and reminds us he spent a lot of time with Third Aunt's ninety-year-old father. "All old men are the same," he says. "They always have to save face." I make a mental note to remember that when dealing with my father and Abah.

* * *

By now I know the protocol of reciprocal meals. On each of our visits, Bernie hosts us at the club or a restaurant, then Amah and Abah invite us for dim sum in town, then the aunts and uncles throw us a banquet on Cheung Chau. Before we leave, we have to return the favors by hosting a banquet for Number 10. On Cheung Chau, we typically get off easy on planning because Third Aunt and Josie go to the fish market and pick out the main course while it's still swimming in a tank. They carry the fish to a restaurant where they know the owners, give instructions for cooking, and order the rest of the food. Amah pays for the meal and later tells Fred what he owes.

This meal is hosted by the aunts and uncles in honor of my parents, who don't understand how important they have become by virtue of their eldest daughter marrying the eldest son of the eldest son of the Lau family. How could they? They are part of the American big bang. My father was an only child of Russian immigrants and the youngest cousin in a family that dispersed in America. My mother was the much younger child in a Norwegian farm family, her older siblings spun off to cities in other states.

The restaurant is one of many nondescript eating establishments along the waterfront, chosen by locals because they know and trust the owners. The decor is homey and casual, the rustic kind of place Number 10 prefers: round tables covered in thin sheets of plastic, red plastic chopsticks, and blue-and-white plastic plates and bowls, just like at Number 10. Bring your own tissues for napkins. Second Uncle asks my parents to sit beside him and Third Aunt, so they can speak English together, and I heave a sigh of relief and gratitude. Third Uncle explains the food, the politics of Hong Kong, and the family dynamics. My mother and father manage their chopsticks with reasonable dexterity, only slightly disconcerted about the food being heaped on their plates by Third Uncle, who warns them about bones and serves them the less dangerous pieces of fish and chicken. My parents are not big eaters, so I'm happy to see that they don't leave piles of uneaten food on their plates. If they had, the hosts would have assumed that the food wasn't good.

When the meal ends, my father does his best to accept the hospitality of Number 10, thanking them repeatedly for the meal. I recognize in my parents' awkwardness my own fumbling inability to accept the gift of kindness. Fred and I ride the ferry back with them and put them in a taxi to Kowloon, then take the subway and a green minivan to Bernie's place, where the door is always open to family. We have another long day of sightseeing ahead.

* * *

On the ferry to Macau, my father sleeps in his classic pose: head tipped back and mouth wide open. I'm talking to my mother, who is sitting between me and my father, when I notice two Chinese men in their late twenties holding a camera. They're kneeling backward in their seats directly in front of my father, whispering to each other in Mandarin. They lean over the seat so that the camera lens is only a few inches from my father's prominent nose and snap several pictures of the sleeping gweilo with the white mustache and hair. "Hey!" I say, rage flicking on high like a gas burner. The men quickly turn and drop below the high seat backs, but I can see between the seats they're looking through their shots, and I can hear them snickering.

"What's going on?" asks Fred, who has been dozing on my other side.

"Those guys were taking pictures of my father," I point at the offending pair.

"Those guys?" and when I nod, Fred leaps to his feet and stalks up the aisle. He jabs his index finger at the two men with the camera and shouts at them in Mandarin. He sounds like a cop who is part pit bull. The men raise their hands in front of their faces and cower. Fred points at their camera while they both look down.

When he returns to his seat, he says, "I fixed it. No problem."

"What did you say to them?"

"I said it wasn't cool to do that. They tried to argue with me and say they didn't do anything wrong, so I told them it was illegal. That scared them. Then I made them delete all the pictures they took."

"And they believed you?"

"They're from the country, so they don't know anything. They thought the gweilo was a funny picture."

Anger still pulses in my ears and chest. I'm surprised at the surge of protectiveness I feel for my father, from whom I've always kept an emotional distance. How dare they? Then I think of all the times we snap photos of foreigners on our travels — people as curiosities, people as art, people we capture to take home and admire or laugh about or frame. A creeping sense of turnabout shame holds a hand mirror to my self-righteousness.

When my parents leave the next day, I'm grateful for their visit and how well they crossed over into our Cheung Chau world with no major faux pas. I wonder when I will see them next.

*

17

Friends and Strangers

WHAT I miss most in Hong Kong is friends, but I was missing friends in Hawaii. The camaraderie of grad school over, my EWC friends drifted off to other grad programs, took jobs on the mainland, or returned to their home countries. Hawaii felt more and more like an airport departure lounge. In Hong Kong, we have Fred's family and friends. They're thoughtful and solicitous, yet I feel unknown. Although some of his family members met my parents, they don't know my daughter or my siblings. They met my dissertation advisor turned friend, who paid us a visit, but none of my other friends. They know my tastes in foods, that I like to read, and that I don't like noise and crowds. They don't know my sense of humor or my core beliefs and values. Friends forged out of common experience, who stick with you when you change lives, differ from circumstantial friends. The latter is the person you end up talking to at a party where you are the only non-Cantonese speaker who didn't get why everyone else is slapping the table and wiping their eyes. The camaraderie is comforting in the moment, but it's not heartwarming.

I miss friendships in which I can let down my guard, let go of my dignity, and vent. I can do none of these things in Hong Kong except by email, and even that I edit. My longtime, artsy friends knew me as a chain-smoker, a sloppy drinker, a spendthrift, a fool for bad boys, and a sucker for lost cats. They know I once shook Lyle Lovett's hand and forgot my name when he spoke to me, and that I wrote my boyfriend's art history papers. When I was an overwhelmed single parent, they were my daughter's other mothers. None of them have ever been to Asia or felt its pull. They are quick to sympathize over the cultural fissures I describe but mystified by my attraction to a place and people so foreign. They don't understand my efforts to belong where it seems obvious I don't.

Trying to fit in and be nice is harder work than remembering not to use profanity in front of my mother. If I swear in front of Amah, chances are she won't have any idea what I'm saying, but she will know in a second if my smile slips or I roll my eyes. How did I end up in a family where nearly everyone went straight through college, earned good grades, found a decent job, married someone successful, and had perfect children who will do the same? I married Fred, once his family's screwup for flunking exams, becoming a music major, and getting divorced. A rebel within his culture, he finds merit in my unconventional American life story, evidence of a fellow bohemian soul. I suspect my choices and defections would just look irresponsible to the rest of his family if they were privy to the details. I feel sorry for myself for not fitting in, although it also occurs to me that being in the background hides my flaws. Being a supporting character in someone else's story, with no history and only simple lines, is good camouflage.

My lack of friends leaves Fred as the sole sounding box for all my frustration and loneliness, Fred who adapts anywhere and is happy to be back in Hong Kong for the first extended stay since he left for school two decades ago. Without a buffer, I am on the brink of becoming the kind of sodden-blanket wife he left. I catch him looking at me sometimes like he can't figure out what to do with me, this woman who wants to be alone but not alone, to be with people but not *those* people, to eat out but not in *those* places, to have adventures but without noise and bright lights.

* * *

In a small conference room at Hong Kong University, there are maybe a dozen people arranged around the conference table, a collection of graduate students and music professors and me, reduced to the category of "trailing spouse." A grad student fiddles with the screen and a video projector on the table, trying to get the image focused and aligned. Gauzy curtains cover the windows. Fred, a visiting professor for a semester, is about to give a talk on some aspect of Chinese music. With his aloha shirt and ponytail, he stands out from the rest of the faculty, who are all dressed in Hong Kong "smart casual." He's in performance mode, joking around and making small talk with his colleagues. I've come along to be part of the audience and to meet a student who needs tutoring on her master's thesis. The seminar room buzzes with conversation of which I am not a part, even though it's in English, the lingua franca of HKU. I am wallpaper with eyes.

A tall European woman strides unapologetically late into the room full of Lilliputians. She is not wallpaper. I've been trying to master the casual elegance of Hong Kong women's scarves since I arrived, and she has it down. Her long, gold-flecked hair spills over a perfectly draped purple scarf that sets off her black wool cape, long black skirt, and black boots. *Here is someone*, I think, *who dresses for herself.* When she turns to find a chair, I notice she's wearing a single silver earring in the shape of a hand of Fatima and a pair of rimless glasses. She is not young and is more handsome than beautiful. I admire her all the more for carrying herself with such style and confidence. She wears no makeup and holds her head like a woman who knows how to command a room. I find her stunning. I think *artist*, and *I want to know her.* I watch her out of the corner of my eye during Fred's talk.

After the talk, she makes her way around the conference table to Fred and me and introduces herself as a PhD candidate in the music department and a folk singer. She says she moved to Hong Kong from Australia with her husband, who teaches sociology at HKU. Her name is Rani, short for Ragnheider, which means "rock heather" in Icelandic, her mother tongue. I decide this means we should be friends.

* * *

I meet Rani at Pacific Coffee in the International Finance Center — IFC, one of the few places in Hong Kong I can find by myself. She makes me wish to be tall in my next life. In the past, I sought tall boyfriends and husbands, who made me feel relatively safe even if they were lousy at protection. My girlfriends are all close to my size. Heart-to-heart is easier if your hearts are on the same level. At five feet eleven inches, Rani is the tallest woman I know and a self-proclaimed Viking.

She invites me and Fred to dinner at their flat in Pok Fu Lam — over the mountain from HKU in one of several faculty housing towers with views of the water. When we arrive, Rani opens the heavy wooden door and, with her arms spread wide, says, "Hello, little people!" We step into a pocket of polished dark wood lined with books and contemporary art, a view of the sunset-lit ocean beyond a wall of glass. Brazilian jazz plays; candles flicker on coffee and end tables. A dining table surrounded by royal blue bentwood chairs is covered by a white cloth and set with Scandinavian china and flatware. "Oh, this is gorgeous!" I say. Coming from the country austerity of Cheung Chau, I am flooded by twin tides of envy and resentment. *So this is how expats live.* I already felt small. Now I feel deprived. *If I could live in a space like this, I could be happy in Hong Kong. Who wouldn't be?*

More interested in food than atmosphere, Fred sniffs the air like a bloodhound. Rani gestures toward her kitchen (*a real kitchen!*), saying, "I have a roast and potatoes in the oven," (*Meat that isn't chopped into small pieces! Potatoes instead of rice! An oven!*) "but first we must have some drinks. Börge?"

When her husband emerges from a back room, I have the distinct impression that everything about him is collapsing. He is thin and not quite as tall as Rani, and his shoulders have the scholarly slump of someone who spends the majority of his time leaning over a desk. Rani stands with her back in the open stance of a singer. He looks rumpled. His close beard and brown wispy ponytail might have once made him appear youthful, but that effect is undercut by the downward pull of his mustache and the deep lines that cut across his forehead and between his nose and mouth. Pale-blue, watery eyes peer at us through wire-rimmed spectacles.

Börge has strong opinions that he's eager to impart over the wine and appetizers. He hates our stupid president, and he thinks most Americans know nothing about the world. He's happy to meet another China scholar, although he hates China's politics and doesn't visit the country if he can help it. The university is full of stupid administrators who are delaying his contract renewal and don't understand the importance of his work on crime and punishment in China. He breaks into fluent Mandarin with Fred, then reverts to clipped and formal-sounding English. Like Rani, he is fluent in at least five languages, starting with his native Norwegian. *Tiresome blowhard*, I think as I listen to Fred verbally spar with this man who enacts the Hawaii stereotype of haole behavior. I watch Rani fold herself inward with Börge in the room, and think about the bargains women make for security, followed by *Thank god I found Fred.*

While we devour the excellent roast and potatoes, I ask Rani about her dissertation. She explains, "I used to be in a music group in Iceland that performed traditional folksongs. I've done many interviews with folksingers, and I'm writing about how Icelandic folk music is changing."

"Where are you with the writing?" I ask, remembering too late that this is the wrong thing to ask anyone in the dissertation process. How many times had I ducked that question? That I'd finally reached the stage of working on the index to my book has made me cocky. For that, I will be struck dumb by ten years of writer's block.

"Nowhere," Börge interjects, turning to her. Acid and conde- scension drip in his voice although he's smiling. "I keep saying you must stay in your office and write, but you don't. You have to write every day. I don't think you want to finish."

"You work with statistics. I work with people. It's not the same!" she protests.

"You still have to work every day. You wanted the office at home when we moved here, but you don't stay in it. I work in my office at school, and I can still write several pages a day."

"That's how you work. I have to move around and think first. I still have boxes and boxes in my office from when we moved here from Cambria."

"You always find a reason not to write," he says, dismissing her with a wave of his hand and clearly used to having the last word. Uncomfortable, I change the subject to ask how they met. Börge's smile becomes shark-like. "She was destitute, and I rescued her," he says. "She had no money, so I took her in and became a father to her girls." He leans back with his arms folded as Rani busies herself gathering the dishes. I will later hear a very different version of this story from her, but, for now, she lets this one linger while she clears the plates in preparation for dessert and port.

*   *   *

On a weekend when Börge is out of town, I stay overnight at Rani's flat. I'm in heaven. She and I sit at her dining room table finishing bowls of Icelandic fish soup made with cream and dill. The night before, I'd luxuriated in her six-foot bathtub, proportioned for giant Europeans, and slept on a real mattress. I'm staying in their domestic helper suite, a far cry from the tiny cubbyholes helpers occupy in typical Chinese flats. The half bathroom and guest room are the size of our living room on Cheung Chau.

Despite being a PhD student, Rani seems free in ways I haven't managed since I went back to school. Or at least when Börge isn't around. I ask her the question I ask all my married friends. "How do you manage your money?" Money issues had bored wormholes in my first two marriages, so it was mostly my idea when Fred and I agreed to keep our finances separate. This arrangement worked great when we both had money, but not so well now that I don't. I'd gone from a regular faculty paycheck to a graduate fellowship, and from that to the little I earn as a college lecturer teaching a single online course per semester. Fred covers our major expenses and is forthcoming with cash when I need it, but he doesn't understand that I hate asking for handouts. I have my credit card, but I still have to pay the bill. I'm fishing for solutions.

"I get an allowance every month," she says.

"Really?" This sounds even more childlike than my situation.

"I tell Börge what I need for the household and spending money, and he deposits it into my account each month. That was the bargain I made before I agreed to come to Hong Kong."

"And that gives you enough to do what you want?"

"Oh, I made sure it was enough so I have extra. I have to get away. And Börge doesn't approve of the choices my girls make, so I send them money from my account. That way he has no idea."

"Doesn't he have to see your finances for taxes?"

She laughs. "He doesn't need to know everything. There are always ways to hide what I spend." After years of concealing what I spent from my second husband, I'm not so sure this sounds like a strategy I want to emulate. An allowance, on the other hand, is an idea I hadn't considered.

"Doesn't Fred give you an allowance?"

"We agreed to keep our money separate."

"But you also agreed to give up everything and go to a foreign country for him. Doesn't he owe you something for that?"

"I never thought of it like that." Uncomfortable, I change the subject. "It was wonderful to sleep on a proper bed last night. Ours is like sleeping on a concrete floor."

"Why don't you buy some foam for it? I think I saw eggcrate foam at IKEA. We can go look today."

"How will I get it home?"

"In a taxi!" Two things I hadn't thought of. What is wrong with me? I used to be so independent. Within an hour, we're off to IKEA.

* * *

When Rani and Börge come to Cheung Chau for a day trip, Rani takes a deep breath and exhales. "It smells just like Iceland!" she exclaims as we stroll together past tanks full of live fish and shellfish, baskets full of dried shrimp and starfish, and rows of dangling mullet with their heads wrapped in white paper. Rani's delight makes me realize I've grown so used to the fishy aroma of Cheung Chau that I no longer notice it. We go inside Gon Yungtai, a small restaurant near the pier famous for its fishballs. "Look, they have fried fish skin!" Rani exclaims, looking at the next table. "Shall we get some?"

"Of course!" says Fred, always game for eating. He orders for us all, and soon we have a bowl of fish skins in the center of the table — another delicacy made from something I'm used to discarding. Fish and chips, yes, but fish chips? The crispy, slightly curled strips are odd and delicious. As we polish off the bowl, our fishballs arrive, floating in bowls of fragrant broth and topped with spring onions and chopped cilantro.

Börge and Rani find everything about Ko Shan Village enchanting. Börge seems more animated and less cantankerous than usual. We take them through the wet market, past the dai pai dong restaurants, the funeral enclosure, and the old women who sit on a bench every day, gossiping and picking at their feet. Then we head uphill to Number 10. Along the way, Fred tells stories about his footloose childhood on the island, where he was poor but surrounded by family and friends. He tells them about running to catch the ferry, about weekday boarding in a tiny room with his sister and his aunt because it was cheaper to rent a room in the city than to pay for the ferry every day. He tells them how the landlady taught him how to cook when he was only eleven and about waiting in line for the single bathroom shared by all the boarders on his floor. I see him transform before their eyes into a Chinese version of Huck Finn, a reminder of how he charmed me in Hawaii. On their long Scandinavian legs, Rani and Einar stride effortlessly up the stairs, making me feel like a small dog scurrying at the end of a leash, taking two steps to their one.

At Number 10, the Vikings are served tea and treated with deference. They put me to shame as Rani fearlessly employs her limited Cantonese and Börge converses in fluent Mandarin. Amah and Abah are impressed, and I am as envious of the Vikings' ability to fit in here as I am of their expat world in town. I wonder how many gweilo have come here over the years. Fred's first wife, my parents, and I are probably not the only ones, but there can't have been many.

* * *

Along with my sole expat friend, I acquire a Chinese friend. I meet them at different times in the same place, the conference room of the music department at HKU. Yeeman, the student I've agreed to tutor, is as tiny as Rani is monumental, as childlike as Rani is a woman of the world, as locally connected as Rani is international. With her asymmetrical haircut and artsy black clothes, Yeeman looks like an ultra-chic twelve-year-old. One of those pencil-thin Asian girls who makes me, a size four in my world, an extra-large in hers. She studies film music and struggles to shape her ideas into words. We meet while Fred is teaching, and while trying to untangle her sentences and undangle her modifiers, I sense a kindred spirit.

Maybe I am drawn to Yeeman in part because I miss Sorrel so much. In the years since I moved to Hawaii, the world of communication has transformed from mail to email, so no more letters. Now that Sorrel is busy with her blended family, she seldom calls except on my birthday and Mother's Day. Although I have yet to learn that every departure shivers the strands of family, tears holes in the web, I sense her distance as a price I must pay for my choices.

Yeeman comes to our sessions in tears more than once over something that's happened in a class or interactions with other students. Along with sentence structure, I teach her the hard lessons I continue to learn about being an extra-sensitive person and an empath in a world where we need to have tougher skin.

* * *

Grateful for my help, Yeeman invites Fred and me to accompany her and her parents across the China border to the city of Shenzhen. Once there, they treat us to dim sum; then Yeeman and her mother and I go for massages. "Cheap-*lah*!" they say. I can't wait — two hours for half the price of a one-hour massage in the

United States. After weeks of being sardined in crowded metros, buses, and ferries, and bombarded by the general pandemonium of Hong Kong, the soothing release of a massage sounds like heaven. I am also, based on what I hear from Amah, a little leery. Amah and Abah visit blind masseuses in Shenzhen who are dirt cheap and on call twenty-four hours a day. Yeeman assures me that her mother, who doesn't speak English, says this place is high class, not at all the sort of place Amah would go. I don't expect scented candles and soft music, but I'm hoping the lights will be dim and the hands gentle.

In the spa's lobby, I notice that I'm the only foreigner. Yeeman translates the menu board behind the counter: "We have to choose between Thai or Chinese massages, the amount of time we want, and if we want to be separate or together." I hate pain, and I know Chinese think it's therapeutic, so I choose Thai. Yeeman and her mother choose Chinese. Because I can't communicate if I'm alone, I'm relieved they ask for a communal room. The girl at the counter hands us white cotton pajamas to change into, and I already know from my one massage experience in China that we're not going to be nude. I'm not so relieved when we're escorted to a narrow room with three platforms placed a foot apart. On each platform is a thin mat. At least the lights are dim.

I'm on the platform nearest the far wall. Next to me is Yeeman's mother, a quiet woman who teaches yoga in Hong Kong. Yeeman is nearest the door. Three slight young women enter and motion for us to lie face down. Within minutes I hear Yeeman and her mother moaning in contentment. The girl who is pressing her small hands into my shoulders and back is tiny and lithe, and when she straddles my legs I feel as if a large cat is sitting on top of me.

The cat grows teeth and claws. What begins as probing pressure quickly becomes angular, pointed, sharp. Her elbows swivel into pressure points, her fingers drill and stab into muscles that would yelp if they could. As she works her way down the sides of my spine and then each leg, fireworks go off where she digs in fingers, thumbs, and elbows. I gasp, and she giggles. She says something to me in a baby voice incongruous with the creature into which she has transformed. No one translates. She uses her body weight as leverage while she twists my arms in directions they aren't designed to go. I imagine tearing sounds deep in my muscles. Searing heat radiates each time she manipulates a joint. I look in desperation toward my roommates, but they both appear to be asleep. How is it that my extra-sensitive friend is so oblivious to physical pain? I'm certain my masseuse has dislocated all my limbs, and I feel faint from the pain when a mantra comes to me: *I've been through childbirth, I can live through this.* I chant this in my head for the next hour.

*   *   *

Years later, when Yeeman moves to Honolulu to study Japanese taiko drumming and we become closer friends, I will relive this day. She will tip her head to one side and ask why I didn't speak up or ask the girl to stop. The only answers I can come up with are that I was too embarrassed to admit I didn't know what I was in for and I didn't want to be a bad foreign guest. Tiny Yeeman, who pounds enormous Japanese drums in Hawaii, will shake her head in incredulity.

*   *   *

Börge and Rani send a pair of Norwegian guests to tour Cheung Chau and meet us. They're a young blond couple with an equally blond toddler in a stroller, so we stick to the waterfront and lower streets. The wife, an amateur photographer, carries a large, fancy camera with an extended lens. At one point, when we stop at a street shrine, we turn to see her squatting beside a stairway with her shirt pulled up to nurse her toddler. Local people pass by, and I see their eyes slide sideways in disapproval. As Fred meets my eyes, I can hear the *Aiyaaa! Crazy gweilo!* he is thinking. At home in America, I would have defended her right to nurse in public. Here, I am caught between my Western feminism and my desire to blend in, so I turn my head in embarrassment.

In the funeral enclosure, we see stacks of paper offerings — a car, a racetrack, a mahjong table with three players, and an arched bridge. The visitors are fascinated: *Look at that! So strange! So bizarre!* Fred does his best to explain, although I can tell he's getting irked. All this picture-taking and explaining with strangers has crossed a line: He hates his culture being exoticized. He doesn't want to be a personal tour guide or representative of the "Orient" for friends of friends. When the visitor hands her camera to her husband so he can photograph her holding the baby in front of the funeral offerings, Fred mutters to me about the cultural cluelessness of gweilo. "I can't believe it! You don't do things like that in a funeral space!"

The woman takes some last shots on the way to the ferry — of a man folding dumplings outside a restaurant and of the old women who sit on the bench across from the wet market and gossip all day. She mimes to all of them to get their approval, and the man nods, unsmiling, and continues with his dough. The women don't understand what she's saying, and when she snaps photos, they turn their backs in unison, tossing loud Cantonese remarks over their shoulders. The photographer is non-plussed for a second, then shifts her camera toward the boats in the harbor.

After we see them off at the ferry, I ask Fred what the old women said to her, and he chuckles. "They said *Who do you think you are taking my picture, white ghost? I'm not here for your entertainment! Go back home and take pictures of yourself!*"

18

Chinese Christmas

THE Christmas season is my favorite time of year. I love the decorations, the music, the baking, the shopping and wrapping, the gatherings, the smell of greenery. When I was growing up, our house sounded, looked, and smelled like Christmas for weeks. We played Christmas albums and decorated our eaves with colored lights, our door with a wreath, and our living room with cedar boughs and a nativity set. The centerpiece was always a seven-foot fir tree festooned in lights and ornaments. My mother baked cookies for weeks. When we were old enough to stay up until midnight, we went with our parents to Faith Lutheran Church for the candlelight service on Christmas Eve. On Christmas morning there were gifts under the tree and filled stockings for the four of us, each with a mandarin orange tucked into the toe and a candy cane hooked over the edge.

Since leaving home, I'd tried every year to recreate the Christmas magic of my childhood. No matter how broke I was, we had stockings, decorations, a tree. Sorrel and I strung cranberries and popcorn and pasted chains of colored paper. We constructed ornaments out of dough and paper and glitter. I stitched stockings and filled them with trinkets and candy. I know how to do Christmas, but my moves have made it more and more challenging. Arkansas had snow, and Houston had shopping, so the initial adjustment was reinventing the holidays without my family. Hawaii, where it's summer all year and a giant Mr. and Mrs. Santa sport aloha wear and rubber slippers, required additional adaptations. I settled for a Cook Island pine, the tropical equivalent of an alpine, on which I placed ornaments that reminded me of Texas, Hawaii, and China. I hung stockings on the bookcases, and I coached Fred on the nuances of American gift-giving, including not providing so many hints he spoils the surprise.

Christmas in Hong Kong feels off. There are decorations in the stores; but instead of red, green, and gold, they tend toward pink and purple and look like the wedding decorations in restaurant ballrooms. There is Christmas music in the glitzy malls, but even the classics sound like digitized marching music, repetitive and mechanical. At Number 10, Third Aunt erects a squat artificial tree in the living room and decorates it with a collection of ornaments from their travels, but there are no presents underneath and no other decorations in the house. No one in the family shops and wraps. No one bakes in a house without an oven. I wonder if this holiday is an adjustment for Josie as well since she comes from a mostly Catholic country where Christmas is the biggest holiday of the year.

While I mope about missing Christmas this year, Number 10 plans for the winter solstice on December 22. I ask Fred how and why they celebrate, and he replies, "Everybody gets together. The solstice is as important as Chinese New Year."

"I thought New Year was the biggest festival."

"There's actually a Chinese expression that says Winter Solstice is bigger than New Year: *Dung daai gwo nin.*" I'm learning that there is a Chinese saying for everything.

"I don't get it. What do you do when you celebrate the solstice? Is there an offering?"

"There's always an offering on special holidays."

"But what do you do on the solstice?"

"We eat. Everybody gets together and eats."

"But isn't that what you do for every holiday?"

"Of course."

This discussion is going nowhere, and it's clear I must wait and see what, if anything, makes this gathering unique. The answer comes in the form of a seemingly random question from Third Aunt. "At home, what do you like to cook?" I fish around in my memory for something distinctive that I make and come up with "I like to make gumbo."

"What's gumbo?"

"It's a chicken or seafood stew from Louisiana that's served over rice."

"Good. You can make that."

And there it is. Potluck, like in Hawaii — except I just committed to cooking gumbo for a family that prefers to eat Chinese food wherever they go. And instead of the usual seven house members and us coming to dinner, the extended family of around thirty people is coming. Gumbo is a legacy from my previous life in Texas. In Hawaii, I made two giant pots of gumbo for our wedding party. Here, I have a two-burner propane stove. Why didn't I say I don't cook or come up with something simple? My alarm must show on my face. "Don't worry," says Third Aunt, patting my arm. "Just make enough for everyone to have a taste."

We borrow a big pot from Number 10, and I channel my panic into thinking about ingredients. After I create a list, Fred and I consider when and where to shop. We have a couple of days, so we start with spices. Where am I going to find Cajun spices? We go to the local grocery store across from the pier where the aisles inside are so narrow that customers have to slide sideways single file and walk around if they meet someone coming through. The spice collection is a promising four shelves, but on closer inspection holds only white pepper, black pepper, red pepper, lemongrass, and MSG. I know I can't use cayenne because no one in the family likes hot food. I insist that I need bay leaves and paprika, although Fred says that no one knows what gumbo tastes like anyway, so it won't matter what I put in it. I take pride in my cooking, and this is my first chance to show the family what I can do in the kitchen. Okra this time of year is unlikely, and filé powder is a distant and unattainable dream. I leave the store with only chicken broth.

Going to the fancy supermarket in IFC where the expats shop takes half a day, but we make an emergency run and score paprika, bay leaves, and thyme. On the way home we stop at the Cheung Chau vegetable stands to pick up garlic and the holy trinity of Cajun cooking: green peppers, celery, and onions. This just might work.

On the morning of the twenty-second, we search for chicken. We walk through the wet market with its pig shanks and dripping ducks hanging from hooks above counters full of pig heads, feet, ears, and entrails. On our second round, we find a stall that has chicken parts and not just whole chickens with feet and heads attached, which neither of us wants to deal with. The butcher wraps up a package of the tiniest chicken legs and thighs I've ever seen. "Why are they so small?" I ask Fred. "They look like they came from pigeons!"

"They're local chickens. Probably not pumped up with all that stuff they feed American chickens."

"True, but we're going to need a lot of these to make up for them being so tiny. And what about sausage? I need smoked sausage."

"Can't you use Chinese sausage? Plenty of that here." He points to a nearby stand with strings of sausage links draped on hooks. I try not to think about how long the meat has been hanging there with no refrigeration.

"You mean *lap cheong*? Isn't it sweet?"

"Yeah, but nobody's going to know the difference. They might even like it better."

"It's supposed to be smoked, not sweet." After one more search through the meat stands, I give up and we buy *lap cheong* and hope for the best. At least I can cook in our flat instead of at Number 10.

In our little kitchen, Fred offers to chop the onions, peppers, and garlic because I can't get any of the ancient knives to cut. He tries them and then hikes down to Number 10 to borrow a cleaver with which he whacks them to bits. He then helps me make the roux in the big pot. A few hours later, we descend the stairs to Number 10, Fred carrying our pot full of the strangest gumbo I've ever made. I've done my best to cover up the sweetness of the sausage with the garlic, but it tastes wrong to me, and I'm worried that, after all our work, no one will like it.

As usual, we hear the Lau family gathering before we get to the front gate. Third Aunt directs us to put the pot with all the other food that is amassing on the buffet. We find a ladle and stack up some bowls. Fred instructs everyone to spoon the gumbo over a scoop of rice.

At the end of the evening, the pot is empty and, although there were no compliments, I heard no complaints. I congratulate myself for having introduced one small thing from my other life into this family where I'm always a guest.

*   *   *

Rani invites us to a holiday meal at her flat, and I'm buzzing with anticipation because I know that she loves Christmas as much as I do. When she opens the door, the scents of roasting meat, cloves, and fresh evergreen envelope us. It's clear my Norwegian-American memories and her Icelandic traditions come from the same place. Candles flicker, and in a corner of the living room is a fir tree festooned in sparkling lights and glistening glass ornaments. I close my eyes and inhale. "Your house smells like Christmas heaven."

Fred inhales and groans in anticipation of a good meal. "Mmmm. Smells so good!"

"I'm cooking a ham and spiced cabbage, and I have a lovely Icelandic rice pudding for dessert, but first we must have some mulled wine." The warm mugs she hands us are fragrant with cinnamon and allspice, heady and delicious. We sip while snacking on cheese and crackers and spiced nuts. Even Börge seems jovial.

At dinner, we enjoy red wine with thick slices of ham, mounds of waxy potatoes and red cabbage cooked with anise. Rani serves sugar cookies to go with the pudding. I lose any impulse to disparage the colonial privilege of their spacious apartment as I bask in the twinkling lights, the familiar food, the books and art, the leisurely conversation in English. After dinner, Börge pours port into fluted crystal glasses, and as its syrupy warmth spreads, I don't care if I'm a hypocrite. It's Christmas, and this level of comfort is just what I've been craving. For the three or four hours we are in Pok Fu Lam, the season is salvaged.

The afterglow of the port and company lasts through the trek back over the mountain (*over the river and through the woods...*), across the water, up the hill, past the barking dogs, and up the stairs. It settles into cranky envy when we open the door to our plain little borrowed space. *If only I lived in a fancy expat apartment with a Christmas tree and art and a kitchen and a bottle of port, I could be happy here in Hong Kong.*

* * *

Buoyed by our gumbo success, or at least the lack of failure, and more determined than ever to create some semblance of Christmas, I propose to Fred that we cook Christmas dinner for Number 10. Volunteering to cook is a tactic Fred successfully uses with my family. On our first visit to my parents' house on Whidbey Island, my mother cooked a salmon dinner for the four of us. Each diner received three broccoli florets, a piece of salmon the size of a pack of cigarettes, and a teacup-sized dollop of instant white rice. My father doused his salmon with catsup and his rice with soy sauce. Although the salmon was dry, just the way my mother likes it, Fred polished off everything on his plate. Then he leaned over to me and whispered, "Is there more?" I'd been helping in the kitchen, so I could answer with authority that this was it. At least he hadn't asked out loud. My health-conscious mother was serving up basic foods, unembellished and in medically recommended portions — her triumph over my father's proclivity for hamburgers and fries. When we got back to the cabin next door, where we were staying, I knew exactly what Fred was going to say: "I'm hungry!"

On the next trip, he tucked ramen noodles into every available space in his suitcase. At the table with my parents, he dutifully cleaned his plate and politely thanked my mother. Once we reached the cabin, he pulled out his ramen to cook a second meal. This strategy worked beautifully for two years until my sister moved into the cabin and we lost our second kitchen.

Now when we visit, Fred volunteers to cook. We shop on the way to my parents' house, and he banishes my mother from her kitchen or tunes out as she flutters and fusses about why he's using extra virgin olive oil and who's going to eat all those leftovers. "Don't worry, Arlene. They'll get eaten before I leave," he reassures her. Because my father has never cooked anything that didn't come out of a can, my mother finds Fred's prowess in the kitchen remarkable. To them, Fred is a celebrity chef while I'm an everyday Betty Crocker. It doesn't hurt that he remains cheerful despite my mother's interference, a skill I should learn.

Fred is skeptical about my proposal to cook an entire meal for the Lau family, but he's game for anything that might make me happy. From Amah he learns that Josie is off that day, and, other than midnight mass for the Catholic contingent, there are no special plans at Number 10. I get a thumbs-up to do whatever I want. In list-making overdrive, I come up with a menu designed to impress and please: squash soup, Swedish meatballs, mashed potatoes, and red cabbage, to borrow a theme from Rani.

I check the menu with Fred, "Do you think I have enough courses? They always have so many dishes on the table for every meal." Even everyday evening meals at Number 10 feature at least five dishes.

He goes straight to logistics. "They'll think it's weird to have soup first."

"So explain it to them."

"They'll want rice."

"Can't they have one day with potatoes instead?" It seems to me that a little flexibility wouldn't hurt anyone. "Where's their spirit of adventure?"

"Can't you serve the meatballs with rice?"

"It's Christmas! You can't have rice for Christmas. It's not traditional."

"OK, OK!" he says, lifting his hands in defense. "I'm just trying to help!"

"Boiled potatoes, then. In small pieces." I hate being derailed from a plan once I have it in place.

We head to City Super in IFC, where I find a small honey-baked ham and toss it into the cart for backup in case they don't like the meatballs. Picking up the ham, Fred reminds me, "Meat needs to be in pieces they can pick up with chopsticks." I glare at him.

"We can cut it up."

From City Super in Central, we take the subway to IKEA in Causeway Bay, where I've spotted jars of lingonberries. Fred has already nixed Swedish pancakes for dessert because we'd have to cook them in batches and everyone would wander off. I settle for a ready-made pound cake I can top with the lingonberries. I could buy frozen meatballs at IKEA, but I'm on a mission now to make everything else from scratch. Number 10 would never resort to prepared food. I will serve my meatballs in gravy, improving on my mother's cheater recipe, which uses canned mushroom soup (and which I secretly love). I haven't yet figured out how we will cook all of this on the four burners we have between our flat and Number 10.

* * *

On Christmas Eve day, I roll meatballs in our flat. We have to stay up late anyway because we've agreed to accompany Third Aunt and· her family to midnight mass at the Cheung Chau Catholic chapel. I'm eager to go. I have vivid childhood memories of singing Silent Night while holding white candles stuck through paper collars to catch the dripping wax. I haven't been a churchgoer since I was fifteen, but I still savor memories of the dimmed lights and atmosphere of joyous expectation.

Josie walks with us to the chapel. The night air is cool, the dark streets hushed. As we walk past the shuttered shops, Third Aunt greets friends headed in the same direction, quietly so as not to wake the sleeping village. There are only a few Chinese, but more and more Filipina helpers appear, and Josie seems to know them all. They wave and call *"Maligayang Pasko!"* to each other in Tagalog.

When we round the bend, we see the small church lit up like a Chinese restaurant. We enter blinking at the fluorescent lights made more blinding by the dark outside. I think maybe the lights will be dimmed for the candles, but it soon becomes clear that there are no candles and that Chinese Christmas will be conducted at megawatt intensity. The priest is an elderly Brit with white hair and a lackluster voice, which doesn't matter because the brief service is in Cantonese. So are the carols, which very few of the scattered worshippers seem to know, their voices thin and off-key. Fred nudges me in the ribs at sour notes, and, when he catches my eye, my disappointment gives way to snickering. How could I have expected a midnight mass on Cheung Chau to resemble my American Christmas memories?

When we step back out into the dark, it's a few minutes past midnight. Christmas Day. Josie beams as she wishes us "Merry Christmas." Helpers hug each other and call, "Merry

Christmas! Merry Christmas!" In their joyful faces is the glow I missed in church.

* * *

We start cooking at Number 10 in midafternoon. Fred fetches a toaster oven from Josie's room, and we set it up in the courtyard so we can heat the ham. Because two large pots won't fit on the two-burner stove at the same time, we plan to fry up the meatballs and make the gravy in the same skillet, then keep it all warm in a thermos-style pot. We will cook the potatoes and beans in the next shift. I made the squash soup the day before in our flat and will reheat it in the rice cooker. I can adapt.

As we cook the meatballs, we attract a rotating audience. We are a dual curiosity in a household where the men don't cook. As Second Aunt and Amah peer over our shoulders and Third Aunt pops in and out, I can feel my shoulders tighten in a double whammy of claustrophobia and stage fright. I'm getting more nervous about culinary failure by the minute.

At last, the food is ready. Second and Third Aunts have set the table according to our specifications: small plates, chopsticks, and Chinese soup spoons. Fred has carved the ham into pieces that are chopstick-manageable and arranged them on a platter with the beans. The meatballs swim in a bowl of gravy, and the potatoes are in a bowl on the kitchen shelf. We ladle the colorful soup into nine bowls, setting one at each place, and, after everyone slides into their seats around the table, Fred announces that tonight we will eat Western style, soup first. "*Sik faan!*" we shout in unison, and I hold my breath while bowls and spoons are lifted around the table. The old people don't like Western spices, so I've seasoned my soup with only onions and a dash of nutmeg. "*Hoh sik,*" says

Amah, setting down her empty bowl. "Good," says Third Aunt. Third Uncle laughs and says, "They were afraid you were going to use weird American spices."

As Third Aunt collects the bowls, Fred and I get the rest of the dishes from the kitchen. As usual, the family eats with little conversation. Usually, Abah finishes first because he learned to eat in family shifts. When he downs an entire bowl of rice in less than a minute, his children say he is "Wind raking the leaves." Tonight, he stays put until we all put down our chopsticks. Fred announces that we will have dessert in the living room. As Third and Second Aunts clear the table, I note a few lonely meatballs and an empty ham plate.

In the living room, everyone thanks me for cooking dinner. I finally get Fred alone and ask, "So, did they like it? I can't tell."

"They liked it. Everyone really loved the ham."

"The ham?! All that work planning, mixing, rolling, chopping, and cooking for an audience, like I was on a cooking show, and the most memorable part of the meal was the precooked ham we heated in a toaster oven?"

"They're old people. They don't like change."

My pride in my holiday accomplishments now a fallen soufflé, I resolve to stop trying to impress this family if all I can ever be is a foreign sideshow. What really matters to them is that I love and support their golden boy. If he's happy, they'll be happy with me. And if he's happiest when I'm happy, then perhaps I've been going about this all wrong.

19

Year of the Rat

CHINESE New Year is everything Christmas in Hong Kong was not. The temperature has dropped to a bone-chilling, wet cold, but the city has filled with buoyant energy. Flower stalls in Mongkok and the annual flower market in Victoria Park have burst into a riotous froth of blooms. On Cheung Chau and in town, Fred and I see people toting tall, budded peach and plum branches they will coax into bloom in their homes. It's time to shop for new clothes, do spring cleaning, pay off debts, end arguments, and tie up loose ends.

This New Year will usher in a year of the rat in the Chinese zodiac, so cute cartoon rats have cropped up throughout the city along with auspicious characters and images associated with good fortune. In Times Square, three-dimensional metallic gold rats tumble over and through an enormous silver wall of cheese. In America, people who are sneaky and vicious are called rats. In China, the rat gets top billing in the zodiac and is considered witty, smart, alert, and flexible. A child born in the year of the rat promises to become a clever and adaptable businessperson.

*   *   *

In the weeks before Chinese New Year, the rooftop of our flat becomes a nursery. Third Aunt sets up a folding table in the cold and teaches me how to carve narcissus bulbs. She demonstrates how to feel for the lobes packed within each tight and fibrous package, where to insert the tip of a knife — slicing downward but not too deep — to nudge each bulb out of its winter slumber. We perform this operation on dozens of bulbs then place them, tips up, in an assortment of ceramic and glass containers, each filled with small stones and water. The potted bulbs cover the table, the edges of the planters, and the tile floor. When I ask, "Why so many?" she smiles and says she likes to give them to people for the New Year. We've filled so many pots I wonder if she is gifting them to all of Ko Shan Village.

We wait to see if spring works its magic in tune with the Chinese calendar, ensuring prosperity if they bloom in time for the New Year. Whenever I hear Third Aunt on the stairs, I throw on a coat to join her on the freezing roof. We peer at each bulb to see if it is stirring. If we've cut them right and the bulb is healthy, each nodule within it will uncurl like a loosened fist. On the days when she doesn't come, I go up to the roof alone to check on our garden-in-waiting. Soon the first root threads poke through and worm their way over the stones, feeling for the water below.

In another week, the bulbs begin to swell. The first green fingers thrust through the top and sides, yellow-green then spring green, pale then vibrant as the slender stems unfurl and rise in small thickets, each stem with its pair of praying hands at the tip. Next, the hands open to reveal frilled cups and saucers in creamy white dabbed with cadmium orange. It's quite a show. After a decade without seasons in Hawaii, I want to applaud each tiny leaf and petal.

* * *

Although most people get only four days off from work for the new year, the holidays last seven days. By the night before the first holiday, Amah, Josie, and Second Aunt have been cooking for a week — tea ducks, thick daikon radish cakes seasoned with dried shrimp and mushrooms, and sticky *gao*, the traditional new year cake made from brown sugar and glutinous rice flour that looks like firm brown Jello topped with a red date. The women deliver Number 10 bounty to family and friends and pile up provisions for three days of family feasting.

Two days ahead of the reunion dinner, when sons return to their family homes with their wives and children, the Number 10 crew makes Teochew sweets from a recipe passed down through Abah's mother, who lived in Number 10 until she died and now gazes down from the dining room wall. We wear our coats because, with no heat in most Hong Kong houses, inside is nearly as cold as outside. Even Abah and Second Uncle, men who don't cook, have a job to do: they walk up the hill early in the morning to cut large leaves, then scissor them to the size of salad plates. In the house, an assembly line swings into action. Josie sits on the kitchen floor, which is covered in newspapers, mixing and kneading sweet rice flour dough with her hands in a white enamel tub. When she finishes a batch, she passes it to Amah and Third Aunt, who sit on stools in the hall beside a low table covered in oilcloth. They press handfuls of dough into comma or disc-shaped depressions carved in wooden paddles, dab a sweet potato mixture into the center of each bit of dough, and upend each molded shape onto a leaf. I stand against the wall with my camera, documenting each stage.

Second Aunt takes a turn at the molds, then Third Uncle. Cousins are conscripted. When Third Aunt asks, "Heather, want to try?" I wave my hands to protest that I am taking photos, but she insists, "Come, come! Sit here." I put down my camera, drop onto a stool, and take the silky dough into my hands to become part of the team. Third Aunt shows me how to scoop the right amount of dough with the tips of my fingers, how to pat it into the mold so there is room left for filling, how much filling to add. After a clumsy first try or two, I become part of the flow. Third Aunt and I fill the trays. Second Aunt returns to feeding the firebox beneath the tile stove in the kitchen. Amah and Josie place trays of molded sweets in a bamboo steamer basket inside the giant wok. The men carry the hot trays out to the balcony to cool alongside daikon radish cakes that were steamed yesterday.

We produce two hundred sweets by the end of the day, and everyone gets a taste of their hard work. The finished product is chewy and rich, a denser version of Japanese mochi. Mine resemble the rest, and I'm outsized proud of my minor part in this family production. Later, the gap in my photo sequence will be a reminder that hiding behind my camera lens provides a sense of safety but keeps belonging out of reach. If I want to be part of this family, I need to step in and get my hands sticky.

* * *

The night before the holiday officially begins, Fred, Bernie, and the four male cousins who grew up together in Number 10 return home to feast with their parents at the reunion dinner. The tiny kitchen becomes a magic purse from fairy tales, producing nine bounteous dishes for good fortune: fish, chicken, duck, stuffed mushroom and tofu skins, abalone, sea cucumbers, braised bamboo shoots, goose, and a soup. Slices of fried *gao* are served for dessert. As with American Thanksgiving, everyone groans and rubs their distended bellies afterward, myself included. "*Bao le!* So much food!" I exclaim to Fred.

"New Year is all about eating," he replies. "You have to have an abundance of food for good fortune, and every food means something to do with good luck, so you have to eat it all!" For Cantonese, I'm learning, eating is never just about the food.

* * *

The first morning of the New Year, I practice my Cantonese phrases as we walk down to Number 10 and join everyone in exchanging ritual greetings — *Gong hei fat choi! Sam seung sih sihng! Daai gat daai lei!* Happy New Year! May you accomplish all that is in your heart! Great luck and fortune!

We eat a vegetarian breakfast of *jai*, monks' food with its lucky ingredients — including black fungus, mushrooms, bean curd, lotus seeds, and water chestnuts — each symbolizing blessings and prosperity for the upcoming year. My ritual black-eyed peas, adopted during my Texas years, seem paltry by comparison.

While we eat, members of Great Aunt's family stop by. To sweeten the year ahead, they're served tea and sweets from a compartmented tray. They replace the candied coconut or lotus root they accept from the tray with *licee* containing a token amount of money. Then more *licee* change hands. Last night married men gave fat envelopes to parents, and elders gave "waist money," to the wives of the younger generation. Fred explains, "This is to pad your waist," using a Teochew reference to a time when women tucked money into their clothing rather than carrying purses. Today is for giving to extended family a generation below. Amah has a drawer full of red envelopes and a calculator in her head. She hands Fred the *licee* and orchestrates his distribution. He will pay up later. All this circulation of wealth works pretty well if you have a big family, since it is both given and received. If you are unmarried, you rake in cash on holidays, but if you're married then you have more cash going out than in. In ritual blessings, old people instruct young married people to "add more people to the family." For the unmarried, there are jokes about not keeping the elders waiting for their wedding banquets. We are beyond both of these expectations, so we pay up.

Not long after the visitors leave, we add gloves and scarves to our coats and walk to Great Aunt's house, where we repeat what happened at Number 10 in reverse. This time Great Aunt and her son offer us their tray, and we exchange sweets for *licee*. A television variety show blares in the background while we exchange ritual greetings. Then some of us continue down the hill for what Third Uncle calls "the big circle of luck."

This is Fred's first time home for Chinese New Year in twenty-eight years, and he asks why vendors are conducting business when all businesses used to shut down for three days. He remembers lots of people walking from house to house to greet each other, but today the streets are mostly empty. Third Uncle says it's been this way for the last ten years. He says, "Usually the younger generation would stay on Cheung Chau for two days with their families, but they came and went last night because there's no heat in Cheung Chau houses. They're used to the city now, and it's too cold for them in the country." I understand their choice. Fred put off buying a portable heater for weeks, and I've parked myself in front of ours since we got it. Yet I'm sad to hear that commercialism and the pace of modern life are changing the old traditions. The Lau family has clung to old ways longer than most, but I wonder again how many traditions will disappear when the current inhabitants of Number 10 pass on.

* * *

The second day of the New Year, daughters return to their families. Abah's two sisters — the "married-out women" — and their families pack into Number 10 with the rest of the Lau clan for lunch, games, group photos, and dinner. We eat the same food as the previous day, with everyone waxing nostalgic and comparing food memories and recipes. I no longer find it strange that every meal prompts a happy discussion of meals past and meals to come. I'm used to Fred asking over breakfast *What's for dinner?* The more health-conscious wives blot oil off of shrimp crackers and try unsuccessfully to limit their children's consumption of fried *gao*, but it's another no-holds-barred eating day.

Families with small children have brought their helpers along. The five Filipinas chat while sitting at a chilly table in the courtyard, enjoying a rare opportunity to eat together before they're asked to take photos of the Lau clan. Each family has already posed for portraits in front of the blooming plum-blossom branch in the dining room. Now we discard our coats long enough to line up three- and four-deep in the courtyard — the extended family, each nuclear family, each generation, the women, the men — with rows of blooming narcissuses in front. The youngest group breaks into goofy poses for their final shot. In my new hot-pink sweater and black turtleneck, I pose with the group of women who answer to Lau *tai* — Mrs. Lau.

After pictures, it's time for lucky gambling. The older generation gathers for mahjong throughout the year, but New Year is the one time the youngsters get to gamble for luck. The clan crowds around the dining room table to cheer each other on and throw dice. *Aiya! Ho-ah! Whaaaa!* They play for small change; and when someone wins, the cheering is so loud I have to cover my ears. On the most auspicious day of the year, the gods are surely paying attention. Good fortune and a happy fate coaxed by a roll of the dice.

In the evening, a group of us treks from house to house once more, handing out *licee*. We distribute wishes that call on the gods to bring everyone good fortune in the coming year: *May you be lucky on horses, may you get a promotion, may your studies go well, may you be beautiful forever, may you win at mahjong.* Exhausted but caught up in the web of family festivities, transformed from observer to participant, I feel lucky indeed.

20

Blessed Buns

"THEY want the flat now?" Third Uncle and Aunt's eldest son, Gabriel, and his wife, Ida, are expecting twins, but the babies aren't due until June. It's only March.

Fred says, "Gabriel and Ida want to remodel the flat before they move in, so they need it pretty soon. Third Aunt said we don't have to move out right away, but I could tell she was just trying to be nice."

"But we don't leave for China until June. Where are we supposed to go?"

"We can move into Number 10. It's only for a couple more months."

"A couple of months in Number 10? You're kidding, right?"

Despite my adjustments to the Lau family, the thought of spending two months in Number 10, surrounded by family day and night, still makes me feel like I can't breathe. I'm grateful that their door is always open to us, and I should be delighted with the option of no cooking or laundry or cleaning duties. But the option comes with no control over what I eat or when, my underwear hanging in the courtyard, waiting in line for the bathroom, and hiding in our room with my books to avoid being told I'm ruining my eyes. Way too many awkward moments left alone with Amah and Abah or Second Aunt and Uncle without a translator. A couple of weeks I could manage now, but not two months.

Once my initial irritation wears off, a glimmer of hope takes its place: a chance to find an apartment in the city. I envision Rani's shiny wood floors and bathtub. An oven and an elevator. Cozy restaurant dinners. It's not too late for us to have a taste of the expat experience, to balance our village stay by experiencing the best of both worlds. We just have to find a furnished flat and fast. Our first look at the online listings lets the air out of my fantasies. Short-term rentals are scarce, prices sky-high. The days tick by, so we rent what we can find on short notice: an over-priced, under-sized sublet in Discovery Bay ("DB" for short) on Lantau Island. Instead of moving to a building in the city's cosmopolitan heart, we will live in its suburban outskirts in one of the generic high-rises built to accommodate Hong Kong Island's expat overflow.

* * *

Moving to DB from Cheung Chau requires extra hands from a cousin and a three-point operation. We lug our suitcases and bags down the stairs and through the streets to the Cheung Chau ferry. Taking the slow ferry, we sit on the open-air lower cargo deck. Our motley assortment of suitcases and shopping bags, some borrowed from Number 10, and my roll of eggcrate foam from IKEA fit right in with the boxes and crates. Tourists and locals willing to pay more ride on the enclosed top deck with air conditioning or on the modern fast ferry. Down below, passengers slurp noodles, nap, and chat with friends. A nephew once told us he saw a rat running around in the rafters of the lower deck. Everyone laughed and swayed back and forth as it scampered overhead. Now I watch out of the corner of my eye for rats, besides the giant roaches I've occasionally seen.

Once docked, we cart our stuff between ferry piers. Compared to the noisy exuberance of the Cheung Chau ferry, the DB ferry looks fancy with its navy-blue upholstered seats, each with a crisp white cloth draped over the headrest. A sign forbids food and drink on board. "So pretentious," Fred grumbles. The few passengers at this time of day are tall Europeans or Filipina helpers shepherding light-haired children too young for school. The passengers speak in low voices or remain silent. Trying to cram our assortment of bags between the rows of seats, we become conspicuous country bumpkins. When we disembark in DB and cross the plaza to find a taxi, we are the only passengers with baggage. Fred says expats in DB probably don't lug their own stuff.

* * *

From our flat's only window, we have a front-row view of Fanta-syland Castle in Hong Kong Disneyland, located directly across the bay. Every night aerial fireworks crest above its fake turrets, halos of color trailing America's contribution to the haze we breathe daily. That I am in Hong Kong looking at an American icon amuses me. The unpredictable hot water and the sketchy landlord are less laughable, but this sublet was available without a lease and is affordable. We have a cubbyhole bathroom, a living/dining/kitchen room, and a bedroom that is a glorified cupboard. The furniture is basic wicker, not much different from what we had on Cheung Chau.

Installed in our just-for-now lodgings, I am suddenly and deeply lonely. After all my complaints about the clumping factor of Number 10, I feel like we've been expelled from the nest.

On the days when Fred teaches in the city and I don't tag along, I wander in our expat neighborhood: modern apartment buildings with park-like lawns, generic Western restaurants, and wide sidewalks. On any of the narrow streets and stairways of Cheung Chau, I could hear televisions, mahjong games, and noisy conversations. I learned to dodge the piles left by stray dogs, the phlegm left by old men. So much of daily life is lived inside out on the island — vegetables and pastries and clothes are displayed on the sidewalk, and people open their doors and windows for ventilation. In DB the residents are separated by their parks and esplanades, cocooned within their glossy, climate-controlled flats. Through the windows, I catch occasional glimpses of grand pianos and bookcases. When people do venture out, mostly on the weekends, they ride on expensive golf carts or stroll accompanied by well-fed purebred dogs and helpers pushing fancy prams. I feel as if I've been parachuted into a movie set. The scenery all looks very foreign.

Some days I take the minibus down the hill to the Western-style grocery where I can find European and American foods. Weetabix and Nutella. Dinty Moore stew. Fresh Italian parsley and basil instead of five-spice powder. In the Cheung Chau grocery, the condiments are soy sauce, black bean sauce, oyster sauce, and sriracha. Here I can buy balsamic vinegar and truffle oil. There I can get a whole black-skinned chicken with its head still attached. Here I can get a package of detached chicken thighs. I should be happy.

I'm so adrift that I go to the store to be around people as much as to shop. I am often the only adult in the store shopping for myself. The rest are Filipina domestic helpers buying groceries for their employers. I hear them greeting each other in Tagalog and speaking accented English to toddlers riding in their carts.

One day, I am in the canned-goods aisle when a young Filipina pushing an empty cart asks me a question. "Excuse me," she says in a high and hesitant voice. "Can you help me? Do you know how to make chili?" After twenty-five years in Texas, it just so happens I do. I respond with a nod and smile, so she hands me her list. In halting English, she says that she is a new hire who works for Americans. After I find all the ingredients for her, I explain how to cook the onions and meat, how to add the spices and tomato sauce. She thanks me, and I turn to leave. "Excuse me," she says again. "Do you know how to make tacos?" We search for more ingredients, and I give another cooking overview. Amused, I wonder if I have American and Texas tattooed on my forehead or if she just assumes that all Americans eat chili and tacos. Either way, I'm grateful for the conversation.

* * *

On a brilliant, sun-saturated Saturday, Amah and Abah come to visit us in DB. When they step off the ferry, they look small, out-of-place, and very Chinese under their sun umbrellas — one plaid and one brown. We walk together through the wide plaza filled with picnic tables and surrounded by British fish and chips and Aussie steak restaurants. Expat families and day-tourists fill many of the tables. Pointing with his chin, Abah talks to Fred, who laughs before translating, "He says, see, that's what they all like to do." Fred tips his head toward an overweight Australian man sitting shirtless in the sun and drinking from a large bottle of beer. "He says gweilo like to sit out in the sun and drink beer all day." I laugh too, but I feel uncomfortable because I'm not sure which side of the fence they think I live on. Here in this expat enclave next door to Cheung Chau, Amah and Abah feel like outsiders. I have an urge to protect them the way they encircle me when I'm the foreigner in their world.

After they inspect our apartment, we take them out to lunch at a Western restaurant near the pier, where we cut up our hamburgers and fish and chips to share family style. When they leave, I wish we could to go back with them to the noise and familiarity of Cheung Chau.

* * *

We return to Cheung Chau and Number 10 for an extended visit ahead of the annual Bun Festival, arriving before the tourists descend. It's May, and the day of the festival is already scorching hot. The Hong Kong government moved the festival to Buddha's birthday, so it falls on a holiday and maximizes heritage tourism potential. By mid-morning, the resident island population of around thirty-three thousand swells three-fold. Bamboo scaffolds plastered with pink, yellow, and red banners transform the wharf. People throng around snack stands that line the street, reaching for sticks of spiral-cut potatoes and fish balls. *Chi lap lap* (hot and sticky), says Fred, plucking his sweat-splotched T-shirt away from his skin.

On the Pak Tai temple grounds, a thirty-foot scaffold frames three soaring cones covered in white steamed buns like enormous

Christmas trees made of cotton balls. To one side of the towers is a smaller enclosure with three smaller cones.

Fred explains, "The big one in the center is where they have the competition."

"Did you ever climb it?" I ask.

"Not me! I hate heights. Used to be anyone could climb them. It was a free-for-all, and whoever got the most buns was the winner."

"How come they don't do that anymore?"

"There were gangsters, and I heard it fell over one year. Somebody was hurt. No one climbed for a long time, but they started it again. Now you have to train and wear a harness. It's not the same. Look — the buns on the big one aren't even real." He shakes his head in disgust.

Nearby, an elaborate three-sided bamboo enclosure houses an opera stage; its open side faces the steps leading up to the temple. The tile-roofed temple, topped by a pair of rippling dragons that flank a flame-encircled pearl, has new red banners on either side of the entrance. In front, the concrete censer prickles with tall sticks of incense that envelop the square in a cloud of fragrant smoke.

We've been staying on Cheung Chau for two days, during which the plaza has been clamorous with the high-pitched, stylized speech and shrill, nasal singing of Cantonese opera. The singing is accompanied by the clacking of wooden blocks, the clash of cymbals, the silky twining of *erhu, sanxian,* and *dizi* — the Chinese vertical bowstring, plucked lute, and bamboo flute. The stage faces the temple so that the elaborately made-up actors stride on thick-soled cloud shoes, wave long white sleeves, shape elegant hand gestures, and brandish martial arts weapons for the gods within. Fred explains, "The real purpose of the bun festival is the ritual cleansing of the island, the Taoist rituals called *jiao* that the priests do away from the public. The bun tower climbing and the parade is mostly for tourists."

*   *   *

The day of the parade, the street becomes almost impenetrable. The closer we get to the waterfront, the more it feels like the island has been invaded. Starting in the central plaza, the street is blocked off with metal barricades. Folding chairs have been set up for the local ethnic associations and their guests, and at the bend of the waterfront promenade is a grandstand for VIPs and the media. The rest of the crowd is stacked several deep behind the barricades.

We find our seats, which Josie saved for us with umbrellas. When we settle in, Amah insists that Josie hold a large plaid umbrella over my head. Horrified at being shaded like a member of the colonial elite, I conspire with Josie to tie the umbrella to the barricade with some plastic tape she retrieves from the market. Around us, the crowd amasses — locals, visitors, children, cameras, way more white faces and tall bodies than we're used to seeing on Cheung Chau. Amah and Second and Third Aunts greet neighbors, while Fred and I gawk at tourists, guessing where they're from. In front of us is the wet market building, and to our left the funeral enclosure, but there are no funerals during the festival week.

The parade, which symbolically circles the island by winding from the Pak Tai temple to the Tin Hau temple and back, starts with an eardrum-shattering din that washes over the noise of the crowd. While the iconic sound of an American parade is the orderly marching band, the signature sound of a Chinese parade is the thunder and clang of lion-dance troupes with their gongs, drums, and cymbals. There are red, yellow, green, orange, and blue lions, each more ornate than the last. Troupe after troupe stops in the plaza to perform: lifting and dropping the lions' enormous furred and horned heads, twisting their two-manned bodies, blinking their electric eyes, clacking their enormous jaws to the clanging and drumming. As usual, my hands cover my ears. Fred leans over to shout, "*Renao!*"

"What?"

"*Renao!*" That exuberant Chinese aesthetic of hot and noisy that I can appreciate only in theory.

Yard-high gods from Cheung Chau's seven temples glide past in their curtained palanquins, like brides being transported to weddings. We glimpse elaborate headdresses, flashing eyes, and golden visages beneath their forward-facing awnings. Tourists admire the carved structures and embroidered banners. Local people lift folded hands to their chests as the gods pass. Four men carry each litter and temple association members walk alongside, each group dressed in matching shirts. Yelling into my left ear, Fred recounts how long ago the island was threatened by plague and overrun with pirates. When someone brought a statue of Pak Tai from Guangzhou, the threats subsided. Now Pak Tai is revered as the island's protector in the same way that Tin Hau is seen as the savior of Peng Chau. They both get places of honor in the Bun Festival parade, but the dark god of the north leads the others in this parade.

The floats come next. On the way here from Number 10, we had passed an assembly of flatbed carts on which small children dressed as deities and legendary figures were being installed like dolls on tall stands threaded through or under their costumes and culminating in hidden bicycle-style seats. Hoisted ten or twelve feet above the carts, the made-up and costumed children now appear to drift above the crowd, giving the term "float" a whole new meaning for me. On the lower part of each cart, another costumed child completes the tableau. "What if they have to pee?" I ask.

"They're out of luck," Fred says. "Bernie was on a float when he was a kid, and he said it was really hot and long."

"So why do they do it?"

"It's an honor for the parents for their kid to be on a float."

Interspersed with more lion-dance troupes, the floats carry pint-sized imperial scholars, empresses, and fairies. In a nod to the upcoming Beijing Olympics, one float carries a cyclist, and several child jockeys represent the upcoming Olympics equestrian events Hong Kong will host. One child waves the flags of China and Hong Kong. Another twirls her riding crop as she glides past. Each float has a group of adults who either take turns pushing the cart using a handle in the back and or pulling it by ropes attached to the sides. Some lucky kids have an adult who carries a long staff with an umbrella to provide shade. I wonder why their heavy makeup isn't running down their necks. Sweat is running down mine.

Next, the local organizations troop past displaying their banners. They include Taoist and Buddhist monks, school groups, sports teams, temple associations, and regional associations. The groups wave to their friends and families, who cheer as they walk past. We wave and call to Abah when the Teochew Association comes into view in their yellow shirts with "Blue Girl Beer" printed on the back.

The People's Republic of China's contribution comes next: inflatable versions of the "Five Friendlies," colorful cartoon animals representing the five major ethnic groups of China (Hui, Manchu, Mongols, Tibetans, and Han) for the Olympics. "Beijing had to get in on the act," Fred comments. A troupe of Cantonese opera performers appears, perhaps the same ones who have been performing at the temple. Dressed in full opera makeup and brilliantly colored satin costumes, they pair off to perform intricate martial arts techniques and multi-person juggling feats with sticks. Clowns and monks and lion dancers on stilts follow.

When a local soccer team is followed by six Brazilian carnival dancers, the crowd gasps. The tall young women look monumental in their stiletto heels and plumed headdresses. Tourists applaud, and the Number 10 relatives buzz. *Aiyaaa! Gauchoaa! What is this? So out of place! Who let them in?* The dancers strut to samba music piped from a boom box, and when they twirl, their fringe-trimmed G-strings reveal perfectly tanned buttocks. Neon-colored feather boas flip and flutter above barely covered breasts. For a few minutes, the parade comes to a standstill as the media mobs the dancers, snapping photos. A few Chinese tourists slip past the barriers to pose with the women, their fingers forming the V sign. In the sideline seats, questions pulse from neighbor to neighbor, a lit-up circuit board of unsmiling faces. "The wrong kind of buns," I snicker to Fred, pointing with my chin to the balconies. "The locals aren't amused."

That a troop of local Boy Scouts come next makes me laugh.

A few more groups pass before the updates travel back on the gossip hotline. *Diverted before they got to the judges' stand. Told their ferry was waiting, and they had to go. Now.* Fred says, "It's a small island and everyone knows who's on the festival committee." Even though I'm American and have never been to Brazil, I am washed with shame by gweilo association, as if I, too, had stripped semi-nude on the main street. I'm embarrassed in front of Fred's family, in front of this place where I try so hard to fit in.

* * *

After the parade, the Number 10 contingent heads to the Cheung Chau Country Club. The Country Club got its name because it's in the country, not because it's fancy or exclusive. Located a block off the short street that cuts across the low, central section of the island, the family-owned restaurant sits one stairway above the beach and contains a single large room filled with round tables that seat ten to twelve. To get there, we weave through the knots of people jostling to get on the many extra ferries pressed into service for the holiday. We accommodate Second Aunt and Amah's slower pace and constant stops to greet neighbors. I feel relieved to be separating from the crowds and glad that the visitors are returning to the city. I'm happy to be home already, at least for a few days.

When we enter the flamingo-pink interior of the country club, we're hit by the chill of air conditioning and the smell of bleach and cooking oil. Members of the Teochew Association gather around two of the tables near the murky-looking windows that face the water. Glasses of tea sweat on the pink plastic table coverings, and the men who walked in the parade mop the shine from their faces and necks. The club owner's son, wearing a stained apron, sets bottles of Blue Girl Beer on the lazy Susans in the center of each table and chats with various members of the group. Third Aunt and I approach a clump of women who are discussing the parade, and I show them my photos of the Brazilians. Third Aunt translates the general consensus: *So nasty! Not wearing anything! Shameful!* The talk continues through all nine predictable courses, and the men chime in with their criticism: *Invited by that local politician with a son on the soccer team. Always trying to make himself look good.*

*   *   *

We leave the country club at dusk. The Number 10 folks head home, and Fred and I stroll down a backstreet where we happen on one of the many shrines that dot the walkways. This one is red with a green roof, a dollhouse-sized temple. Tonight it is alight with candles and incense.

Across the walkway, two men and a woman kneel as they attend to a makeshift altar on a mat of flattened cardboard boxes. They've arranged many cups of tea and pairs of chopsticks around the edges of the mat and filled the center with bananas, oranges, and bags of nuts. Just inside the ring of teacups are takeout containers filled with rice and bristling with incense. There are stacks of lucky paper at the corners of their makeshift table. After a day battered by crowds and noise, Fred and I find this quiet scene entrancing. We whisper so we won't disturb their reverence. "Why isn't there any meat?" I ask. "Your family always has three kinds of meat for offerings. Is this for the earth god?" There are earth god shrines on nearly every street in Ko Shan Village.

"Remember, it's the *jiao* festival and Buddha's birthday, so the offerings are all vegetarian." Yesterday, the whole island had gone vegetarian; even McDonalds had complied with veggie burgers. "In the old days, everyone gave up meat for a week," he adds. "A lot has changed."

The couple lights new incense from the old. The candlelight flickers and reflects off the tiled wall of the building, suffusing the entire corner in a warm yellow glow. We watch until the smoke makes my eyes tear, then we move on.

We walk past the temple grounds, where four Taoist priests in black hats and yellow robes sit at a table under an awning beside the spotlighted bun towers. On the table sits a bucket filled with burning incense. As the smoke drifts around the priests, they look like wavering figures from a dream. At the smaller bun towers, men remove the white steamed buns, each stamped in red with the Chinese characters *ping* and *an*, which together form the word for "safety." They pile the buns into large baskets on carts.

"What will they do with the buns?"

"They deliver them to all the local associations the next day."

"People eat buns that have been out here for days?"

"Those buns are blessed by Taoist priests. Blessed buns can't hurt you." As usual, he scoffs at what he sees as my finicky Western hygiene.

"I forgot that you're immune to everything."

"Haha!" he replies. "I can eat anything and your people always get sick. Too clean."

When we reach the walkway near the pier, the smoke and the dim lights make seeing difficult. We glimpse people eating at tables along the shore, buckets filled with incense, and a few photographers, but the tourists have all gone home.

* * *

The next day we hear the dinging of the bun delivery cart as it nears Number 10. Abah, reading the *Apple Daily*, a local newspaper, holds up a photo of the Brazilians on the front page. The article reports that the dancers were well received by the crowd and were a welcome addition to the parade. At our Number 10 dinner that evening, Third Uncle tells us the local politician who sponsored them had every one of his campaign posters defaced. He says, "It doesn't matter what the papers say. The locals made their point loud and clear." I laugh with the rest of the family. Fred and I may live in expat land, but we're from Cheung Chau.

21

Lost and Found

AFTER moving out of our sublet on DB and spending our final week at Number 10, Fred and I board the Cheung Chau ferry with our carry-on suitcases. We're on our way to Hong Kong University to meet the professors we will lead to China before we return to Hawaii. We slide into seats near the window; and as the ferry pulls out of the harbor, several long, slender boats with red and gold painted sides and elegantly carved dragon heads on their prows slide between us and the anchored fishing boats. "So soon?" I ask. "I thought the Dragon Boat Festival wasn't for a week."

"It's on June 9. They're probably doing a practice run for the race on Sunday."

"I'm sad that we'll miss it. We've seen almost a full cycle of festivals."

"We'll see it some other time. Besides, there's a typhoon watch, so it might get canceled if the storm hits us bad."

As with every festival in Hong Kong, this one has special symbolic food. We've seen *zongzi,* leaf-wrapped packets of stuffed sticky rice folded into perfect triangles or rectangles, stacked and piled in the markets. The festival commemorates the death of Qu Yuan, a Chinese poet and minister from the Warring States period who threw himself into a river after someone falsely accused him of treason in 278 BCE. Villagers tried to spare his body from being eaten by throwing rice balls into the river. Now there are annual boat races and *zongzi* in his honor.

"We need the extra money to pay for all our traveling," Fred says, referring to the brief side trips to Cambodia and Japan we've made while in Hong Kong. To replenish our funds, we'll head for China with an East-West Center group. It's Fred's summer gig, and I'm his assistant. The trip will be our second with the EWC Asian Studies Development Program, which takes American professors on field studies in China. Counting my initial trip to China, in which I was a participant, it's my third field study. Most EWC trips start in Honolulu, but, because Fred and I are in Hong Kong, this group will meet at Hong Kong University's fancy guesthouse. The first leg of our trip will be an introduction to Hong Kong. Sad as I am to miss the summer festivals, I'm eagerly anticipating three things: feeling smart and useful, being around English speakers, and sleeping in a comfortable bed. I've even dared to wish for a bathtub. I'm a daily soaker, so nine months of showering has left me feeling parched and cranky.

The focus of this year's trip is ethnic minorities in China, the same theme that brought Fred and me together in Hawaii ten years earlier and one that overlaps my academic expertise in folklore and tourism. My job for the trip is to present a cultural-etiquette orientation, to talk about cultural tourism, the subject of my soon-to-be-published dissertation, and to serve as a cross-cultural guide along the way. In exchange for my tickets and lodging, I'm also along to add a woman's touch to the otherwise male leadership of the group. I'm happy to have a role that pulls together my academic training and life experience, a welcome change from being the family extra and trailing spouse.

We've parked our big suitcases at Number 10, and we disembark from the ferry with our twenty-two-inch carry-ons stuffed with everything we'll need for the three-week trip to Beijing, Yunnan, and Shanghai. Traveling by taxi to HKU instead of our usual hike through IFC to get to the subway, I feel privileged and pampered. I savor that feeling again as we check into our room in one of several comfortable guesthouses staggered up the hillside and surrounded by trees. "Nice," I sigh, sinking into the soft bed.

* * *

At HKU, we catch up with Peter, our friend from Hawaii and the program coordinator. Participants trickle in all day from various parts of the United States, and we meet them in the dining room for an evening banquet. The introductions are warmed by bottles of red wine; and while the participants tell the group who they are and where they come from, I can't stop thinking how enormous most of them look. They loom over the Chinese waiters like hippos and elephants who've wandered into the small-mammal section of a zoo.

When I give my after-dinner talk on Chinese etiquette and travel expectations, I play to the academics' desire to be travelers and not tourists. I leave out all the times I've whacked into cultural barriers or embarrassed myself, and stick to basic rules and principles. Use serving chopsticks so no one gets sick. If they're not provided, touch only the food you will take, and never root around in the platter with your personal chopsticks. Don't pile food on your plate, and never take more than you can eat. Try everything and act enthusiastic to avoid insulting your hosts. Don't be surprised at the vast quantities of food served at banquets — excess is symbolic of hospitality. Don't be surprised by staring, direct questions, spitting, squat and trench toilets, line-cutting, and smoking indoors. Don't expect toilet paper and napkins to be provided everywhere — carry tissues. Bargain assertively but respectfully. Don't be thrown by what Americans deem schlocky tourism; see it as an opportunity to consider how the Chinese construct themselves for outside consumption.

The participants nod and ask a few questions and, like undergrads, promptly forget everything I say. In the coming weeks, Fred and I will repeatedly flinch as their Americanness bumps up against Chinese cultural norms. Fred will flash angry impatience while I, once there myself, will cringe in recognition.

* * *

Back in our room, Fred and I share initial impressions and speculate about whether we will have some or all of the same elements we had in our last group of twelve: a whiner, a shopaholic, a wanderer, a know-it-all, a laggard. We make bets on which participants might be prone to roommate disputes or not-so-secret liaisons. Not for the first time I say, "It would be easier to take kids than professors. At least if kids are bad, you can send them home."

Fred agrees, "Academics are the worst because they don't listen. They think they already know everything." Remembering our impetuous behavior in the East-West Center program where we met makes me wonder if we might be describing ourselves.

"We aren't like that, are we?"

"Ha! Of course not!"

During his time as a visiting professor at HKU, Fred made special friends of the secretaries. As he does in Hawaii, he joked with the staff and brought them food. In return, they helped him in all the behind-the-scenes things that only secretaries know. The first event of our field study is a fancy dim sum meal in a hotel near Times Square, the location and menu secretary-orchestrated and -approved. Hong Kong dim sum doesn't disappoint. The succession of delicate dumplings, tasty stuffed buns, and saucy noodles dazzles our participants so effectively we will later wonder if we should have ended our trip in Hong Kong instead of Shanghai.

* * *

When we take the group to Cheung Chau to show them a side of Hong Kong that outsiders seldom see, I am reminded of the expression "herding cats." Before we can board the ferry, we spend an hour and a half trying to help a rumpled philosophy professor in his seventies tap into an ATM near the ferry terminal, an effort hindered because he has forgotten his ATM number. He eventually hits on the right combination, but by then we've missed the fast ferry, and the rest of the group has wandered off to take photos of the harbor. By the time Fred and Peter round them up again, we're among the last passengers to board the slow ferry.

Cheung Chau is our trial run for the rest of the journey. We've implemented a buddy system inspired by a professor of

Japanese popular culture on our last trip who was late every morning and disappeared every night. When the missing participant's roommate entered the bus one morning and Fred asked where his buddy was, the roomie responded with "How should I know? Am I my brother's keeper?" to which Fred responded, "*Yes!*" Now when we disembark near the pier, Fred reminds everyone to stay together before the twelve of us start our trek around the island.

I relish my chance to shine as a cultural expert. We parade past the *dai pai dong* and through the wet market, a group of large white spectators who stand out from all the locals going about their daily business. The gruffness in Fred's voice tells me he's struggling with his role as indigenous anthropologist, the fraught business of trying to de-exoticize his everyday world without becoming an object of curiosity for the American professors. I smooth and explain. Where I've previously felt like an intruder looking in, I'm now an interpreter, an intermediary. I point out the funeral enclosure, inactive at the moment, and I answer questions about local folklore and culture. Fred relaxes as we leave the tourist zone near the waterfront and head toward the less-populous side of the island. Away from the crowded streets, he no longer feels self-conscious about being part of a spectacle or worries about running into people he knows. He leads us to Cheung Po Tsai Cave, where he tells the story of the notorious pirate who stashed his loot at this remote location. The participants stop to take pictures at every scenic point. Fred glares at the two philosophy professors who bring up the rear. Deep in conversation, they don't appear to be listening to anything he says.

As we round the island and start back toward the pier, Fred and Peter walk in front, discussing logistics. They announce that we will stop at the *dai pai dong* for a local-style lunch, and Fred calls Amah so she can walk down the hill from Number 10 to meet the group.

Happy to be out of the sun, the participants flop onto plastic stools under the awnings. I take a quick count and then count again. We're two people short — the philosophers have vanished. "Where are Dave and Susan?" I query the group. "Weren't they right behind us?"

"Maybe they were just walking slow," someone offers.

"Maybe they're still taking pictures," says someone else.

"I saw them last at the waterfront."

"Maybe they took a wrong turn."

None of this helps, and the missing professors don't appear. Now that I think about it, the last time I saw Dave, already on our radar after the ATM incident, he was pointing up into the trees while his wallet was inching out of his back pocket. I'd nudged Fred, who warned Dave about monitoring his money and belongings. They might be safe on Cheung Chau, but we're heading for crowded megacities after this leg of the trip, so he will need to be more alert.

Fred and Peter huddle just as Amah turns up. Fred quickly explains to her that we've lost two of our people, and when she says, "*Aiyaaa!* How can you lose professors?" he snorts in exasperation. He calls over the restaurant owner to order milk tea all around then shouts, "OK, Peter and I are going to go find them. Nobody leaves until we get back!" His bluster doesn't scare me, but I can see it has the desired effect on the others. No one else will be wandering off, at least not soon. Two weeks from now, in the Cang Mountains of Dali, we'll look down from a gondola to see the architecture professor doing tai chi on an oversize chessboard far below. Now, we sit in shade that is only slightly cooler than the air beyond and sip our milk tea. Amah tries out her limited

English to little avail. I attempt to answer questions about Chinese customs while we wait. And wait.

It takes Fred and Peter an hour to retrace our steps around the island at a fast clip. When they return, they are dripping, irritated, and alone. No philosophers. "Maybe they headed back to the city," someone says.

"Without telling anyone? They better not have," Fred snarls. He calls the university guesthouse, but they haven't heard from them either. Fred and Peter confer again and then announce that we're heading back. At the pier, Fred flags down a local policeman to describe the missing pair. The cop shakes his head and looks uninterested.

During a subdued group dinner at the HKU guesthouse, Fred gets a call from the front desk saying that our AWOL members have arrived. Fred and Peter go to the lobby to talk to them, and when they hear about how the lost-but-resourceful philosophers took the ferry back to Hong Kong, where they enjoyed a lovely Italian meal, Fred's restrained fuming erupts into profanity we can hear from a room away. This time, I am happy to not mediate. The errant participants will believe Fred is angry because they didn't follow his instructions. While that's true, I suspect that the major offense was making him lose face in front of his mother.

* * *

That night, in our room atop a steep hill, rain lulls us to sleep. In the morning, it's still raining when Fred gets a call from a participant staying in a room lower down the hill. He has stepped out of bed and into water. I turn on the television as Fred opens the door to Waterworld. On the weather channel we see that the typhoon watch has been upgraded to a warning. It's our day to depart, and the forecast is hot and steamy, wet and unpredictable. Typhoon season.

Fred's glasses fog over when we step outside. As we slosh our way to the dining room, water pools in the uneven walkways, and rivulets stream from one level of the hillside to the next. During breakfast, Fred and Peter periodically leave to check the weather news on a screen behind the front desk.

As instructed, everyone brings his or her suitcase to the entrance, where a bus will pick us up and take us to the airport. I slop through puddles, wearing rubber shoes that stick to my feet but allow the rainwater to escape. Others squish along in waterlogged sneakers. Water rises in the entry, so we keep moving the suitcases closer to the higher end. Where is the bus? We have a plane to catch, and we don't want to be late.

When the bus arrives we pile in, lifting our suitcases inside so we can make a quick exit, but there will be no quick anything today. As the bus pulls out of the circular drive and enters the main road, the rain becomes a deluge. We creep past cars abandoned at the edges of a road turned raging river. The streets wind and twist down the hillside, but the water gushes straight down in a series of waterfalls. The submerged bus tires create a wake. We try one direction and then another, snaking past abandoned cars. The driver, connected to the latest information by a headset, announces that Pok Fu Lam Road is closed because of floods, which means we cannot get to the airport in time for our flight. Then he tells us that the airport is closed. We wonder if we will have to turn back, if we *can* turn back. Fred talks on the phone with someone, making frantic plans in Cantonese. The secretaries? He announces a change of plans: we'll go to the train station instead of the airport. The trip is on.

On our last day in Hong Kong, we're literally washed out of the country. In three weeks, after we've toured Beijing, the Tibetan plateau, Yunnan, and Shanghai, we'll return to pick up our belongings from Number 10, but returning to Hong Kong to visit will never feel the same as living here.

PART III: 2011–2014

22

Chinese Borscht

We've been back in Hawaii for three years, and we're leading another EWC group to China. This time we're traveling in Heilongjiang, and the theme of our field study is borders. To our west is Mongolia, southeast is the Sea of Japan, north is Russia, and North Korea is to our south. We are just two degrees of latitude north of my hometown in Washington State and 4,760 miles from Seattle, where my Russian grandparents lived out most of their lives and raised their only child, my father.

Our summer trip is a welcome break from a re-entry fraught with failure and compromise. Although I sailed through my PhD program and my dissertation was published as a book, I didn't land the academic position I was convinced was waiting on the other side of all my mid-life efforts at reinvention. Our unsuccessful bids for a spousal hire at the University of Hawai'i left Fred angry at his colleagues and me embarrassed and resentful in front of mine.

This past January, I accepted a position as the curator of Iolani Palace, a historic house museum interpreting Native Hawaiian history. Although I love museums and was excited about the opportunity, I couldn't stop thinking of an eight-to-five job as a booby prize after all my years of teaching. I was also a beginner. I'd taught museum studies courses, yet I had zero practical experience. After six months of self-study, I am beginning to suspect most of the staff knows less than I do. I love the work, but that I'm one of only three haoles working under a Native Hawaiian director who distrusts haoles and resents PhDs means every workday is mined with potential explosives. I come home exhausted and tearful. I pare myself down to half my size trying to temper my whiteness and not offend. Soon the other two haoles will quit. Because his schedule is more flexible, Fred has gone into full caretaker mode — cleaning, doing laundry, and cooking dinner almost every night. He does his best to hear out my frustrations, but after weathering the previous two years of my unemployment depression, he wants to hit anyone who insults me or makes me cry.

* * *

The Russian café we find on a side street offers pelmeni and borscht on its sandwich board menu. My mouth waters in anticipation of succulent, meat-filled dumplings simmered in chicken broth, a memory of my grandmother's dinner table. Fred says, "I expected you to order the borscht."

"Grandma Diamond never made borscht, but we had pelmeni. Actually, she didn't make those either. She got them from her brother Peter's restaurant in Seattle, the Troika. She had English names for everything. She called these 'little meat pockets.'"

The Chinese waitress brings us a bowl of pelmeni, and the small pillows of noodle dough look and smell like home. I bite into one and am disappointed. The dumplings are plump with ground meat and onions but have a grassy undertaste. "Cilantro? Why would they ruin them with cilantro?"

"It's run by Chinese. Chinese like cilantro." Fred pops the pelmeni whole into his mouth and nods in approval as he chews. "Wontons," he says. His claim that everything comes from China is a running joke in our mixed Hongkonger–American marriage.

"More like ravioli. These have noodle dough and wontons have wrappers."

"Ravioli are just Italian wontons. They're all made from wheat, and noodles came from northern China. Marco Polo brought them to the Italians."

"Lots of cultures have dumplings and turnovers. How do you know it wasn't a simultaneous invention?"

"Look at the name. Pelmeni is probably a derivative of the Mandarin word for noodles, *mien*."

I roll my eyes and eat another little meat pocket.

* * *

We've given our EWC group the day off, so we can explore this city where my grandparents once lived. After lunch, we wander through the streets of the old city. According to my guidebook, Harbin was new when my grandparents arrived there in 1920. Built by Russians on the China stretch of the Trans-Siberian Railway route, the city is a hybrid cultural anomaly, a fitting location for the start of their Jewish–Russian mixed marriage.

Fin de siècle, Art Deco, Art Nouveau, and Romanesque facades, attesting to Russian fascination with European styles, loom in the background like a jumbled stage set. Modern Harbin is a Russian city with no Russians except for a few tourists. Whenever one of us spots a Western face, we say, "Sighting," our usual code.

On a shady street in the old Jewish quarter, we pass a cemetery full of headstones carved in Hebrew and a synagogue repurposed as a youth hostel, its walls covered with posters for concerts and coffee shops. I read aloud from the guidebook that Catherine the Great restricted Jews to the Pale of Settlement in present-day Ukraine, Belarus, and Lithuania. In Ukraine, where my grandfather's family lived, Jews were restricted to certain professions and plagued by brutal pogroms. Many sought refuge in foreign cities like Harbin. By the 1920s, there were as many as twenty thousand Jews in Harbin, most of them from Russia.

We find our way to the Harbin Jewish Museum, housed in the upper two floors of a restored synagogue constructed of blocky gray stone. Sunlight streams through leaded glass windows and spangles the stone floor with six-pointed stars.

Carved in shiny black marble, a plaque lauds China's embrace of Jews while Europe was persecuting them. "All this racial harmony talk seems simplistic, doesn't it?" In the institute on Chinese nationalism where Fred and I met sixteen years earlier, we'd analyzed how China's "harmonious nation" rhetoric has been used to justify forced development and assimilation of ethnic minorities. My propaganda alarm is on alert.

"Chinese like Jews," Fred says. "They think they're good at business and intelligent." When I try to explain my mixed pedigree to Fred's family, they say things like *No wonder she's so smart!* when they hear I had a Jewish grandfather.

"That's stereotyping," I say.

"So what, if it makes you look good?"

The walls of the museum display black-and-white photos of upper-class Jewish life in Harbin. Jews playing pianos and at the theater, Jews in front of stores and banks, Jews relaxing with their families at the beach. I don't recognize my working-class ancestors here any more than I do in histories written by European Jewish literati. My grandfather was a tailor from a family and a city of tailors.

I cannot find my grandparents in this synagogue. A shiksa, my grandmother would have been unwelcome. A non-believer, my grandfather would have stayed away. More than once my grandmother said, *"Your grandfather was a rebel, eating ham and everything. He didn't like religion much."*

* * *

My grandfather and his brothers left Ukraine before the 1917 revolution eradicated imperial Russia. I can only guess at the reasons.

Here is what I know. Isador Diamond made three long sea voyages. In 1911, he boarded a ship bound for America from the Russian city of Libau, now in present-day Latvia. On the manifest of the *S.S. Lithuania*, his race was marked "Hebrew." He journeyed across the Atlantic to America and across America to join his brother and sister on the west coast. He traveled back to Russia to work as a translator for the Red Cross after America entered the First World War.

On the manifest of the *Katori Maru*, the Japanese ship that carried him on his last voyage, from Shanghai to the United States in 1921, he and Ksenia, his Russian Orthodox bride, were first listed as Caucasian. Then someone scratched that out and re-inscribed them both as Hebrew, obscuring her life thread in that error.

On the journey, they stopped in Japan. *It was a Japanese boat, and they like to stop in their own country*, my grandmother would say. Their American date of arrival is stamped October 12, but she remembered that they stayed anchored in Puget Sound over Friday the thirteenth. *Everyone was kept onboard an extra day to avoid bad luck.*

I know our family name was changed from Dimeretz to Diamond by the first brother to emigrate. Until someone on a genealogy website unearthed his father's 1916 naturalization papers, my father was unaware that Isador had grown up as Itzko. The change of both names is not surprising. In English, Chaikl, his older brother, became Michael, and his wife Rifke became Ruby. Itzko and Isador could both be shortened to Izzy.

In America, Isador's older brother would get rich off the family knack for sewing, but my grandfather would be content to stitch the steady seam of a long and quiet life.

*   *   *

In Harbin, Russian-themed shops display traditional matryoshka dolls, like the one my grandmother gave me, beside nested Soviet leaders: big Gorbachev down to tiny Lenin. The tourist stores sell expensive vodka, camouflage gear, and night-vision binoculars. On side streets, we peek into shops stuffed with enough fur coats to depopulate the animal kingdom.

My grandmother learned her first English in Harbin. *The missionaries would read fairy tales to the children, and I would listen so I could learn. I recognized the stories.* She would have a lot to say about her heritage distilled down to dolls, booze, furs, and reminders of war. I imagine her clucking her tongue in disapproval. *Oi, oi, oi.* She never wanted to hear about my parents' visits to places she had been. *I saw China when it was Chinese.* For her, the past was gone, and good riddance.

* * *

On a trip to Seattle, Fred and I visited the widow of my grandmother's nephew. Helen and her husband, Alex, were born in Harbin, and she is our only link to my grandmother's family, the Tulintseffs. For lunch, Helen served what my grandmother called "big meat pockets" and everyone else calls piroshki: delicate blinis filled with ground beef and onions, each packet folded into a perfect rectangle and fried until golden, made from my grandmother's recipe. In another Diamond family tradition, we doused them with catsup. One bite and my eyes brimmed with the longing to be small and safe in my grandmother's kitchen.

Helen led us to a row of headstones at Evergreen Washelli Memorial Park and pointed out Alex's grave. I remember him as gentle, refined, and soft-spoken, a contrast to my boisterous and brash father with his jokes, sarcasm, and bow ties. I stopped at the graves of George and Vera. "George was number three of your grandmother's younger brothers," Helen explained.

"We don't know much about the family on this side," I said. "We never saw them."

Helen turned away for a moment, then said, "Alex always felt bad about the way they treated your grandmother."

"What do you mean?"

"They never approved of her marriage," she said. "Alex was young, so he shunned her too, but she and your grandfather helped him to come to America. Later he realized that it was wrong and apologized to her." In my gut, a pilot light of anger sparked.

I recalled my grandmother's story about her brothers: *We lived on Russian Island and, on the way to school, my brothers made me row the boat. Sometimes they knocked me into the water with the oars.* Good-natured pranking or precursor to the cruelty they would inflict on their sister for loving a Jew?

"Your grandfather was buried over there," Helen said, pointing across the road, "in the Jewish section. When your grandmother died, your father had his ashes moved to be with her." I had been to the rural Lynwood cemetery to visit their graves; their urn plots so small they are located next to the baby section with its balloons and stuffed animals. Neither of them buried with family, the divide extended into death.

* * *

Approaching the heart of the old city, we spot a gilded cross atop a verdigris onion dome. The edifice swells as we enter the square, until it appears the plaza is wearing an enormous, sparkling crown. A fat cross, each of its arms supporting a turret spiked by a smaller glimmering cross, Saint Sophia Cathedral is an imposing paperweight on a vanished past, a palimpsest of the city's change from Russian to Chinese hands. Inside, beneath ribbed and painted arches illuminated by a crystal chandelier and in front of faded frescos of haloed saints and leather-winged angels, stand portable exhibit walls. Now a museum of architecture, this crown jewel of Harbin's Russian era is consigned to narrate the story of its form but not its former function.

My grandparents are absent here as well. My grandmother grew up in the Russian Orthodox church that wouldn't marry her to a Jew. Here, as in the synagogue, her un-belonging settles onto my shoulders, constricts my heart. Was her rejection of religion due to exile or defection? I recognize both as part of my inheritance. She used to say, *Who knew that this mixed marriage would last so long?* As a child, I wondered what she meant. The way I saw it then, they were both white and Russian, so what was mixed? Now, I wish they could meet Fred. They would call him an Oriental and accept him anyway. Although I imagine my grandmother and I laughing about the everyday challenges of marrying and becoming a foreigner, I know our stories are not the same. The costs of our crossings are relative to our times. I grew up in a post-miscegenation era, with mass-communication and airline travel. My grandmother left home forever, with letters her only connection to home. *My mother and I held each other and cried every night,* she said of the days before she left home. She gained a Jewish family, but her defection added loss to loss.

*   *   *

On our last night in Harbin, Fred and I return to the Russian café and order the borscht. The waiter brings us steaming bowls of beef and cabbage floating in tomato broth, and a plate of rye bread. "Wow, this is the same kind we had when I was a kid in Hong Kong," says Fred.

I poke at my soup, which smells like American spaghetti and is the wrong shade of red. "Chinese borscht. The Russian kind is made with beets." I know this from my Russian cookbook, not experience. My dad hated beets, so my grandmother never made borscht.

"I don't know about that, but we got borscht from the Russians. Your people."

"Hah! See, not everything comes from China!"

"We improved it," he can't resist adding with a smirk.

23

Paper Money

Mʏ father and Second Aunt die within a few months of each other, and Fred gets a full account of Second Aunt's funeral from Amah. Second Aunt took her last breath with Second Uncle and their children and grandchildren by her side. Her body was moved to a special hospital room, where family members transferred her body into the waiting coffin. Fred guesses, based on his memories of funerals when he lived at home, that there was incense and a Taoist priest to mark her passage and to close the coffin lid, and that while family members went home to change or sleep, they took turns staying with her body.

He remembers that when his great-grandmother died at home in Number 10, she lay on a platform in the center of the living room, where incense was lit on a makeshift altar. Visitors came and went. Paper offerings were burned in the yard while family "guarded the night," taking turns sitting with the body until it was time for the funeral. Taoist priests conducted the rituals in the living room.

I picture scenes I witnessed on Cheung Chau. Coffins being unloaded from the lower ferry deck. Mourners dressed in white and gathered in the "Pavilion by the Water." Processions winding up the hill to the cemetery, bells ringing so everyone in Ko Shan Village could hear them pass.

* * *

There are no comforting rituals to fall back on when my father's heart gives out. In the hospital bed, he is doll-like. At five feet nine inches, he was never tall, but like Fred, he had a big voice and personality that made him seem larger. Now he has a white stocking cap on his head and tubes entering his nose and mouth. Lindsay, the older of my two younger brothers, didn't say the words "life support" on the hour-long drive from Seattle-Tacoma Airport to Providence Hospital in Everett; he just said our father wasn't conscious, although I can see that the situation is beyond that. I don't feel my father in the room. Surrounded by heaps of purses and bags, my mother and two of my siblings — Holly and Brent — sit on a bench by the window. Our miniature father is center-stage in his high bed, hooked up to monitors and screens and a machine that makes a rhythmic whooshing sound. I'm sure I remember him saying he'd signed a do-not-resuscitate form. No one is crying.

My mother fusses over medical details. *Maybe I shouldn't have told him to take that walk. He was in his recliner, and I thought he*

*was having a seizure. Maybe it was the blood thinner. He didn't have
a pulse, but Holly knew CPR and kept him going until the ambulance
came. They put in a stent and a pacemaker.* What no one asks: *What
if this was his time to go, and he meant to die in his chair?*

I stop my thinking here because I know that, however much my
father might have wanted a fast ticket out when it was his time to
go, he wasn't ready. Despite a failing body that demanded frequent
naps, slowed his steps, and bent his back, he was still planning to
stick around. He'd been counting on visiting Hawaii again; my
parents had planned to arrive in exactly two weeks. He'd invited
us to share their condo in Kona, and we'd purchased our tickets.

When I call Sorrel in Texas to tell her what's happening, she
wants to know if she should come. I say I don't know. I don't
know if he will revive. If he doesn't, I don't know when he will
go. I don't know if he's already gone. I don't know if she can get
here in time. I can't think. I'm having trouble being a mother and
a daughter at the same time.

I go with my mother back to my parents' condo in Everett. She
says she's fine, but her voice is a husk. We eat frozen food. I can
feel her fear, and I think maybe, just this once, we'll speak from our
hearts, but it's a language we don't share. We talk about nothing.
I wish Fred were here; then I'm glad he's away at a conference.
Blood and breath and family: all too hard to explain.

*   *   *

Waiting in the ICU, I have the odd sensation that the hospital
machinery is breathing for us all. Our family isn't used to spending
this much time together in close quarters. My distracted mother
chats with Brent and Holly's kids, occasionally flitting toward the
bed to check monitors.

A detached moon, she barely looks at my father. *Why doesn't she talk to him or hold his hand?* I wonder if she's controlling her emotions for us, wearing a mother mask while the wife quivers inside. Perhaps we're all too embarrassed to say the things we might if we were alone with him, the things we would never say if he were awake. Together, we're like the climate and colors of the ward: carefully neutral.

Holly, Lindsay, and I — each only a year apart — try to lighten the mood, just as our father would have done. Our gallows humor appalls the others, but we can't stop. We chortle about how he would want to know the cost of all that machinery and would have turned it off on us long before this. When a family friend drops by, Lindsay says, "Looks like he's about to sit up and tell a joke, right?" And the friend, who's taken our father's hand in his, laughs and says, "I keep expecting him to open his eyes and tell me how to vote!"

When a former neighbor who's a physician stops by, Lindsay and I ask him the question the nurses won't answer: *What are the chances?* He asks how long our father was without oxygen, and I understand from his deep inhalation and his sympathetic smile that he knows we are biding time, that we must be the ones to decide. The pacemaker keeps my father's heart going as a machine inflates and deflates his lungs.

Taking Lindsay aside, I say, "Dad would have hated this!"

He nods and says, "I know." Despite our past feuds, we click into lockstep.

The two of us walk to the nurses' station to ask the questions we can't ask in front of our mother: *Would he be able to breathe on his own? Is there any brain activity?* The nurses are kind-faced and factual in their answers. The time spent waiting for paramedics to arrive at my parents' Whidbey Island home, even with

Holly doing CPR, was too long to not have taken a toll. Even if our father opens his eyes and breathes on his own, he won't be who he was. It's up to us how long to keep the machines running. "Mom can't make this decision alone, and we can't make it for her," I say before we return to the room. "I think she needs to talk to a pastor, and since only Brent goes to church, let's get him to call."

When the pastor arrives, he gathers us around the bed and asks us to hold hands while he says a prayer of release. We bow our heads, even those of us who haven't done so in decades, and somewhere in the message about faith and salvation and resurrection, for an extraordinary moment, the believers and the unbelievers unite in saying goodbye. When the pastor finishes the prayer, all eyes are streaming, and we pull each other into a wet tangle of hugs. We feel finished, but we aren't. Lindsay goes in search of the head nurse. We wait some more.

When the nurse finally comes, my mother, Lindsay, and I follow her down the hall to a conference room. We sit on one side of the table, the nurse on the other.

"What's next?" we ask her.

"I'd like to do another CAT scan," she says.

"Will that tell you anything you don't already know?" I ask.

"Not really," she admits.

"Then there really isn't any point, is there?"

"It all depends on what you want," she says in a calm and neutral voice she must practice.

I turn to my mother, and ask, "What do you think, Mom? Are you ready?" With her unfixed eyes and expressionless face, she reminds me of the American Girl dolls she collects and that line her mantel and stair landing. She gazes at each of us as if the answer might be written on our faces, and then says, "Yes, I guess so," in a tired voice. We return to the room and wait some more, but this time we know how it will end. Time is suspended. Our voices are hushed, solemn. The monitors pulse and breathe and pulse and breathe.

At long last, two nurses arrive to remove the apparatus that has kept my father's body lifelike for three days, more than he would have wanted but enough time for us to get right with ourselves. We're asked to leave the room. When we re-enter, we collectively hold our breath as my father's chest rises three times, each inhalation deeper than the last, the final exhalation a sigh. Then silence. He becomes a wax figure — head tipped back, eyes closed, mouth gaping — almost like he looked when napping in his recliner, but not quite. I think of the deleted photos on the boat to Macau — of the white-haired, sleeping gweilo with the Roman nose and mustache. Brent and I inherited variations of that nose. With our father gone, we will look only like each other.

In the heavy silence, we don't know what to do with our hands and faces or what to say except goodbye, and it's too late for that. The nurses have vanished again, and we linger a moment before drifting in clumps out the door, our arms around each other. I imagine our father's last breath circling the room behind us and sifting down like fine dust.

* * *

Two days later, we crowd into a small room inside Our Savior's Lutheran Church, where the pastor asks us to sort through our memories. Our father wasn't a heart-to-heart sort of dad, so we contribute comic stories and mental snapshots. Someone remembers him waterskiing with a cigar in his mouth. We add that he liked cheeseburgers and fries, mostly forbidden by our mother. In mid-life he loved cruising around in his purple TR6, his golden retriever, Stocky, sitting a head taller than him. In his later years, he could be spotted in parades driving his Model A alongside his gray-haired car-enthusiast friends in their ancient cars. My mother smiles but has little to say. Sorrel, who'd arrived too late to say goodbye, adds the only sober note when she says her grandfather was the only stability she'd had as a child. We paint him in the shape of our loss, tailor him to fit the setting. Our stories are sparks but not the flame.

* * *

The next morning, Lindsay drives me and Mom to Sunrise Crematorium, a green building near the waterfront that looks like a small warehouse. We're here because Lindsay told the nurses our father was a penny pincher. When we enter, a pudgy woman with teased black hair, tattoos, and a gold front tooth meets us in the lobby. Her badge says Rayleen. As a soap opera blares from a TV in the room behind the short counter, Rayleen waves us to chairs around a small conference table and chatters about the weather. This is not the somber atmosphere I expected. I catch Lindsay's eye and we raise our eyebrows. Rayleen waves a hand across shelves filled with everything from flowered and pewter urns to wooden boxes. There are small price cards in front of each, and I note that some urns are quite expensive. "You can pick from any of these," says Rayleen.

"What do you think, Mom?" I ask, turning to her. My mother, already small, looks like she has shrunk by half in the last four days. Sighing, she glances at the shelves.

"Oh, I don't know. You kids pick something."

Lindsay, channeling my father, jumps in. "Which one's the cheapest? Our dad didn't want us wasting money on his funeral."

"This one right here." Rayleen pulls down a plain-lidded box made of yellow pine.

"That'll be just fine," says Lindsay. I take a deep breath while I decide if I want to risk contradicting my brother when he's in take-charge mode. I've gone along with his not-wasting-money spiel, but this is too much.

"Mom," I say, trying to nudge her out of the fog that has swallowed her, "This is forever. Do you really want to think of Dad's ashes sitting in a box like this for all time?"

She blinks at the box as if she's only now seeing it. "Well, I suppose not." She's deflated, and even this tiny decision seems an effort.

I glance over the shelves again, mentally discarding flowers and kitschy cuteness along with high prices, and choose three solid-colored, sedate-looking ceramic urns. I place them on the table in front of her and ask, "How about one of these?"

After a pause, she says, "Maybe the green one."

* * *

Brent is the one who picks up the ashes two weeks later, and when he does, he emails me to ask if I know the source of the poem on the bag. "What bag?" I write back. I have a dim memory of a folded cloth on the shelf next to the green urn. "Why? What does it say?"

He writes back, "It says 'Until we meet again at the Rainbow Bridge.' I thought maybe it was from Norse mythology."

I don't know, so I call Sorrel, who hoots with laughter. When she can catch her breath, she says, "They use it in pet funerals! The rainbow bridge is where dead pets go!"

When I share this info with the rest of my siblings, we decide that our father would find this inscription hilariously appropriate for a former veterinarian. To myself, I think the least Rayleen could have done is tell us the green urn was for pets if it was. Was she snickering when we left? Then I wonder if Sunrise also cremates pets, and if my father's ashes might be mixed in with those of dogs and cats. Would he mind? Probably not. He was a veterinarian, after all. He'd just turn it into a good story.

* * *

Before the first of the two memorial services for my father, my siblings and I stand together while our mother greets her friends. Brent suggests that I, as the eldest, should be speaking. Lindsay, anointed executor by our father, says "Why not?" even though he'd assumed the role was his. We can both speak. And we do — he from notes and me from the inspiration of five minutes. What comes to me is something I didn't realize until that moment: that the things about our parents that drive us crazy as kids are sometimes what we come to see as gifts. My father, a child of immigrants who left their ancestral homes forever, who felt left out most of his young life because he was deprived of both Jewish and Russian traditions by his parents' mixed marriage, had a gift for creating community. He brought people together — all of those in each of the filled churches, and all of us, who had laughed and cried together when he died. Perhaps this kind of belonging is something everyone else in my family already knows, something I had to learn by leaving home and becoming part of a family on the other side of the globe. As I look at Fred sitting in a pew beside my family, I'm grateful to have married a man who embodies my father's best qualities.

* * *

Amah says a funeral for an old person like my father or Second Aunt is a "laughing funeral" because the deceased has lived a long life, and family is there to attend to their final passage. Second Aunt's eldest led the procession from the funeral enclosure up the hill to the crematorium, and it was he who pressed the switch on the cremation chamber. He returned to pick up and inter her ashes in the columbarium. He will pray for her soul in the Mormon Church to which he has converted, and her husband, daughter, and younger son will burn incense and colored paper to honor her in the years to come. We will visit her niche in the cemetery columbarium when we return to Cheung Chau.

Fred may have this in mind when he questions me as I pack for a trip home on the anniversary of my father's death. "What're you all going to do when you get there? Just stand around?"

"Probably," I say.

"Hold hands and sing a song? Tell jokes?"

"Probably. There isn't even a place to leave flowers."

"So weird." He shakes his head at our lack of ritual. On Cheung Chau there would be twice-a-year occasions for grave cleanings and offerings. The dead would be fed, clothed, and revered. Even the columbarium has receptacles for paper burning and flowers.

"I know, I know. Makes me appreciate all that incense and bowing when we go to Cheung Chau."

"At least we know what to do."

*　*　*

It's just as he predicted. My siblings and I shiver and fidget with our mother in front of the low wall beside Our Savior's Lutheran Church. The columbarium lines one side of a covered walkway, a recent addition to the church complex. There are only a few niches, and most of the names are familiar to my mother and siblings. The weather is damp and cold, and having just flown in from Hawaii, I'm shivering. Brent carries a flower arrangement, a mound of white chrysanthemums with glossy salal leaves and berries. There's a single red rose at its peak. He shows our mother how the rose, in its own little vial, can be lifted out and replaced by an extra chrysanthemum provided by the florist.

"I guess the rose is for you to take home, Mom," he says.

"What are we supposed to do with the flowers?" I ask. I look around at the two concrete benches and a planter in the walkway. "Leave them on the bench?"

"I keep thinking maybe they could make room in this," my mother says, touching the concrete planter. We'll have this conversation each time we visit in the next few years. The churchgoers will say they'll look into it.

"Some places have little vases that hang on the wall," says Holly. "That's probably what the rose is for." After a pause, she says, "I'm thinking of putting up a plaque for Hayley." My father's death date was her deceased daughter's birthday. When my father died, someone said they were now together in heaven. Later in the day, Holly tells me how hard it is for her to go to cemeteries and how she wishes the family would talk about Hayley. How much it hurts that no one talked about her after she died. I remind her how surprising it would be if we knew what to say.

"Maybe someone can hold the flowers and take a picture next to Dad." Lindsay is eager to be out of here, so he grabs the flowers and poses next to the crypt. Brent snaps a shot on his phone, and I wonder who in the world would want such a photo.

I say, "If we were in Hong Kong, here's what we'd do." I stand in front of my father's niche and bow deeply three times with my hands together in front of my chest.

"And Dad would be telling you to knock it off," Holly says. She's right.

*   *   *

Bundled up against the wind, I stand alone on the deck of the Mukilteo ferry on the way back to what is now just my mother's house. Brent and Lindsay are back at their jobs. Holly and Mom are getting coffee in the ferry's warm café, and in a minute I will join them. I think about how inept we are with death and how our father's passing has brought us together anyway. I wish I had some paper money to burn for him. He would have found that pretty funny since most of my life I was borrowing money from him. *Consider it a down payment on what I owe you,* I'd say. I imagine what we might have burned at his funeral. A purple sports car, some poker chips, bow ties, a case of red wine, some burgers and fries, and a box of cigars. A doctor's bag and a stethoscope, just in case people bring their pets over the rainbow bridge. Shorts and sandals, so he can be comfortable. And, because he loved to travel, a suitcase and a permanent passport to worlds unknown.

24

Filial Piety

BEING my mother's travel companion for two weeks in Norway is my big chance to make up for lost time and distance and be useful in the wake of my father's death. We've never traveled together, but with my father gone for six months, my mother and I both need a distraction. I fly from Hong Kong to Seattle. We fly together to Oslo, where we meet our American tour group. After all my trips with the Laus, I feel certain I can do this. I've watched how my sisters-in-law take care of Amah and Abah, and I am eager to show my mother I can be a caring and dutiful daughter and a pleasant traveling companion.

There are twelve of us on the tour bus. Linda, our tour leader, is a robust blonde nurse my mother knows from the Daughters of

Norway. My mother sits to my left, in the window seat. Everyone says it's sweet that we're traveling together; but when we're alone, we're awkward and strange after all the years apart. Farther back in the bus is Dorothy Ann, eighty-eight like my mother but a head taller. Dorothy Ann has brought along her daughter and three granddaughters. Having done this before, they are as chummy as high school friends. They titter like a flock of birds at dusk in the back of the bus.

Dorothy Ann's brood shares a sizeable room in the first farmhouse where we lodge. We hear peals of laughter from down the hall; they say they're having a slumber party. Their obvious enjoyment at being together reminds me of the Lau family on our trips together. Our room, with its twin beds and a tiny en-suite bathroom, seems too quiet. I fish for conversation starters and ways to stop my mother from fussing over details. I assume I'm here only because she wants to travel while she can and because my father is dead. Envious of all the first-choice companions, I feel like a booby-prize roommate.

Norway is the most breathtaking place I've ever seen. It's the natural beauty of Washington State — with its mountains, islands, evergreens, and water — intensified, magnified. Air so crisp you could bite it, snowcaps Rorschaching clouds, inky blues and greens, quiet so vast and deep it's as I imagine sound in outer space. We feast on salmon and herring, berries and cream. I wonder how my ancestors ever left, but someone in the bus reminds us, "The Norwegians who went to the United States were poor: the younger brothers with no land, the families that couldn't make a living." My ancestors on both sides dropped into America through the colander of the Old World.

At most of our tour accommodations, our rooms hold a platform with two folded duvets and two pillows. I coil into myself like a garden snail when I see that my mother and I must sleep side by side in a space smaller than I share with my husband. I roll as far as I can toward the edge and try not to move. How can mothers and daughters, once connected, become so averse to touching? Fred and his siblings wouldn't think twice about sleeping side by side with each other or their parents. My mother snores. When I turn, I see her head tipped back, her mouth open, and I flash back to my father slack-jawed after his last breath. I try to scrub the cadaver image from my mind, but it leaves a stain of fear. She's next. I'm only twenty-six years behind.

We have a free afternoon in Trondheim before we head south-west to the fjords. My mother and I go to the cathedral, where she urges me to climb the narrow stairs to the roof because she did that with my father years ago. I choke back my claustrophobia in the windowless spiral staircase and am rewarded with a spectac-ular view of the city. I return to the nave, where she waits, and admit she was right. In the decorative arts museum, we peruse the Scandinavian furniture she always loved, and I always said I hated, and then we visit an exhibit of Norwegian and Chinese paper cutting — Norse mythology and Chinese dragons, like seeing my two lives scissored into art. On the way back to our hotel, we pass through a cottage garden where I recognize some flowers — salvia, foxgloves, verbena — and ask her the names of others. My mother the master gardener knows them all. She taught me to love books and animals and plants and stars. With so much in common, I still feel like a weed in her rose garden.

*　*　*

Confucius outlined three levels of filial piety: being a credit to our parents, not disgracing them, and being able to support them. In other words, live up to their expectations, don't embarrass them, and give back in their old age. I've failed on all three counts. In the wake of losing our father six months ago, my siblings stepped into caretaking for our mother, starting when she lost her balance and crashed into a wall. Now one brother drops in every week to oversee her finances, another looks after house maintenance, and my sister handles tasks from shopping to computer emergencies. From Hawaii, all I've done is worry and offer unsolicited advice.

Now I try to be attentive, but my mother doesn't want a caretaker. My siblings have watched my parents' senescence in incremental time. A gentle slope. As the child who's lived away all my adult life, I see drop-offs; I'm startled by my mother's stooped shoulders and bent back. We were once the same size, and now she barely reaches my ear. I take her arm on the stairs, as I've learned to do with Amah, but she pulls away. I urge her to stay hydrated, and she bristles. She loses the expensive water bottle I bought for her, then argues, "You know, you can't believe everything they say. Some of us don't need to drink that much water." I try to move her when she stops in the middle of the sidewalk to take photos and is nearly run over by bicyclists. She fumes, "People just don't see little old ladies." Old people might need a hand, but my mother doesn't want mine. Accustomed to interdependence, Amah and Abah welcome the attentions that come with age as benefits. My mother values independence and hates being considered old.

She garners admiration for her youthful spunk when she accomplishes a two-mile hike through a national park. Without water, I note. *Your mother is so cute. So youthful. So nice that you can do this together.* She smiles demurely. They remark how her blue eyes sparkle against her white hair. She reminds me of a rebellious child.

In the mountain town of Roros, we visit a copper mine. Dorothy Ann stays in the museum above, but my mother, despite a recent fall and fracture, gamely straps on a helmet and descends into the dark mine shaft with its steep stairs and slippery slopes. Halfway through the tunnel, a guide offers to accompany back anyone who doesn't want to go the whole route. I hint she should go back, but my mother insists on forging ahead. That is, until someone else decides to go back. Then she changes her mind and says she thinks she will do that too. Her idea, not mine.

We have extra seats in the bus, so people spread out. I'm craving downtime, quiet space in my head, but my mother sticks beside me and regales me with stories of her travels to Norway with my father and everywhere else in the world. I sigh and squirm, hearing her stories as a grating reminder that my extrovert father, like Fred, was the life of the party, the source of the fun. I'm too busy feeling like an understudy to consider how traveling so soon and alone must make my father seem both close and far to her, how she has no words for the way his sudden departure has turned her life into a puzzle missing all its edge pieces.

Instead, she complains that we don't stop for lunches, that we don't have enough historical information, that the doors in the hotels open out instead of in. I think I'm gaining a deeper under-standing of my father's deafness. How he used to tighten his jaw and say, "Yes, Arlene?" in mock patience when she interrupted his reading. Then I remember explaining to Fred that what he hears as my complaints are just observations. I cringe to think my mother and I share the same annoying habits of being critical and thinking out loud. Maybe I've inherited the worst from both sides of the gene pool: my father's impatience and my mother's perfectionism. That would make me double-dip defective.

My mother needs my help but won't admit it. She misplaces her airline tickets, loses toiletries in her carry-on bag, and has trouble figuring out foreign currency. She relies on me to fill our spare time with activities. I'm used to my husband and his siblings taking care of their parents on trips, but I'm not used to doing it myself. I'm annoyed with my mother for leaning on my father all these years and at my father for letting that happen. I'm embarrassed when I think about how I let Fred take care of money and tickets when we travel because it's easier to relinquish control. I'm angry at my father for dying. We weren't close when he was alive, but if he were here, he'd take charge. My mother and I would both feel protected.

When we move between the bus and wherever we're staying, I trade luggage with my mother because mine is lighter and has better wheels. I'm left tugging her old-fashioned suitcase, as weighty as our politeness. On a day we have to walk a few blocks to our hotel over cobblestone streets, I offer to pull both. She insists she can pull mine by herself. It sticks and rocks on the cobblestones. I slow down to keep pace with her, and when we fall behind the rest of the group, the youngest of Dorothy Ann's granddaughters runs back to help. My mother hands the suitcase over to her with a grateful smile. Muttering to myself that now I look like a terrible daughter for not assisting my mother, I think I finally get the Chinese concept of saving and giving face. Hers has been saved, mine lost.

"Why wouldn't you let me help you?" I ask when we finally close the door to our room.

"I don't see why you had to be so bossy," she says, her face turned away from me. *Bossy?* I haven't been called that since I was a kid, at least not to my face. The toxic tide of my adolescence wells up: *over-sensitive, dramatic, troublemaker, bossy.* I bite back what I want to say about her depending on me to manage everything, just as she was with my father. I suggest she walk in the garden that afternoon while I steam in the sauna with Linda and another woman. When we overheat, we pull hotel robes on over our bathing suits and walk across the street to the fjord. I am the first one to plunge into the icy water.

When I return to our room, my mother sits on the bed across from me and says, "I'm sorry I snapped at you. You know I love you, don't you?" And because I've built a wall around my heart and topped it with broken glass, I can only look away and blurt, "I know," and busy myself with my suitcase.

My efforts at Chinese filial piety have fallen flat, but I still need the toolbox from my Chinese life. I hear Fred saying, *How come American kids expect to be understood? Why do you think being filial is about you?* Whenever I complain that my family doesn't talk about feelings, he reminds me that nobody says *I love you* in the Lau family either. *You don't have to say that stuff*, he says. *Everybody already knows. It's what you do that counts.*

That evening, my mother and I move on as if nothing has happened. We compare notes on our afternoon while sipping chilled Chablis in the outdoor bar of our hotel. We watch the sun sink below the fjord and pose for a selfie we send to Fred: mother and daughter enjoying a special moment together in a special place.

Neither of us knows this will be her last international trip. A year later, Fred and I will plan a tour with her in mind, but a fall, worse than the last, will keep her at home, and we will travel with my siblings instead — an option I would never have considered before traveling with the Lau family.

*   *   *

For Christmas that year, I make my mother a photo book of our trip. I organize my pictures according to our route, interspersing landscapes with shots of cheerful companions and scrumptious food.

I enlarge a shot of the two of us smiling in front of snow-capped mountains for the cover. Sifting through our shared experiences, I wonder if generational difference is just another form of cultural divide. How many encounters did it take for me to climb over my internal fences between America and Hong Kong? I've learned that getting past difference takes thinking like an anthropologist and then not. It takes time, proximity, acceptance, compassion, and a big dose of humor. It takes humility. I need those same tools on the journey back home.

25

Happy Family

On the occasion of Amah and Abah's sixtieth wedding anniversary, we accompany Fred's immediate family on a week-long bus tour around the Japanese island of Kyushu. The trip was Abah's idea. He said if everyone came to Hong Kong for just a banquet, we would disperse. On a tour, we'd all be together. Our trip is the post-banquet honeymoon after the fancy Hong Kong banquet. The sixteen of us together in one place again are Amah and Abah's anniversary gift.

It was the opposite of what my family would choose. For my parents' sixtieth wedding anniversary four years earlier, my father invited me and Fred, Holly, and my brothers and their wives on an Alaska cruise. It was a generous and surprising offer, but, unlike the Hawaii trip for my graduation, complicated by not including grandchildren and great-grandchildren. Brent and Maren, whose kids were the youngest, stayed home, and the rest of us sailed off for a week of more concentrated time together than we'd had since we were children, in a space much smaller than Hawaii. We scattered like airborne seeds during the day and drifted back together each evening for meals. After traveling with the Laus, I first savored then questioned the long pockets of time in which we were free to wander. Some of us drank too much, talked too much or too little, disappeared for long stretches, turned off phones, wondered what was really meant by what was said or not said, needed too much downtime, or felt guilty about needing downtime. In other words, we acted like our usual independent selves. After years of aiming myself out and away like a loosed arrow, I realized I was not the only one relearning how to be part of an organism, its circulating elements interdependent and peripherally aware. My family prefers sizable dollops of personal space in its togetherness.

On the bus with the Lau family, I lean against the window with a scarf wrapped high on my neck to block out the noise without obviously covering my ears. This trip it isn't Fred's family driving me crazy with their chatter, although there are moments when the tour guide has to ask them to tone it down. The nieces and nephews are now college age, and I love traveling with them. No, this time it's Oscar the tour guide eroding my sanity. Large, round, Chinese Oscar who has lived in Japan and has a mission to educate backward Hongkongers about the niceties and refinement of Japanese culture. Oscar, who probably dreams of being a stand-up comedian, fills every potentially contemplative moment of the journey with witty monologues in Cantonese, tainting my cnjoyment of the exquisite landscapes and quaint towns we pass through, puncturing my reveries. I understand nothing of the content without Fred's occasional translations, which makes Oscar's habit of referring to himself in the third person even more annoying. What I hear is an endless loop of *blah blah blah Oscar, blah blah blah Oscar.* "I'm going to put a plastic bag over his head if he doesn't shut up," I mumble. I want to contemplate the view undisturbed.

It is late December, and through the bus windows I watch fine snow dust Fukuoka and steam plumes rise from the many hot springs we pass along the way. The landscape looks like nowhere on earth I've ever seen. It looks like nowhere on earth.

"Just tune out, no one else is listening," Fred says. True on that count, at least from my vantage point in the middle of the bus. The young people share earphones and listen to music. Amah and Abah doze while the others pass snacks and talk among themselves.

"What's he talking about anyway?"

"He's saying that Japanese don't like the way Chinese make noise in restaurants and hotels. They're horrified by the way Chinese fight over the bill in a restaurant and yell in the halls."

"Me too. Are you sure all the people up front are Cantonese? They're so quiet they could be Japanese. I suppose he's talking to us."

"The Happy Family," Fred chuckles. Oscar has taken to referring to the Lau family, who he reminds repeatedly to get back to the bus on time and to quiet down when he gives instructions, as "the Happy Family." Strangers fill the front third of the bus — married couples and two mother-and-daughter dyads. The rest of the bus is three generations of Lau family travelers: Amah and Abah, the four siblings and three spouses, six young-adult offspring, and the girlfriend of Mimi's oldest daughter. The Laus have to traipse past all the others each time they're late, and, despite being a veteran of family tours, I'm embarrassed each time Oscar calls them out. I cut my eyes at Fred, who lifts his eyebrows in amused resignation.

Then I notice how Amah says hello to each of the women in the front as she boards, how she clowns apologetically when she and the others are late — *Sorry! Sorry!* How most of the other travelers smile in indulgence at this old couple from the country with their big family while I worry about comportment. I've been with my Chinese family long enough now to know that they aren't perfect, yet I remember neighbors on Cheung Chau saying that the Lau family is one of the few old-style, traditional families left. How fortunate they are to have such a close extended family. Are the other passengers on the bus admiring us?

When we get our hotel room keys in Fukuoka, Oscar's etiquette lessons are forgotten. The voices of Susanna, Mimi, and Amah bounce up and down the hall as they consult: *Where are you? Our room is here. I think you have my key! What time is dinner? He said we should wear our robes and slippers! Do you want to go to the baths later?* As Fred laughs, I duck into our room, remembering why I refer to the Lau family as the Loud Family.

We show up to dinner in the hotel dining room dressed alike in our blue-and-white-striped cotton yukatas with navy belts and vests, white tabi socks, and wooden sandals. My usual self-consciousness has vanished, leaving a cozy nonchalance in its place, as if my edges have been redrawn with a wet brush instead of a fine-tipped pen. We sit on floor cushions at a long table, the old people at one end so they can stretch out their creaky legs. As the many small dishes are served, extra plates of sashimi drift our way because most of the family eats nothing raw. Fred and I share a jug of sake. We all pose for pictures.

* * *

An hour after dinner, most of us meet in the hall to go to the onsen on the first floor of the hotel. Amah, Mimi, Susanna, two nieces, and I turn left to the women's side, while the men turn to the right. Mimi's oldest daughter and her girlfriend are missing because they went before dinner.

Once I am naked in the onsen, I carry my hand towel but don't know what to do with it. I remember only that the instruction guide in our room, replete with graphics for foreigners, said not to leave anything on the edge of the pool. It's not like I can cover much of myself with a hand towel, anyway. It's not my first time in an onsen, but being unclothed in front of my in-laws is such a new level of shedding my American propriety and personal reserve that the incessant narrator in my brain is speechless. All I can imagine her saying when she gets her wind back is *Huh? We're doing what?*

Unclothed, the women in Fred's family — young, old, and in-between — are still the same constellation. Mimi and Susanna fuss over Amah as they lead her down the steps to the pool, supporting her elbows so she doesn't slip on the tiles. Amah drapes her towel across her head while she soaks. The nieces lean together against the edge of the pool, chatting and floating. I steep with them until I'm flushed and dripping, then walk outside to the outdoor pool, where the air is chilly and there's a waterfall. Cut pomelos and jasmine blossoms float in the water. I sit on a rock ledge just below the surface of the heated water, my upper body fanned by the cool air. Wrapping my towel around my hair, I resist the impulse to submerge when the others join me.

I wonder how naked can feel so natural in some settings and so uncomfortable in others. I once saw my mother dash through the house naked when she'd taken a shower and forgotten a towel. My sister and I turn our backs if we have to change in the same room, yet I have friends who think nothing of being naked with sisters. My sister-in-law goes to a spa with her mother, yet I haven't seen Sorrel naked since she was ten, when she started insisting on closed doors and privacy. Appalled I'd been to an onsen in Japan with my graduate advisor, she was horrified I'd been to one in Washington with my sister-in-law. The idea of family or strangers bathing together is inconceivable to her. As I dress with the women in my Chinese family, I wish she could experience the small courtesies of mutual nakedness, the camaraderie of women, the ease and acceptance possible once we've shed our clothes, how artifice falls away in water.

*　*　*

On New Year's Day, the bus drops us off at an outlet shopping mall. While the rest of the family bargain shops, Fred and I wander from store to store. The Christmas decorations remind me I've missed Christmas again to be here. Picturing my siblings and their families eating together, my mother missing my father, my daughter and her kids with their stockings and tree, I feel like I'm stuck in a glass snow globe on a faraway shelf. My American family knows me in ways my Chinese family never can. As do my American friends. Although the foreign has become familiar, and my family sometimes seems foreign to me, we still share a culture, a language, a history of shared experiences. We share all the Christmases past, and I know that as far as I roam, they will always make room for me at the table. With them, I don't need Oscar to tell me how to behave. I don't need a matching outfit to tell others with whom I belong. I just need to pay attention and be willing to fit back in.

I stroke my left wrist, missing the jade bracelet I wore for so many years before it cracked in two during a playful tussle with Fred. "See? It protected you," he said. "It broke your fall." Later, he offered to get it repaired.

I smiled and said, "No thanks. I don't need it anymore."

Epilogue: Trailing Spouse

As I ride the East Rail Line from University station to Shatin in Hong Kong's New Territories, an area north of Hong Kong Island that stretches from Kowloon to the China border, I'm struck by how much the city and I have changed since 2015. Hong Kong, along with the rest of the world, is in the midst of a pandemic, so everyone wears a surgical mask. People around me no longer appear foreign. Likewise, I no longer feel like a foreigner, despite my American passport. I used to panic about ever finding my way around in the crush of people and interconnected buildings and transportation systems, and I now navigate familiar routes with practiced ease. I'm still language challenged, but I'm no longer afraid to use my limited Cantonese to greet the minibus drivers and tell them where to let me off. In the past, Hong Kong's crowds made me feel so claustrophobic I had anxiety attacks; but when I disembark at Shatin station today, I will weave through the shoppers at New Town Plaza like a pro and manage my errands with relative calm.

Fred and I moved from Honolulu to Hong Kong in 2018 when Fred was offered a full professorship at his alma mater, the Chinese University of Hong Kong. We live on campus in a roomy faculty flat, and I have mixed feelings about having become the expat with the shiny parquet wood floors and maid's quarters I once envied. Unlike many of the foreign and local faculty, Fred and I have not purchased a car or hired a helper, managing quite well despite being a bus ride and two train stops from the nearest supermarket. Before the pandemic, we traveled internationally and hosted friends and family in our guestroom. These strange days, our longest journeys are to the island of Cheung Chau to visit Fred's family, a trip that takes us two hours by train, subway, foot, and ferry. At our last family gathering, the obligatory photos included a whole new crop of cousins.

Hong Kong has changed too. In 2019, our city was convulsed by protests and violence. The campus where we live was under siege for three days and then cut off from the rest of the city for a month while our vandalized train station was out of commission. Hong Kong is now muffled by masks and silenced by a new security law that criminalizes dissent; yet the city continues building, rumbling, bustling, and evolving at breakneck speed while more traditional places like Cheung Chau amble forward at a slower pace.

My experiences with the Lau family showed me what I'd missed by straying so far from my own family, and in the past few years I've spent more concentrated time with my family than I have in decades. Before Fred and I relocated, one of my brothers and his wife traveled with us to a Lau family wedding. After our move, two of my granddaughters came to Hong Kong for an extended visit. Last year, I spent five months helping out at my mother's house on Whidbey Island while my sister underwent chemotherapy. This new sense of togetherness is bittersweet now that travel is prohibitive due to quarantine requirements on both ends.

On the train, I avoid touching the steel poles or grips, preferring instead a no-hands balance stance. I've discovered the key to stability is to bend my knees. Flexibility seems to be the repeated answer to the challenges of my cross-cultural life. Between stations,

I people watch and type notes on my phone because it turns out my mid-life transition was always leading me here, to the page. I may have come to Hong Kong this time as a "trailing spouse," the unofficial term for a "dependent" partner sponsored by a family member with a Hong Kong job, but time and space add up to opportunity. These days, I'm using both to reinvent myself as writer.

Acknowledgments

I would like to acknowledge that "Chinese Borscht" previously appeared in the Hong Kong Review.

I am grateful for the support and guidance of the partners at Camphor Press: John Ross, Michael Cannings, and Mark Swofford. As someone new to the publishing process, I couldn't have asked for a better team. Thanks to John and Mark for making the editorial process such a collaborative pleasure and to Michael for patient guidance and working with my cover design idea. I'm grateful to Ida Wong, a member of the Lau clan, for making that idea a beautiful reality.

This book would not have happened without my writing teachers and editors. I signed up for my first writing class with Joelle Fraser on a whim, and I emerged with the seeds of this story. I completed most of the first draft in a course by Brooke Warner and Linda Joy Myers. When I detoured into short essays, Nicole Breit's and Rachel Thompson's courses helped me return to my manuscript with new eyes, as did Becky Blake, my book coach for completing the final chapters. Many thanks to Laura King for her thoughtful editing and to Yvette Cantu Schneider for getting me past my umpteenth revision.

Writing is solitary work, and much of my solace has come from connecting to other writers. I've been cheered on by my friends Claire Chao and Susan Blumberg-Kason; and without Susan's help,

I might not have found Camphor Press. The encouragement of Teri Lyn Helm, Yolande House, Cynthia Wessendorf, and Rachel Laverdiere, along with the many generous writers in my online writers' groups, kept me moving forward.

Several people read early drafts or parts of this book: Jenny Miller Garmendia, Mari Yoshihara, Sandra York, Maren Diamond, Rina Chung, Mara Miller, Jessie McDonald, Yolande House, Rachel Laverdiere, Nicole Breit, Karen Zey, and Susan-Blumberg-Kason. Thank you for seeing past the flaws.

I'm blessed to have friends who have known me through multiple reinventions and believed in my creative abilities long before I did: Sandra York, Lisa Goodman, Frances Russell, and Cheryl Mount Dubroc, my long-haul soul sisters. Eddie Gallaher nudged me toward this new phase and departed way too soon. I still talk to him.

An East-West Center grant led me to China and my husband, and an EWC fellowship provided me with an international cohort and global perspectives. Thank you to Betty Buck, Roger Ames, and Peter Hershock for giving me a taste of Asia before I ever got there.

Most importantly, I am forever grateful to my American and Chinese families, the former for keeping the door open and the latter for opening theirs. Neither signed up for being represented in a memoir, and I deeply appreciate their support for my compulsion to make art out of my life when they might have preferred to keep their private moments out of a book. And, finally, my two dearest loves should get service awards for their indulgence in that regard and others: Sorrel, for making room in her heart for all my changes, and Fred, for hitching his fate to mine and everything else that has made this journey possible.

About the Author

Heather Diamond grew up in Everett, Washington. She earned a PhD in American Studies from the University of Hawai'i and has worked as a bookseller, a university lecturer, and a museum curator. She is the author of American Aloha: Cultural Tourism and the Negotiation of Tradition, and her essays have appeared in various literary magazines. She lives in Hong Kong with her husband and cats. She blogs at heatherdiamondwriter.com.

.

CPSIA information can be obtained
at www.ICGtesting.com
Printed in the USA
JSHW031949250521
15188JS00006B/26